The Point is to Change the World

Andaiye (September 11, 1942–May 31, 2019) was one of the Caribbean's leading radical political figures, social and political thinkers, and public intellectuals. She spent all of her adult life in left and women's politics in Guyana, the Caribbean and internationally. In Guyana, she was a member of the Working People's Alliance (WPA), serving on the party executive and as party coordinator/editor, international secretary and women's secretary through the period of political turbulence and anti-dictatorial struggle that culminated in the assassination of Walter Rodney on June 13, 1980. Part of her political work was editing some of the last writing by Walter Rodney. From the mid-1980s Andaiye's activism was largely with women in Guyana, the Caribbean, and globally. She was one of the founders of Red Thread, a women's organization in Guyana, worked with the Women and Development Unit of the University of the West Indies, was attached very briefly to the regional integration organization (CARICOM) as Special Advisor to the Secretary General on Women & Gender, helping prepare Ministers of Women's Affairs for the 1995 Beijing Conference on Women, and was a member of the Regional Executive of the Caribbean Association for Feminist Research and Action (CAFRA) in the mid-1990s. Internationally, she was associated with the Global Women's Strike (GWS) and Women of Colour in the Global Women's Strike. A cancer survivor herself twice over, Andaiye was a founder of the now defunct Guyana Cancer Society and Cancer Survivors Action Group. For many years, she wrote a weekly newspaper column titled "Woman's Eye View," and she has written and published articles and chapters on women in Guyana and the rest of the Caribbean.

Alissa Trotz is Professor of Caribbean Studies at New College and Women and Gender Studies at the University of Toronto. She is also affiliate faculty at the Dame Nita Barrow Institute of Gender and Development Studies at the University of the West Indies, Cave Hill, Barbados. She is a member of Red Thread Women's Organization in Guyana and editor of "In the Diaspora," a weekly newspaper column in the Guyanese daily, *Stabroek News*.

Black Critique

Series editors: Anthony Bogues and Bedour Alagraa

We live in a troubled world. The rise of authoritarianism marks the dominant current political order. The end of colonial empires did not inaugurate a more humane world; rather, the old order reasserted itself.

In opposition, throughout the twentieth century and until today, anti-racist, radical decolonization struggles attempted to create new forms of thought. Figures from Ida B. Wells to W. E. B. Du Bois and Steve Biko, from Claudia Jones to Walter Rodney and Amílcar Cabral produced work which drew from the historical experiences of Africa and the African diaspora. They drew inspiration from the Haitian revolution, radical black abolitionist thought and practice, and other currents that marked the contours of a black radical intellectual and political tradition.

The Black Critique series operates squarely within this tradition of ideas and political struggles. It includes books which foreground this rich and complex history. At a time when there is a deep desire for change, black radicalism is one of the most under-explored traditions that can drive emancipatory change today. This series highlights these critical ideas from anywhere in the black world, creating a new history of radical thought for our times.

Also available:

Moving Against the System:
The 1968 Congress of Black Writers and the Making of Global Consciousness
Edited and with an Introduction by David Austin

A Certain Amount of Madness: The Life, Politics and Legacies of Thomas Sankara
Edited by Amber Murrey

Cedric J. Robinson: On Racial Capitalism, Black Internationalism, and Cultures of Resistance
Edited by H. L. T. Quan

Black Minded: The Political Philosophy of Malcolm X
Michael Sawyer

Red International and Black Caribbean Communists in New York City, Mexico and the West Indies, 1919–1939
Margaret Stevens

The Point is to Change the World

Selected Writings of Andaiye

Edited by Alissa Trotz

PLUTO PRESS

First published 2020 by Pluto Press
345 Archway Road, London N6 5AA

www.plutobooks.com

British Library Cataloguing in Publication Data
A catalogue record for this book is available from the British Library

ISBN   978 0 7453 4126 2   Hardback
ISBN   978 0 7453 4127 9   Paperback
ISBN   978 1 7868 0622 2   PDF eBook
ISBN   978 1 7868 0624 6   Kindle eBook
ISBN   978 1 7868 0623 9   EPUB eBook

Typeset by Stanford DTP Services, Northampton, England

The philosophers have hitherto only interpreted the world in various ways. The point, however, is to change it.

Karl Marx, *Theses on Feuerbach*, 1845

Shape and Motion (Martin Carter), by Abbyssinian Carto (2015)
(photographer: Robert Salmieri)

Contents

PART TWO   A DIFFERENT PERSPECTIVE: STARTING WITH
THE UNWAGED CARING WORK OF MAINLY WOMEN WE
REACH ALL SECTORS

PART THREE   THE POLITICAL IN THE PERSONAL

PART FOUR   TOWARDS STRENGTHENING THE MOVEMENT

Last Word

FOREWORDS

Andaiye's Radical Imagination—with Special Reference to Her Engagement with the Working People's Alliance

Clem Seecharan

Andaiye was born in Georgetown, British Guiana on September 11, 1942. Her original name was Sandra Williams but she changed it in the mid-1970s, inspired by the Black Power movement in America and in the region. Of Swahili origin, Andaiye means "a daughter comes home." Her change of name was a definitive statement affirming pride in her African antecedents. Perhaps it also reflected her intention to cast down her bucket in Guyana in pursuit of a radical transformation of the country of her birth. It has been an unfaltering resolve that led her to political activism in the Movement Against Oppression (MAO) in the 1960s; the Working People's Alliance (WPA) from 1978 to the mid-1990s; and from 1986 until prevented by illness, as a champion of women's rights through the Red Thread Women's Organisation in Guyana. Regionally she was active in the Caribbean Association for Feminist Research and Action (CAFRA), and internationally in Women of Color in the Global Women's Strike (WOC/GWS). Hers has been one of the most compelling contributions by a Guyanese in sustaining a culture of protest and change—animated by a radical imagination. Its magnitude is better appreciated when juxtaposed with the fact that Andaiye has been ferociously battling cancer since it was first diagnosed 30 years ago. She is not just an inspirational and transformative figure in Guyana, but a regional and international champion of working class and women's rights.

Her father, Dr. Frank Williams, was the personal physician of President Forbes Burnham, leader of the People's National Congress (PNC), so I was curious to learn of her family's reaction to her anti-PNC politics over several years. Andaiye responded thus:

> My parents remained close to Burnham until Walter was killed, but never cut relations with me. Indeed, WPA people (including Walter) remained welcome in their home. In a broader sense though, some of my blood relatives and almost all my non-blood family and old friends opposed my politics (or at least were afraid of how it could affect them) and broke relations.

Many Africans in Guyana would have disavowed Andaiye's radical critique of the Burnham regime for racial reasons: for letting the side down. Others (as she notes) were afraid of victimization and loss of security. This fear was exacerbated by the violence the Burnham state had unleashed on the WPA, defined as an instrument of subversion of a recalcitrant minority partly from within the African middle class. The regime had become increasingly dictatorial after Burnham's PNC engaged in extensive rigging of the general elections of July 1973. And given the closeness of the relationship between Andaiye's father and Forbes Burnham, it must have taken an "aristocracy of will" (as George Lamming puts it) for a comparatively young woman like Andaiye to return to Guyana in 1978 (aged 36), a Marxist committed to radical change—the liberation of the country from Burnham's authoritarian rule.

What was the political environment that shaped young Andaiye and Walter Rodney (both born in 1942), as well as Rupert Roopnaraine (born in early1943)? When they were about 11 years old, the short-lived radical government of the People's Progressive Party (PPP), led by Cheddi Jagan (1918–1997) and Forbes Burnham (1923–1985), was elected to office and then ejected by the British government after 133 days, in October 1953, because of its alleged goal of establishing a communist state. It is arguable, therefore, that these young people absorbed the spirit of rebellion and triumph, as well as its speedy decline into ethnic bifurcation. The early nationalist movement though ambitiously radical, was fragile on account of the deep-seated racial insecurities between the two principal segments of Guyanese society, African and Indian. The idealist Marxist strain of the movement was reflected in the politics of Cheddi and Janet Jagan (1920–2009), Sydney King (Eusi Kwayana; 1925–), Rory Westmaas (1926–2016) and Martin Carter (1927–1997). Indeed, Carter's trenchant poetry of resistance was a seminal force that framed the political horizon of many young Guyanese. It did not necessarily lessen mutual ethnic incomprehension, but it bred a radical temperament discernibly more pronounced than anywhere else in the British West Indies. (Forbes Burnham never did empathize with the Marxist wing of the original PPP.)

Andaiye observes that the rebel seed, paradoxically, was also planted by the biases in her colonial education. She recalls that even the sea battering the Georgetown coast, kept out by the sturdy sea-wall, though stained brown by virtue of the silt of the great Amazonian rivers disgorging into the Atlantic, was redefined by her primary school teacher as "blue"! She tells how she was made to see her black skin:

> I knew, very early, the use of the word "black" as disparagement ("Stay out of the sun, you want to turn more black?": said especially to little black girls.) I didn't understand yet what the injunction had to do with gender, but it did: blackness lowered your "market value." It was not an asset in marrying up.

Andaiye's name change was a statement that Africanness was worthy of retrieval and celebration. It follows that this means of self-affirmation helped to fortify her own fight for working class rights and the rights of women to equality of opportunity. Later, inspired profoundly by Selma James, she also would champion the recognition of the invisible unwaged women in the home. I was impelled to go online to learn more about her name. What I discovered encapsulates her personality so immaculately that I feel as if this name were held in reserve, in racial memory, specifically for reclamation by Sandra Williams:

> People with the name Andaiye have a deep inner need for quiet, and a desire to understand and analyse the world they live in, and to learn deeper truths … [They] are dynamic, visionary and versatile, able to make constructive use of freedom.

During the time that Andaiye and Rodney were students at the University (College) of the West Indies (UWI, Mona), colonial Guyana had descended into ethnic hatred: a virtual racial war between Africans and Indians. It was exacerbated by Anglo-American complicity in fomenting chaos in order to dislodge Jagan (the perceived communist) and install the "moderate" Burnham, before independence. British Guiana was immersed in the Cold War. Home-based scholars and public intellectuals struggled to conceive a progressive alternative that might rescue Guyana from its bedeviling racial futility. Contributors to *New World Quarterly* and *New World Fortnightly* provoked nuanced scholarly perspectives on the plantation societies of the British West Indies, towards the end of empire. This was instrumental in the making of Andaiye's radical temperament.

Andaiye's intellectual growth was enriched by her experience in the United States (between 1972 and 1977) where she lectured in a program for "disadvantaged students" (SEEK) at Queens College, New York. This was enhanced by political support for the civil rights, black power consciousness, anti-apartheid and Latin American anti-dictatorial movements. She sees enlightened activism as the medium for subverting orthodoxies and oppressive structures. This is always allied with her critical evaluation of contemporary society, impelled by a passion for change. Walter Rodney was obviously a seminal example.

But it is arguable that her exemplar of political engagement is the apostle of self-sacrifice, Eusi Kwayana—eschewing material security for the often elusive and precarious idealism of political and social transformation. Eusi is clearly pivotal to her own political vocation which offered minimal financial protection: working unwaged as coordinator of the WPA from 1978 to 1986, and within Red Thread from 1986 to 1989 and from the mid-1990s to 2006. Listing several people who'd assisted him with his last book, *A History of the Guyanese Working People, 1881–1905* (nearing completion when he was assassinated in

THE POINT IS TO CHANGE THE WORLD

June 1980) and outlining what he would acknowledge each for, Rodney ended, tersely but powerfully: "and [to] Eusi Kwayana for [the] example."

Andaiye concurred entirely:

> [Eusi] was and is an example of a will to engage, a willingness to change when he saw he was wrong ... [He showed] a willingness to apologise, and he did so, publicly. In 1978, in a talk to the Guyana Sociological Society called "Racial Insecurity and the Political System," he apologised for dealing with race in 1961 in an insensitive way.

She was, of course, alluding to Eusi's advocacy of partition of the colony if power-sharing constitutional arrangements, between Africans and Indians, were not devised before independence was granted. And Eusi did express remorse for his *modus operandi* on the question of racial insecurity in the early 1960s, acknowledging the "abrasive manner in which I raised the racial issue ... in language reflecting the grossness of the times."

The range of writings in this book reflects Andaiye's life of challenge, conflict, despair, serious illness but also empathy, courage, resilience and an inviolable sense of possibilities—something to hold on to. It is infused with an unconquerable feminist strand that had not hitherto been conceived in Guyana in the manner Andaiye did. Her writings are indispensable to the history of women's fight for equality and the reclaiming of their humanity in Guyana. To comprehend these diverse articles is to enter into a universe of scholarship and activism that most people in the region rarely encounter. This collection is a benchmark for the study of the Caribbean radical imagination. And it is permeated by her fortitude and magnanimity in daring to seek to change entrenched attitudes against the disadvantaged. Moreover, her commitment is always guided by what drew her initially to the WPA in 1978: "a daughter comes home" because of "the possibility of multiracialness."

Andaiye's version of the WPA's part in seeking to undermine the dictatorial Burnham state corroborates Walter Rodney's, in his writings as well as his speeches at mass street meetings in mid- to late 1979. The latter took place in the context of "the civil rebellion" after he, Roopnaraine and Omowale were charged with the burning down of the building housing the Office of the General Secretary of the PNC and the Ministry of National Development, on July 11, 1979. Shortly thereafter the WPA declared itself a political party, and though not officially the leader, Rodney was generally recognised as such. And, even then, it was also widely assumed that, without Rodney, the incipient movement had little chance of becoming a credible political alternative to the Burnham dictatorship.

Yet, strangely, Andaiye suggests that the leadership of the WPA—even in this period of their most robust challenge to the Burnham regime (1979–80)—had no strategy for the acquisition of political power. They manifested no definitive conception of the realities of gaining power and its daunting responsibilities, despite the declaration that it was a political party committed to eliminating Burnham's authoritarian rule "by any means necessary."

> **David Scott** [in *Small Axe*]: So as the WPA is solidifying as a political party, the project as you all are discussing it, has as its objective the overthrow of Burnham. That's the talk then. That what is required is the revolutionary overthrow of the Burnham regime.
>
> **Andaiye:** Yes ... The reason for the hesitation is because it was couched in the language of "*Burnham must go, and he must go by any means necessary.*" But the WPA functioned a lot, not only pre-party but afterwards ... very much on a need-to-know basis. And therefore there would *not* be general talk in the WPA about "overthrow" [emphasis added].

Given what she says about functioning on a "need-to-know" basis, Andaiye could have been unaware of the specifics of the insurrectionary plan to which Rupert Roopnaraine refers when he says that shortly before Rodney's assassination, the WPA was doing more than talking about freedom or liberation from the Burnham dictatorship. They were allegedly preparing for a violent assault on the regime. This is what Rupert told Clairmont Chung:

> We were at the time attempting to equip ourselves, essentially ready ourselves, and ready the masses for an insurrectionary attack on the state. I make no excuses about that ... But we were at the time attempting to put ourselves in a state of readiness to make an assault on the state. It's no secret we were accumulating weapons. We were accumulating equipment of various kinds, and a certain amount of that was coming from the military ... [But] Burnham had penetrated so much of the WPA ... it was a very dangerous game we were playing. In point of fact, we found ourselves at all hours of the night, in strange places, doing dangerous things because those were the things it was necessary to do, it seemed to us at the time. The miracle is that more of us didn't get killed. (Chung 2013: 112–113)

On the question of race, Andaiye is critical and self-critical of the fact that not long after the creation of the WPA, the WPA leadership allowed the "withering away" of the two race-based cultural organizations, the African Society for Cultural Relations with Independent Africa (ASCRIA, led by Eusi Kwayana) and the Indian Progressive Revolutionary Associates (IPRA, led by Moses Bhagwan), which had joined forces with other organizations in the formation of the WPA in 1974. She contends that it was a mistake to terminate or prematurely lessen their crucial grassroots initiatives in the promotion of ethnic security as a prelude to the formidable project of national reconciliation. There had been an earlier and equally fatal precedent: the failure of the original PPP, a coalition of anti-colonial nationalists of diverse ethnic and ideological strains, to tackle the fundamental problem of ethnic incomprehension, the source of chronic ethnic insecurity.

Andaiye reflects on Rodney's initial views on organizing in this ethnically diverse society with entrenched suspicions. For him, this required, in the short run, the sustaining of organizations that would address the peculiar cultural needs and fears and aspirations of each segment. He considered this a prerequisite to the ultimate goal of realizing a robust Guyanese national culture. Rodney conceded that this could be counter-productive: "If you organize separately, this may well be construed by each group as something exclusive and hostile." Therefore, in order to negate the probability of further polarization because of such ethnic organizations, it was essential to devise integrative mechanisms, to "act in the kind of fashion and use the kind of language which makes it clear to the other group what the national aims are."

This lofty proposition was far from fruition when Rodney returned to Guyana and joined in forming the WPA in 1974. But Andaiye thinks that like others, he saw the WPA as the instrument to accelerate the process of national cohesion, so that with its formation, race-based organizations were no longer required. In retrospect, she acknowledges that the problem of ethnic insecurity had not been "irreversibly changed" and consequently, it should have continued to receive the concentrated focus originally provided by ASCRIA and IPRA, while synchronizing their peculiar cultural agenda with the wider political objectives of the WPA. She observes that even during the "civil rebellion" of 1979, the problem of racial insecurity remained unresolved (see Essay 6).

She notes that shortly before the assassination of Rodney, on June 13, 1980, he had written thus: "the firmest unity is unity in struggle." This prompts Andaiye to pose the fundamental question of how does one sustain that unity when the chronic ethnic insecurity still simmers, when the "struggle" has lost its momentum.

Andaiye makes a compelling critique of a lacuna in the WPA agenda reminiscent of the original PPP. What she does not say, however, is that parties like the WPA, rooted in Marxism-Leninism, are inclined to treat the ethnic issue as "epiphenomenal"—at a secondary level, subordinate to the paramount issue, the class question:

Looking back, I believe that IPRA and ASCRIA should have continued as autonomous organizations inside the WPA because the conditions they had fought to change before the WPA came into being had not irreversibly changed with the formation of the WPA. In my view, if ASCRIA and IPRA had remained alive as autonomous political organizations within the WPA, they would not only have been positioned to help work against the renewed descent into race violence and the further entrenching of opposing race narratives (after the PPP was elected in 1992), but to ensuring that the WPA remained a force in touch with and representing the separate and shared interests of Africans and Indians, well beyond the time it lost that strength.

Rodney, in his speeches and in his booklet *People's Power, No Dictator* (published by the WPA during "the civil rebellion" of July–November 1979), was clear that they were in pursuit of the termination of Burnham's rule. Burnham was antagonized by the WPA's attack on the regime, and its threat to seek to remove it "by any means possible." Besides, as Andaiye points out, Burnham was deeply "angered" by Rodney's characterization of him as "King Kong," imbued with a peculiar kind of "Midas touch," the obverse of its conventional connotation.

Burnham denounced the WPA as the "worst possible alternative"; moreover, he rebuked the leadership of the WPA (he refused to accord Rodney any validity by using his name) that his "steel was sharper" than theirs; and that they should therefore make their wills. The subsequent assassination of two activists of the WPA, Ohene Koama and Edward Dublin, in November 1979 and February 1980 respectively, was widely interpreted as a prelude to further violence targeted clinically and ferociously at the WPA leadership. Burnham could handle Jagan's Indian-based, largely moribund, "communist" opposition; in fact, it was perceived as pivotal to the longevity of his rule. But for a young African-Guyanese like Walter Rodney to mount such irreverent resistance to his regime, meant that drastic violent measures were necessary and totally defensible.

Rodney had endeavored to undermine the mystique of omnipotence that Burnham had assiduously cultivated over many years in power. In *People's Power, No Dictator*, he speaks of the vulgarity of the dictatorship warranting language that mirrors its crudity:

> Our language must express not only ridicule but anger and disgust. The dictatorship has reduced us to such a level that the situation can be described only in terms befitting filth, pollution and excrement. Even our deep-seated sense of modesty cannot stand in the way of rough words to describe the nation's shame. That is why the WPA repeats the legend of King Midas who was said to have been able to touch anything and turn it into gold. That was called the "Midas Touch". Now Guyana has seen the "Burnham Touch"— anything he touches turns to shit!

On June 6, 1980, one week before he was assassinated, Rodney made his last speech, in Georgetown. He did not spare Burnham on this occasion either:

To speak of freedom in these days, the enemies of the people of Guyana are threatening to charge us with treason ... If they say it is treason to plot to overthrow the King, *then we are all treasonable* [*sic*] ... They call themselves the *Kabaka* [a reference to Burnham]—a feudal, backward word. They talk about their reign. Now they talk about treason. But we understand where they are going. What they do not understand is where we are going!

A Commission of Inquiry (COI) into the death of Rodney did not materialize until 34 years after his death, in 2014. Yet, strangely, it did not call Rupert Roopnaraine as a witness although he was still living in Guyana; neither did he submit a memorandum to them, as far as I know. He attended the hearings on the day Eusi Kwayana was a witness before the Commission. If his statement quoted earlier is accurate, then with the WPA infiltrated by the Burnham regime, the latter would have construed the WPA as being in a state of war against them. Therefore any violence unleashed against the WPA could be rationalized as defensive, a case of apprehended insurrection to protect the nation. However, the COI concluded that Rodney's assassin was Gregory Smith (an electronics expert formerly in the Guyana Defence Force), who had befriended Rodney; that he had constructed the deadly device that killed Rodney; moreover, that Burnham was fully aware of, and connived in, the plot to kill Rodney. Yet Roopnaraine and Clive Thomas had never met Gregory Smith (neither had virtually all of the other leaders of the WPA).

The report of the COI was completed in February 2016, but the president of Guyana (the leader of the party of Burnham) refused to grant it the official seal by publishing it. It is obvious why he took that decision:

> We accept that Gregory Smith was encouraged in providing that device [that killed Rodney] by prominent members of State agencies ...
>
> We have no hesitation in holding that Gregory Smith was responsible for the death on 13 June 1980, and that in so doing he was acting as an agent of the State having been aided and abetted so to do, by individuals holding positions of leadership in State agencies and committed to carrying out the wishes of the People's National Congress administration. ...
>
> We conclude that Prime Minister Burnham knew of the plan and was part of the conspiracy to assassinate Walter Rodney.

*   *   *

There are many imponderable questions thrown up by Andaiye's critical account of her work in the WPA, at a contentious juncture in Guyana's post-independence political history. Scholars will be provoked into reassessing the diverse strands of the complex politics of the time, as a consequence of loose ends that emerge from some of these very fine, provocative essays. There are limits as to what is knowable because much of Guyana's post-independence documents are irretrievable—shredded or hidden away. But this book goes far beyond the labyrinthine politics. It is the story of a brave woman who has refused to be silenced. She has never recoiled from speaking truth to power.

I give the final word to Andaiye. It captures the indefatigable spirit of this Guyanese hero:

> As late as 1989 when I was diagnosed people still didn't say the word cancer; they said "the big C." With very few exceptions, friends and family who were told of my illness initially responded with such fear that it fell to me to console them, and often, I was the only one who would name the disease. When I was first in hospital in Barbados, my aunt came into the room on tiptoe although she could see I was awake, and whispered when she spoke, as decent people did in the presence of death.

POSTSCRIPT

Andaiye died in Georgetown on May 31, 2019. Moses Bhagwan, her former colleague in the WPA, sent me his tribute. He speaks for me and many more:

> Her death is not a surrender. She has simply relocated into an eminent domain of our country's history as one of the most exemplary, most gifted and the bravest. She is ... permanently there, as a beacon for those who want to fight against diseases of the mind and of the body, for a higher quality of life and for a decent country to live in.

Walk good, Andaiye!

Clem Seecharan is Emeritus Professor of History at London Metropolitan University, where he was Head of Caribbean Studies for nearly 20 years. He is the author of several books, including *Sweetening "Bitter Sugar": Jock Campbell, the Booker Reformer in British Guiana, 1934–66* (awarded the Elsa Goveia Prize, 2005, by the Association of Caribbean Historians). His latest book is on Cheddi Jagan and the Cold War. He was awarded the D.Litt. by the University of the West Indies (St Augustine) in 2017.

REFERENCE

Chung, Clairmont. 2013. *Walter Rodney: A Promise of Revolution*. New York: New York Monthly Review Books.

Between Home and Street:
Andaiye's Revolutionary Vision

Robin D. G. Kelley

There is no frontier between home and street.

Andaiye

I first heard of Andaiye in the fall of 1992, around the time of Guyana's historic elections that ended the 28-year reign of the People's National Congress (PNC)—21 of those years under the dictatorial rule of Forbes Burnham. I had recently joined the University of Michigan faculty and spent most of my time at the Center for Afro-American and African Studies (CAAS). That's where I met Nesha Haniff, a dynamic scholar who worked on women, gender, sexuality, and education in the Caribbean. It was when the topic of the elections came up that I learned that Nesha was Guyanese. I'm not trained as a Caribbeanist, but the maternal side of my family is Jamaican and Cuban, and back then I considered myself pretty well-informed about Guyana. Walter Rodney was my hero; reading his book *How Europe Underdeveloped Africa* convinced me to pursue a doctorate in History. I knew something about the Working People's Alliance (WPA) and Eusi Kwayana. I had seen Rupert Roopnaraine's haunting film, *The Terror and the Times*. I owned a dog-eared copy of Clive Y. Thomas's *Dependence and Transformation: The Economics of the Transition to Socialism*. I'd even written an undergraduate paper on the rise of Afro-Guyanese communal villages following the formal abolition of slavery. And in 1984 I had the honor of working on Rodney's papers as a research assistant at UCLA. His widow, Pat, had temporarily left his papers with my dissertation advisor, Ned Alpers, after Rodney's assassination on June 13, 1980.

So imagine my excitement upon learning that Nesha was not only Guyanese but had ties to the WPA. I rattled off some names in an effort to establish my *bona fides*, but she just as quickly disabused me of my romantic notions of Guyanese politics, which were still stuck in the early 1980s. Near the end of her impromptu lecture she quipped, "If you want to know about Guyana and the struggles there, you need to know the women. No one talks about the women. You heard of Andaiye? Used to go by Sandra Williams? Look her up. She's brilliant." Unfortunately, I did not heed her advice. (Later I realized that I'd encountered her name in the acknowledgements of Rodney's posthumously published *History of the Guyanese Working People*, but I did not know enough to "look her up.")

Twelve years later, David Scott, editor of *Small Axe*, published a 95-page interview with Andaiye in a special issue of the journal devoted to Guyana. In an uncanny moment of *déjà vu*, I had just joined the anthropology faculty at Columbia University and David, a Jamaican like my mother, was my new colleague and interlocutor on all things Caribbean. Similar to Nesha, he deepened my understanding of Caribbean history and revealed the complex and contradictory dynamics at the core of the region's political radicalism. The interview with Andaiye, excerpts of which are reproduced in this volume, is stunning in its scope, depth, and sheer honesty (see Essay 4). Her wisdom as a skilled organizer, a political strategist, a student of history, as well as her analysis of gendered labor, violence, and neoliberalism, situated her in my mind as one the Caribbean's brightest stars—which is saying a lot since the Caribbean is renowned for producing some of the world's greatest radical thinkers. Indeed, it is not an exaggeration to say that this volume will occupy a vaunted place alongside the writings of C. L. R. James, Frantz Fanon, Aime Cesaire, Sylvia Wynter, Edouard Glissant, George Lamming, Kamau Brathwaite, Stuart Hall, and certainly Walter Rodney. And like her distinguished predecessors, Andaiye and her brilliant collaborator, Alissa Trotz, did not put this book together in order to gather dust in a library. The title says it all: *The Point is to Change the World*.

The title comes from Karl Marx's eleventh and final thesis on Feuerbach (1845): "The philosophers have only interpreted the world in various ways; the point is to change it." To be clear, Marx was not arguing that action takes precedence over analysis. Rather, he was challenging his old comrades, the Young Hegelians, who believed that a change of ideas—their ideas—would change reality. Marx, by contrast, was insisting that the problems of philosophy cannot be solved by passively interpreting the world as it is, but only by remolding the world to resolve the philosophical contradictions inherent in it. Struggle produces new philosophy, not the other way around. Action produces our reality which then demands new analysis, which in turn possesses material force. Andaiye embodies and exemplifies this idea in every way. The profound insights contained in the essays, speeches, letters, interviews, and diary entries that make up this book were all produced in struggle. Those ideas have shaped movements committed to changing social, economic, and political reality in the Caribbean and for women around the world, which in turn, created new conditions and new horizons of possibility.

One of those horizons of possibility she identified occurred in the period between 1979 and 1983—beginning with revolutions in Nicaragua, Iran, and of course, Grenada. The New Jewel Movement's (NJM) overthrow of Eric Gairy's regime on March 13, 1979, marked a sea change, not only for the left in the Caribbean but throughout the hemisphere and around the world. From her unique perspective as a founding member of the WPA, Andaiye vividly recalled how the promise of socialist transformation in Grenada emboldened the movement in Guyana to take on the Burnham regime. But those heady days faced a head wind of reaction. In Jamaica, Michael Manley's efforts to build socialism through parliamentary measures and redistributive policies funded through deficit finance collapsed under the weight of mounting debt, internal violence, and IMF-imposed structural adjustment policies. The neo-liberal revolution reached new heights with the elections of Margaret Thatcher and Ronald Reagan. Then Walter Rodney was assassinated in 1980. Two years later, Suriname's military dictatorship directed the murder of Bram Behr, the popular journalist and Communist leader, along with 14 of his comrades. And then, in a coup to overthrow the NJM leadership, Maurice Bishop was killed, along with seven other leaders (including his long-time partner and minister of education, Jaqueline Creft). The coup paved the way for the US invasion of Grenada, completing the counterrevolution.

Andaiye's critical analysis of these events reminds us that the Caribbean stood at the very epicenter of what was arguably the last horizon of revolutionary possibility before the consolidation of the neoliberal order. But she always resisted the tendency to mourn or lament what could have been, or to blame these defeats entirely on US imperialism. Instead, she engaged in sober criticism and self-criticism. She pointed to the weakening and decline of mass organizations in Grenada under Bishop, which she attributed in part to the anti-democratic character of the Marxist–Leninist cadre party. As early as 1982, elements of the Caribbean left had begun to break with Bishop over the lack of democracy in Grenada. Seeing the writing on the wall, as it were, the WPA abandoned its plans to become a cadre organization and opted instead to remain a mass party with a robust electoral strategy.

She considered how the WPA might have better handled racial tensions between Indian- and African-descended people by encouraging more autonomous organizing across sectors. She examined how class and gender dynamics within the movement privileges middle-class and male leadership over working-class and women's leadership. The lessons she draws here are especially relevant today, when a growing number of self-styled activist-intellectuals have abandoned the Third World project for a racial politics that reduces the structure of the modern world to a single immutable antagonism: between blackness and anti-blackness. What Andaiye and her WPA comrades came to understand in struggle was that the racial antagonisms between people of African and Indian descent were historical, not fixed nor insurmountable. Finding some bases for unity was not only politically desirable but a matter of life and death. They had neither the time nor luxury to debate whether non-blacks could ever move beyond or dispense with anti-blackness. And as Andaiye makes clear throughout the book, they had to attend to multiple vectors of antagonisms and contradictions across different sectors. Analyzing and addressing the multiple contradictions of gender, race, and class has long been the core of her theoretical and organizing work.

Andaiye dispels the myth that Rodney's assassination and the overthrow of the New Jewel Movement killed the WPA. On the contrary, the WPA continued to organize across racial divisions and even extended its work from the coast to the interior in order to mobilize indigenous communities. She attributed the decline of multiracial politics in Guyana to privileging elections over broad mass mobilizations of labor, civil society, women, and peasants fighting for land redistribution. By the time Guyana's economy was forced to submit to IMF-imposed structural adjustment policies, there were very few political institutions independent of the two political parties, and as a consequence there were no mass organizations capable of resisting austerity.

Early on, Andaiye recognized that the mobilization of women as an autonomous sector was key to advancing a revolutionary agenda. She saw first-hand how the devolution of Grenada's National Women's Organization undermined democracy and produced a socialist vision that excluded, for example, reproductive labor and the problem of gendered violence. And she questioned the gender dynamics within her own party, observing that the enormous demands of organizing "meant that there was not a single woman in its leadership who had children to care for." Thus middle-class women who could afford childcare and domestic service occupied leadership positions, not only in the WPA but also in autonomous women's organizations. In other words, she came to see what many of her comrades could not—the critical importance of understanding reproductive labor in order to advance a more radical critique of capitalism and theory of revolution.

Building on the lessons learned in the 1980s, Andaiye emerged as one of the most incisive and imaginative feminist thinkers in the hemisphere. She became a dynamic and critical force within the Caribbean Association for Feminist Research and Action (CAFRA), and in 1986 co-founded Red Thread Women's Organisation in Guyana, a multiracial women's network independent of any political party. Andaiye became a leading proponent of the international Wages for Housework perspective which brought the unwaged work of reproduction, ignored by the left concentrating exclusively on the "point of production," into political focus. Selma James, founder of the IWFH and Andaiye's close colleague, argued that women's unwaged work was central to the reproduction of capital. The IWFH redefined the working class to include both waged and unwaged workers, an antiracist perspective which put non-industrial and industrial worlds together. This was not a sterile academic theory but an international campaign which developed and expanded over many years by bringing together different sectors and nationalities and their struggles. Its central strategic demand for wages for housework from the state evolved into the Global Women's Strike (GWS), "invest in caring not killing" and "a living wage for mothers and other carers," which drew especially on the movements of single mothers, workers on the land—subsistence, bonded, low waged—and for pay equity. This perspective is not an attempt to reform capitalism in order to achieve something resembling gender equity. It was conceived as an anti-capitalist and anti-imperialist strategy demanding that the reproduction of every human life rather than the market be central to the economy, to every development and to the ecology.

Andaiye combined her experience with the movement Walter Rodney had led, with Red Thread and with the GWS to fuel an analysis of structural adjustment policies which for the first time made the exploitation of women visible and central.

Furthermore, the crisis generated by neoliberalism provoked an increase in state, domestic, interpersonal, community and gendered violence, as well as racial tensions and xenophobia not just in Guyana but throughout the Caribbean. Taken together, Andaiye observes, all of these factors have not only deepened gender inequality but accelerated the exploitation of women, who are now burdened with providing more as social services and subsidies are slashed, men are forced to migrate for work, and women have even less time to organize against the conditions.

She poses a profound question: "What happens to housewives if the fight against the IMF is a fight for the unions? Because you know that today unions don't organize housewives, though they once did!" As the point of reference of the GWS in Guyana, Andaiye believes that women can—and do—organize. She takes the left to task for underestimating the power of housewives to mobilize massively and effectively. She explicitly cites the example of the 1983 food rebellion in Guyana, a struggle led by housewives in alliance with trade unionists in the Sugar and Bauxite Workers Unity Committee.

For Andaiye, the street, the state, the workplace, and the household were not bounded, discrete domains but part of an entire interlocking system of exploitation and contested terrain. She learned first-hand that the incorporation of oppositional movements into official governing and administrative agencies, either at the national or international scale, could have disastrous consequences. Despite three decades of incredible work with Red Thread (the multiracial women's organization she co-founded in Guyana in 1986) and various international women's organizations, Andaiye concluded that the absence of a vibrant grassroots movement led by poor women opened the door for the "NGO-ization of the movement." The policy agenda reflected the perspectives of professional women, which tended "to isolate gender from its interconnections with class, race and other power relations, and to put technocratic 'solutions' in place of transformative solutions." It is a damning appraisal, to which she holds *herself* to account. Knowing Andaiye's principled record of struggle, I cannot agree with her self-critique. Nevertheless, she has a point. NGOs work in concert with the state and international bodies that are consistent with neoliberal policies. The capture of "civil society" by the liberal state creates stasis, an equilibrium of power that does nothing to radically alter free trade policies, redistribute wealth, end austerity, or empower working people to decide on their own destiny. She tells us all of this not as a *mea culpa* or a lament, but as a lesson for future struggles.

Andaiye greatly admired and promoted Clotil Walcott, a working class organizer who, immediately after meeting the Wages For Housework Campaign, formed the National Union of Domestic Employees (NUDE) in Trinidad, bringing together low-waged and unwaged workers (Clotil Walcott got the Trinidad government to pass the first legislation anywhere to measure and value unwaged work). Both NUDE and Red Thread, represented by Andaiye, were part of a bi-lingual network of domestic workers based in the Caribbean and Latin America. Andaiye was a member of Women of Color in the Global Women's Strike (formerly Black Women for Wages for Housework) of which Margaret Prescod was a founder. They had met in the 1960s in New York at a group of Caribbean political people (Maurice Bishop was a member) and remained close friends; in the last 15 years Andaiye and Margaret worked together especially in support of the Haitian movement.

Sadly, Andaiye will never see *The Point is to Change the World* in its published form or witness how new generations of activists will put the book to use. She joined the ancestors on May 31, 2019, surrounded by friends, family, and comrades, aware that the book was complete and on its way to the publisher. Her passing was shocking, but not surprising. Andaiye was a die-hard revolutionary who had come face-to-face with death many times. She was a long-distance runner, fearless, dedicated, and steadfast in her love for the people. But the struggle had taken its toll. She suffered physical violence and bouts of depression. She was among the first on the scene to witness the mutilated and burned body of her dear friend and comrade, Walter Rodney. For 30 years she survived not one but two different bouts of cancer. And in each case, she somehow turned her traumas and illnesses and disease into political lessons. She writes movingly in these pages about what it meant to suffer in community, how the collective work required to sustain her life in those periods of vulnerability gave her a renewed appreciation for affective, caring work. And she excoriated the medical industry for reproducing gendered, raced, and class hierarchies by concentrating authority and "expertise" in the hands of doctors, leaving patients feeling powerless and isolated. The conceit of modern medicine as science, she pointed out, has the effect of silencing patients, rendering their opinions or self-diagnoses invalid. If that's not bad enough, expertise is specialized to such a degree that modern medicine is unable to treat the whole body as an entity, let alone the mind and body together, or the social body.

Attending to the social body … this is what Andaiye has always been about. Unlike so many radicals who either look at what's immediately in front of them or look back to a romantic past (usually dwelling in the French Revolution!), or leap headlong into the dream world of a utopian future, Andaiye had 360-degree vision. She saw all around her, and into the cracks and crevices of life and labor many well-meaning radicals overlook. She knew the social body is everything—the visible and the invisible—and liberation requires the overturning of every form of oppression. The point, indeed, is to change the world. But by reading this book you'll discover that Andaiye's world was always bigger than most of us have ever imagined.

Andaiye presente!

Robin D. G. Kelley is Professor of History and Black Studies at UCLA, and author of several books, including, *Thelonious Monk: The Life and Times of an American Original*; *Africa Speaks, America Answers: Modern Jazz in Revolutionary Times*; and *Freedom Dreams: The Black Radical Imagination*. He recently co-edited Walter Rodney's *The Russian Revolution: A View From the Third World* (Verso, 2018).

The Principle of Justice as a Labor of Caring

Honor Ford-Smith

At the start of her impressive collection of writings, Andaiye explains exactly who her book is meant for. It is meant for activists, she says: folks who want to change the world and "overturn the power relations which are embedded in every unequal facet of our lives." Through essays, letters, journal entries and other writings, she tells the story of an activist life, lived in the context of Caribbean social movements after flag independence. The result is a book which, without a word of jargon, narrates in clear and down-to-earth language, the development of a reflexive praxis of emancipation grounded in context. At a time when right wing populism, economic inequality, environmental destruction and virulent racism are on the rise, this collection offers an inspiring narrative of what it means to fight together across difference for a just and inclusive politic.

Andaiye takes a clear look not just at the society that formed her, but also at herself. With candor, humor and sometimes irony, she discusses her formation over decades, beginning with her own lived experience as a black, middle-class woman at the end of British colonialism. She presents struggles for justice—not as spectacular or heroic acts of courage or salvation—but rather as an ordinary part of the meaning of being human. She is uniquely able to reflect on her own vulnerabilities and treat them as intimate teachers—her brush with madness and her struggle against cancer. She describes the early years of building the Working People's Alliance, the meaning and impact of the murders of Walter Rodney and Maurice Bishop and the fall of the Grenada Revolution. She reflects on the idea of betrayal in its multiple meanings through a discussion of the anti-colonial writing of George Lamming arguing that too often "those we nurture and sacrifice into power, help not us but our enemies." She charts her path through the invasion of Grenada to the formation of the Guyanese women's organization, Red Thread and her own long fight against cancer.

Throughout she is unflinchingly critical and questioning of the global forces that create inequality, but she is also relentless about naming the ways these forces take up residence within us. She makes her criticisms carefully, not irresponsibly and always by identifying the ways in which these mistakes and others, implicate her. Instead of the hubris and self-justifying narratives of political leaders, to which we have become accustomed, Andaiye is uncompromisingly self-reflexive. She is always the woman who is unafraid to ask awkward questions, to sniff out pretentiousness and hypocrisy within and without.

She criticizes the state and left organizations for ignoring the voices and the needs of grassroots women. She calls out radical approaches which remain at their core intrinsically committed to a politics of hierarchy, respectability and reversal and so end up repeating the mistakes they were meant to challenge. She denounces those who spread terror through random violence and racial attacks in Guyanese communities of all races and those who collude with it by remaining silent. She challenges feminists for turning activist impulses into NGOs dependent on international aid, for equating race-consciousness with African-Caribbean experience, for leaving out working class leadership.

From this place of unflinching reflexivity, she asks us to imagine alternatives to the injustice which often seems naturalized in the region. She argues for a deeply accountable politics—one that learns from mistakes; one that is perpetually attentive (as she is) to what folks on the ground are actively doing so as to survive (she gives the example of how women transformed themselves into smugglers); and one that is grounded in a process of action/reflection on such transformative capabilities. This politics of accountability places the needs of the impoverished at the center of how we organize and what we organize for. And it is from this position that she is able to elaborate and advance a radical politics of anti-racism and care.

To the best of my knowledge she is one of a very few people in the region who have attempted to think about what a radical and equal multi-racial society might look like and to develop a practice that addresses how it might be brought into being. Perhaps this was possible because of the particular context of Guyana—and only Guyana, with Indian and African majorities, its hybridity and its indigenous heartland. But I would like to think that she, like Walter Rodney before her, has opened a space for a larger conversation, one which confronts the silences about race and racism in all its complicated and often violent forms. As I read it, the radical anti-racist practice she proposes requires challenging all the racial hierarchies that capitalism relies on, deflecting attention away from racial binaries, without, at the same time reinscribing them. In the case of Red Thread, this meant organizing from the bottom of the racial/class hierarchies to challenge the material and gendered injustices that underlie racial formation. Centering the interests of the poorest women in the way we organize and what we organize for means attending to both the importance of working in autonomous sectors but it also means working to sustain inclusive spaces in which we can struggle together. Through this work and across sectors, folks begin to confront and unravel the way racial ideology contaminates everyday relationships even as they take aim at its larger more opaque and hydra-headed global formations. This means creating an atmosphere in which there is a willingness to accept being challenged around the privilege and pain afforded by racism. It means doing the extremely hard work of listening carefully across these historically constituted differences while challenging and working through colonial ways of seeing. In this way we can begin to unravel racial ideology. This working together, as Alissa Trotz points out, is best epitomized in the work done by Red Thread around and after the floods of 2004—Indo-Guyanese and Afro-Guyanese from settings where racial relations are heavily spatialized organized inside and outside of their own villages. They took on myriad tasks such as compiling and counting their immediate needs, decrying the unequal and politicized distribution of relief. They demanded representation in disaster planning discussions, called for accountability for how relief moneys were spent, researched the ways in which "gender, race, class and disability mediated the distribution of vulnerability (calling for a cancellation of household debt; stressing the need to address historic levels of poverty that existed *prior* to the floods, and differentiated people's ability to escape or mitigate the damage)" (Trotz 2010).

Andaiye represents herself in her writing as a woman who comes to be guided by the *principle of justice as a labor of caring*. This, she suggests, can become a key value in a fight against the layered violences of various kinds which in societies like the Caribbean are often turned inward, and fractured along lines of race, class, age, and gender. One way to think about the kind of politics this approach calls into being is to look at its impact on Andaiye as a cancer survivor. Any of the challenges which Andaiye faced in her life could have been enough to stop anyone in their tracks. But she never burned out. She was very ill, and doubtless battled the aftershocks of trauma, but she was never silenced. The murder of her comrade and its echoes in the WPA and beyond, a brush with madness which saw her briefly hospitalized in a psych ward in the United States, unsteady employment and a perpetually low income, the partial destruction of her home by fire and a life with fatal illness as a companion—any one of these would have been enough to halt many. But Andaiye continued to speak, to write, and to act until her cancer caused her death at the old age of 77.

No doubt she was a remarkable person, but that is not enough to explain her longevity or the quality of her living. The many networks and interconnections involved in her care and, through that care their own, are evidence of how caring labor can outwit death. Her endurance depended on an entanglement with collective community care and through this she was able to keep the doctors on their toes, and create and sustain a long life. But there is something else. Caring labor also gives back to those who do it because, where it is recognized as essential to existence, it enables a resonant community that counters the all too familiar alienation of life in the midst of profound inequality. Absence of care is death and so the work of care calls into being a recognition that life means something because of the meaning we create together.

Andaiye gave something to everyone around her through this ethical practice of a politics of care. Her chosen and often queer family from all places, orientations and backgrounds, reciprocated in ways which built rich interconnections and enduring communities. She co-founded the Guyanese Cancer Society and made public the labor associated with living with the illness. She supported many cancer victims with visits and encouragement and long conversations about treatment. She enabled a discussion about the cost of care linking survival to affordability and she made dry and wicked fun of both the limitations of western medicine as a mode of healing and the excesses of alternative non-western practices. She sent updates to her friends and organized them to support her as she negotiated all that she had to do to stay alive. The medication she needed was often unavailable in Guyana and had to be procured through the rapid mobilization of these care networks. She deployed her ironic wit as part of her armory of survival. "Ah tired telling people thanks," she would say, sighing and rolling her eyes at some gift someone had given her. The slogan "Touch one, touch all" which the women from African and Asian communities chanted together in their struggles against sexual violence speaks volumes about the forms of solidarity generated.

What is remarkable about Andaiye's book, like Andaiye herself, is its liveliness, its accessibility and its unpretentiousness as it offers a thoughtful and compelling portrait of a period and a place that is often overlooked in discussions of the global south. Its portrait of individual actors and moments are compassionate without sentimentality and challenging without predictable or heavy handed didacticism. This important work offers a counter narrative to the inevitability of neoliberal excess in the Caribbean. It also offers an alternative perspective to the limitations of both discourses on development and identity politics at a time when both are badly needed. Now when the history of the Third Worldist moment and what followed it, is being re-evaluated, this compelling voice needs to be heard.

Honor Ford-Smith was founding Artistic Director of the Sistren (Sisters) Theatre Collective and a founding member of the Caribbean Association for Feminist Research and Action. She coauthored and edited *Lionheart Gal: Lifestories of Jamaican Women*; *3 Jamaican Plays: A Postcolonial Anthology 1977–1987*; and her collection of poems, *My Mother's Last Dance*, was published in 1997 (Sister Vision). She is Associate Professor of Cultural and Artistic Practices for Environmental and Social Justice in the Faculty of Environmental Studies at York University, Toronto, Canada, and for the last ten years has worked on the performance cycles *Letters from the Dead* and *Song for the Beloved*, both of which remember those who have died as a result of state violence and the violence of armed strong men in the Caribbean and its diaspora.

REFERENCE

Trotz, D. Alissa. 2010. "Shifting the Ground Beneath Us: Social Reproduction, Grassroots Women and the 2005 Floods in Guyana." *Interventions* 12(1) (2010): 120.

Editor's Note
On the Politics of Precision

This collection of writings began as a conversation with Andaiye over ten years ago in light of her ongoing experience of living with cancer and the urgency some of us at the time felt about gathering up her work. It took on new meaning and focus after a fire in 2010 that destroyed part of Andaiye's home—salvaging material, reconstructing edited essays, hunting down lost references. Karen de Souza, Andaiye's close friend and political associate (first in the WPA, and later Red Thread) describes the process of completing this book thus:[1]

These words and so many more were all tapped out with one finger (in the computer years; pounded out pre-word processor, in the typewriter years). I'm sure at the time they discussed and agreed to compile this book Alissa thought it would be a short-term project—after all, the pieces were already written: they only had to be gathered, selected and organised! Any notion of a short time frame however, did not account for Andaiye's capacity to refine, revise and edit her writing. As it worked out Andaiye largely released the manuscript before going into hospital on May 7, and she declared that she was happier with the edits that she was able to make after the publisher requested that the number of words be reduced. This process reminded me of the almost magical edits she did on the poems of Mobutu Kamara (an activist who Andaiye worked with in the WPA), carving a few crisp and poignant stanzas from the meandering pages that he had written.

This was not just about deciding what to include in the collection; it involved extensive discussion and—with the exception of letters to the press—seemingly unending edits, including of essays that had previously appeared elsewhere. Of one of these, Andaiye announced to us that "it's full of repetition … it's not me who published it, it's you, when you all thought I might die in surgery. I love you all bad but this thing want editing … I can only hope that … my readers could read better than you!"[2] On another occasion after finding errors in a document I had triumphantly sent to her to sign off on, she declared exasperatedly that this was proof that she really could not "ups and die" until the book was finished. And back to the drawing board we went. From her hospital bed in the ICU this past May, Andaiye continued to work, jotting notes and dictating a few things in relation to the manuscript. She was hoping to complete a talk she had agreed earlier in the year to give to students in the summer program run by the Institute for Gender and Development Studies at the Cave Hill, Barbados campus of the University of the West Indies.[3]

Andaiye died in the early evening of May 31, 2019. It is nothing less than agonizing to have finally reached the finish line without her here to celebrate this journey with us, not least because of how much *loving work* went into this volume, how much *work* she put herself, and us, through. That she demanded no less of herself was an example to us all, even as she became steadily weaker; as she put it, "living with the conscious expectation of dying has been one of the most disorienting features of the last four years." In the void left by her passing, I have come to recognize the political significance of her scrupulous attention to detail (she has described this aspect of herself as "obsessive"). A favorite phrase of Andaiye's was that "language is a product and producer of action." Such caring attention, as exemplified in the essays in this volume, represent what we might describe as a *politics of precision* that is simultaneously and inextricably an orientation to justice and a mode of inhabitation.[4]

Precision as an orientation to justice demands the kind of revolutionary discipline described by Walter Rodney where "we don't take ourselves too seriously, or take the system seriously," and where "we move towards understanding that we're working seriously to establish an alternative, as distinct from working seriously to participate in the system" (Rodney 1990: 5). As Andaiye put it, "I was working over and over the book, adjusting and whatever, to make one point—how to change the world." She was deeply inspired by Nina López's description of Selma James's collection of writings as organizing tools rather than simply explanations (James 2012). From the very beginning and all the way through, she grappled with two questions: Who was the book for? To what use might it be put? She hoped that younger generations of activists in Guyana, the Caribbean and beyond would be a primary audience, and was adamant that the grassroots women of Red Thread, the Guyanese organization she co-founded over three decades ago, had to be able to find themselves in it. The title she settled on, *The Point is to Change the World*, is striking in its clarity and simplicity. Most importantly perhaps, it springs from Andaiye's unwavering belief in the self-organized and abundant energies, activities and capacities of working people, starting with those most vulnerable and excluded, the unwaged carers of our society.

Precision as a mode of inhabitation directs our attention to the ways Andaiye sought to listen, understand and move in the world, attuned to what Barbadian novelist George Lamming would describe as the urgent need to revolutionize human relations. But in seeking to answer the question she once posed in this way—"How will we organize to live?"—precision could never be prescription. For Andaiye, a non-negotiable commitment to seeking out the social motion in a particular place and time necessarily required an orientation to flow, a disposition, if you will, to fluidity. It was expressed in part by her legendary self-deprecating humor, what Karen de Souza describes as "her capacity to laugh at herself and to prick the bubble of self-importance of those around her. A story of the WPA's first center told by Andaiye never failed to contrast her title—coordinator—with one primary function, fetching buckets of water to clean the toilet." That relentless scrutiny, starting with oneself, is a consistent theme throughout this volume, offering a radical instantiation of Guyanese poet Martin Carter's injunction that "all are involved! all are consumed!" In her preface and at the end of Essay 26, Andaiye readily acknowledges what she has not addressed; she revisits the anti-dictatorial resistance of 1970s and 1980s Guyana in order to account for earlier and complete misrecognition of the significant contributions of housewives and other carers (Essay 13); her tribute to Audre Lorde offers a moving account of a friendship forged through illness and across differences (Essay 16). From her hospital bed, shortly before she was no longer able to speak, she began a conversation about what to do with her as yet unpublished work; among the instructions she left was that "all those things done for anybody, anywhere that says gender is binary you reject. Amend it where it is a small point but otherwise reject it." In an interview recently published in *Monthly Review*, Selma James offers an analysis of the movement implications of C. L. R. James's analysis that resonates beautifully with Andaiye's practice:

> What happens now, increasingly, in most struggles, is that different sectors speak up and broaden the demands to ensure that they are included and become visible and integral to what the whole movement stands for: women, the nationalities, the races, the ages, the disabled, the sexual choices and iden-tities, the prisoners, the veterans, the children ... C. L. R. does not spell this out but opens the way for what the movements have articulated in action. For him our job as anti-capitalists was to see that even before organizations of struggle announce themselves, their direction is welcomed, encouraged, protected, advertised. (James and Augustin 2019)

And reflecting on the importance of advancing the multiracial power of the Guyanese working people, Andaiye put it this way: "the task is unfinished. It is as true today as it was when [Walter] Rodney made the point, that working to build unity in struggle in the face of all that militates against it is a precon-dition of the *continued* work of *enlarging* our freedom" (emphasis added). In February, frustrated by the state of what she referred to as so-called progressive politics in the Caribbean, she expressed her desire to draft a statement titled "Here We Stand":

saying to all the "left" of the region and the world—we are trying to practice and demand a politics [of self-emancipation] that is anti-imperialist, Pan-Africanist, anti-racist, anti-sexist, anti-homophobic and transphobic etc. For us [there is] no contradiction; it's all about expanding human freedom.

Guyana has entered yet another period of political uncertainty and stalemate with the successful passing of a no-confidence motion against the government in December 2018, in a context in which the multinational oil giant Exxon Mobil has projected it would begin offshore oil production in December 2019. Against this backdrop, Andaiye described herself as "*incidentally*, retired due to illness not age" (emphasis added), noting that "part of the loss of power I've experienced is the loss of work as we normally define it, which in my case was political activism." And yet, in the midst of finalizing edits to the manuscript and her rapidly failing health, Andaiye had begun working with some of us to compile the writings of long-standing WPA activist Moses Bhagwan, and had started to jot notes to offer her perspective "as an old/er woman who used to be an activist in the Rodney led WPA and in Red Thread at a national level but also regionally and internationally":

If we believe that changing Guyana is the work of elites we will continue to rely on new structures of power and/or to create NGOs with foreign funding whose task is advocacy, and which are often hostage to the ambitious. But if we understand that only with people-led popular participation in changing Guyana will we change it, we will aim at building movements which organize, struggle, protest, resist … [this is] not old-fashioned; look at indigenous movements and struggles in other parts of the Americas.

Karen de Souza has rightly noted that "some people described Andaiye's 'longevity' as living on borrowed time, but really, there was nothing borrowed about her years. They were years carved out by her determination, by the amount of work she did, and by the support of her community." Andaiye had once written that

The sicker I get, the more work it takes to survive … the more work it takes to survive, the less I'm seen—or see myself—as doing any work at all. The unwaged work of caring for people the society dismisses as most unpro-ductive, most unable to "work" (those who are immobilized by chronic illness, severely disabled, or older) starting with the work we do to care for ourselves—is the most uncounted and unvalued work of all.

But Andaiye had shown us how to recognize and value this work, what she calls the "conspiracies of mutual caring" organized in the face of, because of and despite the power relations we face. This past May, it manifested in the communities of carers who (like the Caribbean sistren who held her up when she was first diagnosed with cancer), gathered physically and virtually from all around the world, showing up in word and deed, offering love, energy and laughter to her and to each other. Andaiye had said that "No one ever wants to go. The question is whether you reach the point where you can let go. It doesn't mean all fear and anxiety go but that there are other things as well, including the certainty that you are loved." She was not only loved, but she had helped create the conditions in which it was possible to love her in that way.

We are deeply grateful (a word Andaiye would have used very sparingly and always with narrowed eyes, but which is entirely appropriate here) that Andaiye was able to have the final say on the sections and order of the essays. She had read and offered her usual extensive edits on Clem Seecharan's foreword, and I read what Honor Ford-Smith had written to her in hospital. Robin Kelley's contribution came while she was in hospital and she asked us to print it out and put it in a folder by her bed, along with an interview, "Beyond Boundaries," that Selma James had sent her and which has since been published by *Monthly Review* (James and Augustin 2019). Anthony Bogues's afterword was completed after her passing; immense thanks are due to him for immediately responding with enthusiasm and support when we first approached him four years ago about placing the manuscript with Pluto's Black Critique series. Andaiye described the "colors of the sky when the sun in Guyana is rising or setting over the Atlantic, and which have always made me feel at peace" (Essay 15); the coloring inside the lettering on the front cover was taken from images of a Guyanese sunset by Areta Buk and artist Abbyssinian Carto (Andaiye's brother).

In her preface, Andaiye joins Walter Rodney (whose *History of the Guyanese Working People* she edited and which was posthumously published, as this book is) in acknowledging Guyanese elder Eusi Kwayana, for example. We have come full circle—even as we know she would have rolled her eyes at this—as we thank Andaiye, for example.

Alissa Trotz
Toronto
December 2019

NOTES

1. This is how Karen describes her relationship with Andaiye: "My path met Andaiye's in 1979 and we maintained a close connection until I witnessed her last breath. In the 40 years during which I was variously her editor's assistant and proofreader, her technician/computer fixer, solver of software mysteries, witness to some of her lowest moments when she was immobilized by grief and/or racked with illness or the supposed treatment for the illness, I learnt much about the indomitable will that

THE POINT IS TO CHANGE THE WORLD

kept her alive three decades after she was first diagnosed with and treated for cancer. I also learnt about the esteem (not always love) in which she was held both in and outside the Caribbean, and about the widespread commitment to keeping her alive."

2. This was back in 2012 when, 23 years after diagnosis and treatment for non-Hodgkin's lymphoma, Andaiye received a diagnosis of breast cancer and underwent a mastectomy (see Essay 15).

3. The talk Andaiye completed, "The Power Relations in the Personal and the Conspiracies of Mutual Caring We Organize to Fight Them," is an expanded version of Essay 15, and was published by *Scholar and Feminist Online* (16:1, Winter 2020).

4. Having drafted this note on precision, I returned to Selma James's anthology, where I immediately realized that this was also a term that Nina López refers to in her introduction, describing Selma's work as exemplifying "a determination to be precise" and quoting Selma herself identifying imprecision as "the enemy" (James 2012: 9, 11).

REFERENCES

James, Selma and Ron Augustin. 2019. "Beyond Boundaries." *Monthly Review* 71(4). Retrieved from https://monthlyreview.org/2019/09/01/beyond-boundaries.
James, Selma. 2012. *Sex, Race and Class: The Perspective of Winning. A Selection of Writings, 1952–2011*, Oakland, CA: PM Press.
Rodney, Walter. 1990. *Walter Rodney Speaks: The Making of an African Intellectual.* Trenton, NJ: Africa World Press.

Preface and Acknowledgements

This anthology is meant for activists, younger and older, outside of and within the university, in the Caribbean, the Caribbean diaspora and beyond, who know—even if that is all they think they know—that the point is to change the world. It is about the power relations embedded in every facet of our lives and the need to organize together to overturn them. The pieces in it are in varied styles—formal presentations, essays, informal talks, newspaper columns, a radio viewpoint, a ministerial brief, small items of auto/biography, letters to the press. Almost all were written or spoken as the activist I was for 50+ years. I put the anthology together because I hope it can contribute to people who are organizing for change.

Part One, "Learning Lessons from Past Organizing," comes out of years of activism in part of the Caribbean where in the late 1970s to the mid-1980s, particularly in Grenada, Guyana and Jamaica, the movement for transformation was advanced. It includes criticism and self-criticism of the feminist movement centered in the Caribbean Association for Feminist Research and Action (CAFRA) and the left movement which briefly allied the New Jewel Movement (NJM) of Grenada, the Working People's Alliance (WPA) of Guyana, the Workers' Party of Jamaica (WPJ), the Antigua Caribbean Liberation Movement (ACLM) and others. It also analyses the race divides which have derailed the struggle of Guyanese people for much of the last 60 years and examines the pros, cons and challenges of organizing within and against those divides.

Part Two presents "A Different Perspective," one which comes out of the politics of the Global Women's Strike (GWS), and the International Wages for Housework (IWFH) campaign born in 1972 which coordinates it, and whose perspective shapes it. This is a good place to say that while there are some pieces in the anthology that Selma James, the founder of the IWFH campaign and co-founder of the GWS, has never seen and with which she might disagree, her political perspective has been important in the development of mine. James rejects the economism and substitution of party for people that have been imposed in various places in the name of Marxism; instead, she reclaims a Marx that always begins with the individual within the class movement. The body of her work across 60 years has recently been published under the title *Sex, Race and Class: The Perspective of Winning*, writings that in the introduction Nina Lopez rightly describes as "organizing tools." One of the tools which I have found most useful is the piece entitled "Sex, Race and Class" (1974), which describes the "hierarchy of labor powers," at the bottom of which is ""*a hitherto invisible stratum ...—the housewife—to which there corresponds no wage at all.*"

Although, as James has pointed out to me in conversation, this analysis was written 45 years ago and the advent of autonomous movements representing different sectors and of globalization have led to changes in the division of labor, in my view it still points the way to how we should organize if we mean to unify the struggles of all sectors against capital, ensuring that we begin with those with the least power and resources in the capitalist hierarchy (the unwaged worker) so that all are included. Rather than an approach to organizing which begins with prescriptions of where we are going (a vision, yes, but not prescriptions), we see to it that every autonomous sector's struggle is incorporated in the whole, that there is no hierarchy of which sector is the more exploited, or the more important; and that each sector fights for the demands of all. These are the principles on which I argue that we should work not to revive the old Caribbean movement for transformation but to give birth to a new one.

Part Three, "The Political in the Personal," is based on the view that the personal is not just personal: the story of each of us, if we tell it true, carries in it everyone's story; and our collected stories carry in them the power relations of the whole society. The section begins with my personal story of surviving cancer (twice), key elements of which were the relationships that grew with other women involved in the same or a similar struggle, including my friend Audre Lorde. I had first experienced a special form of this kind of relationship in the women's ward of a psychiatric hospital in the United States in the early 1970s. Class, race, and gender relations were stark: almost all the inmates in the ward were working class—black, brown and white; almost all the nurses female, the guards male. How psychiatric hospitals (like prisons) are used and who is locked away in them is profoundly political. The aspect of that experience that gave me back some power in an almost completely disempowering environment was the conspiracy of mutual caring created among and by a group of us as women warehoused in a space where we knew in that way of knowing that has no words, that acting only as individuals we might be completely destroyed. Part Three ends with a section that discusses "Undomesticating Violence," all the kinds of violence whose misnaming as say, corporal punishment or domestic violence masks the fact that they are about the abuse of power, including sometimes the power of position wielded by people ranging from preachers to political leaders.

Part Four—"Towards Strengthening the Movement"—contains a single essay: "Gender, Race and Class: A Perspective on the Contemporary Caribbean Struggle." This is an analysis which leads to a call for organizing in the region against *all* exploitation, discrimination, and subordination, correcting the weaknesses of past and present organizing: the left has never learned to see the concerns of women, and even less of LGBTI+ persons and people with disabilities, as integral to working class interests; and those who organize as women, LGBTI+ persons, and people with disabilities are typically not anti-capitalist and anti-imperialist and downplay the power relations of class. The analysis in Part Four was presented in 2009, but the changes in the world since then make the organizing it calls for even more urgently needed.

The anthology ends with "Last Word," a discussion of some of the last speaking and writing on and for the Guyanese working people by Walter Rodney, with whom I organized in the WPA. The section is called "Last Word" not because it is a summing up of the anthology, and still less to suggest that what Rodney wrote was the last word on any issue; I've heard him argue that people who write should publish as part of a conversation with others to collectively work towards ever increasing understanding of the issues. It is above all this coming together of adherence to ideological principle, careful study, openness to change and commitment to the struggle to change the world that I believe we should learn from him.

*   *   *

When Alissa Trotz, the editor of the anthology, volunteered to help me compile it she thought we could do it in a few long meetings; after all, we were putting together material I had already written, some of it previously published. Instead, for many reasons including my illness, it took a few long years, and we had to call in assistance from several friends: Nigel Westmaas, unofficial archivist of the WPA, to track down dates and documents; Eusi Kwayana (the oldest of us), to jog our memories of details that the rest of us had forgotten; Karen de Souza, to read and proof drafts, and to rescue me from my continued inadequacies with technology; and Carol Lawes, the most meticulous copy editor I've ever encountered, to remove my fears that errors were creeping by all the rest of us. There would have been no anthology without the time, labor, patience and skill they each contributed. Particular thanks are due to Alissa. I also thank Clem Seecharan for an introduction of astonishing generosity.

I don't want to overstate what this anthology does. It has clear weaknesses, some of which derive from my relative distance from political organizing over the last few years. There are obvious gaps in it resulting from the loss of several pieces of work in a serious fire at my home in 2010; periods when I didn't organize (or write) because of serious illness; and the fact that I often did not write in my own name but in the name of the main groups in which I was active in Guyana. There are also gaps or weaknesses which reflect weaknesses in my political work: above all, there is little or nothing about the threat of extinction from global warming, about care of the environment, about culture, and about the cyber movement in the discussion of making the regional movement.

* * *

Sometime in 1980, not long before he was killed, Walter Rodney mentioned how much he regretted not being able to acknowledge by name some persons who had given him useful information for the book he was then completing, *A History of the Guyanese Working People: 1881–1905*, for fear of getting them into trouble. For some reason I asked him who else he wanted to acknowledge and he started with his family, added the several WPA people who had given him practical assistance with the book, and ended, "And Eusi, for example." I wrote in those acknowledgements as he had listed them before the manuscript went into the publishers after his death; and I end this preface with the same acknowledgment with which he ended his: Eusi, for example.

Andaiye
Georgetown
April 2019

Abbreviations

ACLM	Antigua Caribbean Liberation Movement
ASCRIA	African Society for Cultural Relations with Independent Africa
CAFRA	Caribbean Association for Feminist Research and Action
CARICOM	Caribbean Community
COI	Commission of Inquiry
CSSP	Continuous Sample Survey of Population
ERP	Economic Recovery Program
FLS	Forward Looking Strategies for the Advancement of Women
GAWU	Guiana Agricultural Workers Union; later, Guyana Agricultural and General Workers Union
GDP	gross domestic product
GMWU	Guyana Mine Workers Union
GNP	gross national product
GWAR	Grassroots Women Across Race
GWS	Global Women's Strike
ILO	International Labour Organization
IMF	International Monetary Fund
IPRA	Indian Political Revolutionary Associates
IWFH	International Wages for Housework Campaign
JHWA	Jamaica Household Workers Association
MAO	Movement against Oppression
MP	Member of Parliament
NAACIE	National Association of Agricultural, Clerical and Industrial Employees
NHL	non-Hodgkin's lymphoma
NIS	National Insurance Scheme
NJM	New Jewel Movement
NWO	National Women's Organization (Grenada)
NUDE	National Union of Domestic Employees
OWP	Organization of Working People
OWTU	Oilfield Workers Trade Union (Trinidad and Tobago)
PNC	People's National Congress
PPP	People's Progressive Party
PRG	People's Revolutionary Government of Grenada
SAP	Structural Adjustment Programme
SBWUC	Sugar and Bauxite Workers Unity Committee
SNA	System of National Accounts
UN	United Nations
VLD	Vanguard for Liberation and Democracy
WAND	Women and Development Unit (UWI School of Continuing Studies)
WAT	Women Against Terror
WPA	Working People's Alliance
WPJ	Workers' Party of Jamaica
WPVP	Working People's Vanguard Party

PART ONE

LEARNING LESSONS FROM PAST ORGANIZING

SECTION I
THE GOOD AND BAD OF SOME EARLIER FEMINIST
AND LEFT ORGANIZING IN THE REGION

ESSAY 1

*The Angle You Look from Determines What You See: Towards
a Critique of Feminist Politics and Organizing in the Caribbean*
[2002]

A PERSONAL THANK YOU TO LUCILLE MATHURIN MAIR

There is nothing I can add to the wealth of tributes that Joycelin Massiah and Peggy Antrobus paid to Lucille Mathurin Mair in their commemorative lectures of 1998 and 2000. All I can do is to offer a small personal thank you.

Lucille Mathurin was my warden at Mary Seacole Hall. That is to say, she was my warden until she refused to allow me to stay in the hall in my third year as an undergraduate. The precursor to this was that she had called me in—twice, I think—to remonstrate with me about the behavior of a gang of women I used to hang out with. She said that apart from having received complaints from others, serious students, about our raucous talk and laughter late into the night, she herself could hear us from her house nearby. She had also observed that we were cutting classes, and altogether acting as though we had not come to the university to study. I asked her why she was speaking only to me: was it because we often hung out in my room? "No," she answered. It was because I was—not the leader of the pack; that would be claiming too much—but in some way its facilitator.

Years later, when she was, I think, Jamaica's Permanent Representative to the United Nations, and I the International Secretary of the Working People's Alliance (WPA) in Guyana, we met at a Socialist International Conference in Venezuela. Now, our positions were clearly very different, and I have no reason to believe that she approved of the political activities of the WPA. But her face lit up when she saw me and we hugged. "You're glad to see I got more serious, aren't you?" I asked. "So it worked," she laughed. I met her several times after that, especially after I joined the organized women's movement in the region.

I still think she should have let me stay in the hall, but I thank her for refusing to act as an enabler in my determination to party my life away because, deep down, I found life confusing.

So, my old warden. This is for you, with respect and love.

WHY A CRITIQUE OF FEMINIST POLITICS IN THE REGION?

This presentation will continue the tradition begun by the first two presenters of the Lucille Mathurin Mair lecture, of using direct experience in the regional women's movement—most directly in the movement in the English-speaking Caribbean—to raise issues about its future. While it offers a critique of feminist politics in the region, it does so from a different angle than Peggy Antrobus (2000: 25), who argued that it was the loss of energy of feminist politics from the work of feminists in the region as administrators, researchers, practitioners and organizers that was leading to the de-politicization of the work. I want to talk about the flaw within feminist politics and feminist organizing itself.

First, let me say what the critique is not. I understood from the moment I wrote the title and sub-title that they might mislead some into believing that I was going to critique feminist politics in the Caribbean from the angle of the proponents of the "male marginalization" thesis. There is no chance of that. I believe, with many other Caribbean women, that it is in all our interests to recognize and address what is happening to *some sectors* of men in the region, including early school-drop-out and a precipitous fall in the proportion of males in the formal education system at all levels.

But to recognize this is different from accepting a thesis that at least implies that while men are moving to the margins of the economy, the education system, and other institutions of Caribbean society, women are moving to the center. We can only believe that if we ignore how power works; for, at no time in our history have the majority of men or women been at the center of economic, political or social power. And interacting with how the hierarchies of nation, class, and race operate, there is a power hierarchy between men and women— and every Caribbean woman, of any race or age and even class, lives a reality of female subordination.

There are many personal testimonies from young women about the persistence of discrimination. Hear, for example, Gabrielle Hosein (2001: 1): "We grew up seeing how much has changed for women, while also seeing where we were still being left out."[1]

If I believe all this, why am I making this critique? In what spirit? Colleagues of mine who have worked with me as gender experts/consultants/resource persons over the last six years know how frequently I have derailed sessions by trying to explain, not too clearly, what I thought was wrong with what we were doing. What I am trying to say today, more clearly, is what I think is wrong in feminist politics, dealing with it only in relation to the region—in particular the English-speaking Caribbean—which is where I have been part of a certain experience. Thus, the critique is in the first place a self-criticism, though I hope, more useful than only that.

I think the place to start is with how we learn about power and what we learn about power from real life, as distinct from any "ism" at all. As Patricia Mohamed (1998: 7) says, we relate to the world through the way we experience it, and I would add, the way we experience the world should teach us something about how to build a movement, if that is what we want to do.

HOW AND WHAT WE FIRST LEARN ABOUT POWER

To illustrate aspects of how girls and women in the region learned about power decades ago, and perhaps still learn today, I want to begin with a page-and-a-half adapted from something I began writing 25 years or so ago and never finished. The page-and-a-half began like this:

> *If I close my eyes against the bright, yellow sun; and the shivering trees; and the cold, empty rooftops; if I close my eyes I can see my grandmother where she used to be, rocking in her chair and singing herself a cradlesong to still the rage that grew as she grew older.*
>
> *"He that is down/ need fear no fall," she would begin. "He that is down/ need fear no fall/He that is low, no pride …" And her voice would falter as she came to the last line because, as she would say, each day, defiantly, "Pride yuh mus' have. Pride yuh gotta have."*
>
> *Now I whisper to her across time, "Hey, Granny, I en crazy. Jus' down. Not crazy."*
>
> *Then I run to the corner where my mother hides. "Look!" I plead. "She crazy. Little Jackie Horner/Hiding in her corner," I giggle, chanting, singsong, like a child. "Little Jackie Horner/Hiding in her corner …"*
>
> *Then "Ma?" I call softly, to say sorry. And the walls begin to shake, and the floor rise, and my grandmother sighs to the rhythm of our fears.*

I'm not completely sure what this is about (some of what you write you don't know is there), but I know it is about three generations of women: the narrator, her mother, and her grandmother—the grandmother, *singing herself a cradlesong to still the rage that grew as she grew older*; her daughter, the mother, described by the grand-daughter/narrator as *crazy*; and the grand-daughter/narrator herself having to defend herself against the charge (which may be her own) that *she* is crazy. And since I know where the story was going and where it came from, I know that it was to be about the work that each had to do in order to try not to go under. For the grandmother, it was, in part, about the work of coping with the strange death of a young husband, with what she perceived of as desertion by him and shunning by his friends, and with raising eight children without a partner when she had only low-waged "women's skills." For the mother, it was, again in part, about the work of trying to make herself into a normal middle-class wife after a childhood of poverty, of leaving school early, of illness, of abuse from a male relative, of what she perceived of as a lack of support—amounting to desertion—by her mother. For the grand-daughter/ narrator, it was in part the work of surviving into womanhood through a maze of contradictory demands and signals from these two women. No men were involved in the physical or emotional housework of raising any of these women.

But of course, the story is also about how the lives of girls and women are affected by race and color, class and other power hierarchies. I learned the limitations placed on me by race before I learned the limitations of gender: I knew, very early, the use of the word "black" as disparagement ("Stay out de sun, Yuh want tuh turn more black?" said especially to little black girls). I didn't understand yet what the injunction had to do with gender, but it did; blackness lowered your market value.[2]

I also learned early about the inequalities among nations, particularly as these determined the education of colonials. The story that was never finished continued:

> In school the teacher asked, "What color is the sea?"
> "Brown, teacher, brown," we chorused.
> "Brown?" she shouted. "Brown? Is how yuh mean brown? Open yuh book at page 3. Repeat after me: The sea is blue. The sea is blue. The sea is?"
> "Blue, teacher, blue."
> But we knew the sea. It was where daily, boys swam, behind the wall where at Easter we all flew kites, and where, on Sunday afternoons, teenage boys would sit to catch the eyes of teenage girls riding by.
> We had seen what we knew as the sea, and it was brown; brown with the mud and silt washed down by the Amazon. So we ran after school to look again, to stare at the dark, muddy water, and repeat in reluctant acquiescence, "Blue, teacher, blue. The sea is blue."

In my own life as in the life of the grand-daughter/narrator who is only partly me, rage was, though not coherently, about all the ways that power worked against me: I was born in a colony, educated from books which not only ignored me but negated me. I was born black, of parents who were at that time both very low-waged nurses. My parents went away, my mother to continue to work as a nurse so my father could study to be a doctor and I went to primary school where I learned some of the connections between class and race or color: in primary school where no one was well-off or light-skinned, black people (called Negroes then) were superior to Indians, because closer to English ways. I left primary for secondary school where I learned the connections between class, race or color, and gender. Here, where parents of all races were professionals, civil servants and the like, and almost everyone's ways were suitably anglicized, skin color and hair determined where we were on the ladder. Here, an Indian was not inferior to a "Negro," neither, of course, was anyone else with a lighter skin. All this was crucial in the competition for boys: as one lighter-skinned friend told me, "I will get more than you." I understood the earlier admonitions to stay out of the sun. The last, long quote from the story goes as follows:

> At home I asked my grandmother, "Why the teacher say the sea blue?"
>
> "You does ask too many question," she answered, banging the pot hard against the sink. "You does ask altogether too many question."
>
> I looked at her, saw reflected in her face the faces of all the women at whose seeming sureness I tried to clutch: teachers in school saying "Girl, behave well, study hard, sit properly"; and pretty friends admonishing "Girl close dem book, press yuh hair nice, smile sexy"—and I smiled as I rode my bicycle past my domestic worker great-aunt standing on the corner threatening my disguise, smiled as I listened to my mother and her friends instruct me to be a good girl get a husband even while they complained about theirs. "Lord," I prayed when I was fourteen and sixteen, "Let me be—whatever. Dumber. Prettier. Fairer. Surer." And I embraced whatever seemed like solid ground, marveling that I could hold none.
>
> Now I close my eyes against the bright yellow sun and "Oh!" I whisper to the grandmother rocking in the light and shadow behind my lids, "How much further down?"

Race/ethnicity/color; class; nation; gender; age: from childhood I could feel—if not understand—their interaction in my life. And this is how I came to politics. As I wrote in "The Red Thread Story," which I had actually named "A Red Thread Story":

> Each stage of my political life started with a sense of being discriminated against in a particular place—as a citizen of a colony, for instance, or as a person of African descent; and my politics were informed first by a kind of Guyanese/West Indian nationalism, later by ideas of the Black Power movement, then by Marxism. What was consistent throughout this journey was a search for explanations of how power worked and, increasingly, of how each power relation worked in interaction with others. I always knew that I was avoiding confrontation with the power relations between men and women, but it was only in the mid-1980s that I actively began to seek out the women's movement in the region and internationally. (Andaiye 2000: 54)

Why did I finally seek out the women's movement in the mid-1980s?

WHAT PROPELLED ME TOWARDS THE WOMEN'S MOVEMENT

Unlike Joycelin Massiah and Peggy Antrobus, I am not a pioneer of the modern phase of the regional women's movement. Two developments propelled me towards it in about 1985.

The first, in 1982, was a re-encounter with the International Wages for Housework Campaign, founded in 1972 on "a breakthrough understanding of the location of housework in the hierarchy of work and wealth" (Andaiye 2000: 56).[3] I had first heard of the Campaign through Margaret Prescod of Barbados and Wilmette Brown of the United States, who later co-founded Black Women for Wages for Housework. Then in 1982, after a chance meeting with Wilmette Brown while attending a British Labour Party Conference as International Secretary of the WPA, I was invited to speak along with many other women at a conference on race and immigration in London. Later in 1982, I took part in a 12-day church occupation against "police harassment and racism" called by the English Collective of Prostitutes, one of the autonomous organizations of the Campaign, whose basic organizing principle is the autonomy of sectors with different levels of power, including sectors of women with different levels of power.

The second development that led me to seek out the organized Caribbean women's movement came in 1983 as I looked at the internal struggles of the New Jewel Movement (NJM) and asked, "where are the women from the National Women's Organization?" I do not know how many members the National Women's Organization (NWO) had by October 1983 when the Grenada "revo," as it was called, was overthrown. According to Manning Marable (1987: 238), in early 1982, NWO membership had reached 6,500 women organized into 155 local units but by mid-1983 (I would argue, as a direct response to developments in the party) it was rapidly losing members. The structure of the relationship between the NJM and the NWO was Leninist. NJM was a cadre party made up only of the most "advanced" members (i.e., advanced in their reading of the science of Marxism–Leninism), and around it but subordinate to it, were the "mass organizations." Since a cadre party's membership is restricted, in 1983 the NJM's total membership, including candidate or non-voting members, was three hundred (Marable 1987: 227).[4] Marable also says (ibid.: 237), in what I can only describe as a cop-out, "[The] NJM's approach toward women's rights was compromised by its tendency to rely on hierarchical and command-oriented measures." In effect, the NWO had no independent influence it could exercise on the internal struggle which destroyed the New Jewel Movement, because this "mass organization" of women had no autonomy from the party.

These two moments (the spectacle of the NWO's impotence; the re-encounter with the Wages for Housework Campaign) were a turning point for me—the one, demonstrating the need for women to organize autonomously from men because they have different levels of power, and the other, applying the principle of autonomous organizing among women because we, too, have different levels of power among our different sectors.

WHAT FEMINISM PROMISED AND WHAT IT HAS PRODUCED

I am not going to discuss gains and the limitations of gains made in the increased visibility of women's subordination, law reform, increased access to education and so on: both Joycelin Massiah and Peggy Antrobus extensively chronicled the story of the women's movement, and of feminist politics within it, in recent decades. What I am concerned with is whether and how organized feminist politics in the region fulfilled the promise it made when it defined its task. Again, let me clarify that I am drawing heavily on personal experience.

The clearest definition came from the Caribbean Association for Feminist Research and Action (CAFRA) which defined feminist politics as "a matter of both consciousness and action," continuing, "We are committed to understanding the relationship between the oppression of women and other forms of oppression in the society, and we are working actively for change." According to its Mission Statement, CAFRA's goal was "individual and societal transformation."[5] Rhoda Reddock (1995: 3), one of the founding members of CAFRA, discussed how Caribbean feminism related what some call "women's issues" such as domestic violence, to other inequalities produced by the socio-economic system:

> In addition to these "women's issues," a small but vocal band of women have argued, along with colleagues and sisters internationally, that the subordination of women ... cannot be seen separately from the overall inequality, violence, discrimination, and general unfairness characteristic of the present socio-economic system—that women's subordination is only the most fundamental aspect of a generally unfair and violent system based on racism, classism, and of course, sexism. For women's movement activists, the challenge is therefore not simply to remove male dominance, which, by the way, oppresses men as well as women, but the overall social and economic system of which it is a part.

Individual feminists in the region, many of them institution-based, have met the standard of connecting power hierarchies in some of their work, including in their research and advocacy. One example of the latter is the fight waged by feminists working with CARICOM (the Caribbean Community) as consultants in the Beijing and post-Beijing processes for the inclusion of statements on the negative impact of globalization on the Caribbean and on the exploitation of Caribbean women's unwaged and low-waged work. This fight has been against privileged feminists from Latin American countries in meetings of the Latin America and Caribbean region, and feminists from developed countries who were usually both racist and imperialist.

But feminist politics in the region has *not* connected hierarchies in its organizing, in spite of the determination many of us expressed in the 1980s to reverse the drive that previous movements had to control and exclude, a drive that was particularly true of left movements led by Marxist–Leninist parties. Among those side-lined by cadre parties were women. It was no accident, as Charles Mills (undated: 24) says, that the demographic base of the NJM was mainly young and male. Even in the WPA of Guyana, which was never really organized on Marxist–Leninist lines, the Leninist "principle" that a good party member was one who was "every day with the people"—in other words, one who did party work for 26 hours a day—meant that there was not a single woman in its leadership who had children to care for: either our children were grown or we had no children or the children were out of the country. In more rigid cadre parties, women reached the leadership only when they were well-off enough to hire other women to care for their children as well as their own.

While feminism has defined itself as placing great store on inclusiveness, organized feminist politics in the region has not been inclusive. CAFRA, for example, has always been made up mainly of Afro-Caribbean women, with Indo-Caribbean women in a small minority and little or no connection with Indigenous women, the poorest women in the region. Working class women of all race/ethnic groups form another minority. The age range was and still is narrow. How is this better than what we opposed in the left movement? In the form and practice of organizing in the 1980s and later, we studiously ignored the power relations among women, thereby allowing us, women with more power (however derived) to dominate or exclude; consciously or not, deliberately or not—it does not matter.

I do not believe that we thought any further (I certainly did not) than the need for the autonomy of women from men. But in organizing, if we cut gender off from the other power hierarchies—that is, if we work to end the power relations between men and women while ignoring the power relations among women, we will not succeed in transforming the power relations between women and men because we are not aiming at the whole power structure of which the power relations between men and women are only a part.

On the question of who is included in, and who is excluded from, feminist organizing in the region, I want to talk mainly about race/ethnicity and class, and to limit the discussion of race/ethnicity to the low level of participation of Indo-Caribbean women in organized feminist politics. As far as I know, Indigenous women are not present in these politics at all. This part of the discussion again begins with Guyana.

Guyana, as you know, is a country of deep race/ethnic divides. Our three main race/ethnic groups, Indo-Guyanese, Afro-Guyanese and the Indigenous peoples, are largely organized in separate parties. We are divided by geography. Indigenous peoples live mainly in the Guyana hinterland, and the two other groups mainly on the coastal strip bordering the Atlantic Ocean (the blue sea of the story I began with). We are also still divided to a great extent by occupation; for example, large numbers of Indigenous people are subsistence farmers; almost all field workers in sugar are Indo-Guyanese; almost all bauxite workers are Afro-Guyanese. Many businessmen and businesswomen are Indo-Guyanese; few Afro-Guyanese or Indigenous Guyanese are. The Police Force and the Army are largely Afro-Guyanese. Especially on the coast, small daily transactions—say, in the market—can become occasions for mistrust to flare between Indo-Guyanese and Afro-Guyanese. As in societies with deep race/ethnic divides, there are real differences of "culture" and real myths about each other.

Red Thread has never described itself as feminist, but half of its founders would certainly have described themselves as feminist in 1986. The group was created out of a recognition by these founders, all of whom were members or close associates of the WPA, of the need for the autonomy of women from political parties.[6] The founders were middle class, of different race groups, while the majority of members were and are largely working-class Indo-Guyanese and Afro-Guyanese women. In a context of economic collapse, Red Thread was originally based on income generation, a move that facilitated rural Indo-Guyanese women obtaining permission from husbands and other relatives to engage in activities which took them away from their villages, and sometimes even from the country. At that stage, Red Thread therefore included hundreds of women from coastal Guyana, both Indo-Guyanese and Afro-Guyanese. We also worked with Indigenous women on the coast; only in the 1990s were we able to work with Indigenous women in the hinterland, given the distance and the lack of affordable transport.

In relation to Indo-Guyanese and Afro-Guyanese membership, in the early 1990s, when income generation was no longer available as a base from which to carry out other activities, numbers fell, and proportionately, the numbers of Indo-Guyanese members fell. Our much smaller group still has both Indo-Guyanese and Afro-Guyanese women, but I believe that we never drew the lesson we should have drawn from the space that income-generation provided for the majority of Indo-Guyanese women members: that this space, or a similarly including kind of space, had to be fought for.

Regionally, I do not know whether the question of race/ethnic inclusiveness has been seriously addressed at the organizational level. In a recorded but unpublished exchange between myself and Rawwida Baksh-Soodeen in 1995, Baksh-Soodeen spoke about how the present wave of the Caribbean feminist movement had built on earlier movements which addressed class and race hierarchies, and how strong class and race consciousness were by the time that the feminist movement began to re-emerge. However, she added, race consciousness here meant only Afro- Caribbean race consciousness as it was organized and influenced by the Black Power movement. What about class? While it is true that the movement was dominated by women of African descent, it had and has a minority of *working class* women of African descent. Caribbean culture is often described as an "Afro-centric culture." but the Caribbean has always seemed to me to turn its back on much of the daily culture of working class Afro-Caribbean people, other than their music. Moreover, the Indo-Caribbean women in the movement were not working class either. There is no feminist or feminist-led group that I know, including those where working class women are in the majority (like Red Thread), where working class women are in the leadership. It was with this in mind that I said to Rawwida Baksh-Soodeen in 1995:

> We claim too much for ourselves as a movement if we don't admit that in the women's movement in its present phase, we do not deal with class or race adequately … Although many of the people who moved from the Left movement into the women's movement were themselves individuals who had struggled to make sure that race and gender were issues in the Left movement, I would still say that while the women's movement at a theoretical level links the oppressions of race, class, gender and nation, it has not yet found a way at the active political level to link these issues.

I would put it differently now—at the active political level what we need to find are not "links," but the inherent connections among those who are exploited.

THE POWER RELATIONS AMONG WOMEN

So-called anti-hierarchical forms and practices of organizing cannot allow us to find these connections, because what they do is to leave those with most power in control.

It is only possible to confront hierarchies from a base that recognizes that hierarchies exist, and reflects this by having sectors with different levels of power organize autonomously. In this way each sector, particularly those with the least power, can independently analyze its experience, identify its interests, work out its strategies, and bring all of this to the common table. Increasing the power of the least powerful sectors is essential to ensuring accountability from the more powerful sectors and essential to ensuring that women who rise in the power structure stay accountable.

This kind of autonomous organizing of sectors with different levels of power is the opposite of divisiveness. It is the only way that women can be truly autonomous of men, and the only way to undermine all the hierarchies of which women form the bottom rung.

Inside Red Thread, it is not yet clear to us what autonomous organizing of sectors can mean in a small group though already we can see prostitute women separately grouped, and rural women separately grouped from urban women. What we have agreed in relation both to forms and practice is this:

> The principle of autonomous organizing of sectors should be applied, based on an honest evaluation of how power works in the organization, which can only come "from a digging and a willingness to dig" into one's experience as oppressor and oppressed. You have to be sure that the honesty will lead you to a better place and not just expose you to more attack. Little by little the layers peel off. (Andaiye 2000: 93)

For all of us, the question is always what we want to win, and for and with whom. For those of us who want to challenge all power hierarchies, we must begin with the interests of the poorest women—again, not only in theory but in the way we organize and in what we organize for and against. We need to understand work and poverty not as a Beijing "critical issue," but as the material base of a movement for transformation. The point of fighting for unwaged work to be counted, is what counting makes visible about the similarities and differences among women, and therefore about power relations, including those among us. There is no contradiction between organizing with work and poverty as what I have just called "the material base for transformation," and the imperative of fighting against violence and for women's sexual and repro-ductive rights. The difference would be, for example, that when we fight for the right to choose, instead of fighting only for the right to choose not to have a child, we would fight for the right to choose to bear and rear the child, with everything that means about confronting the issues of poverty.[7] But many of our women's groups and feminist groups have turned what began as activist bases into NGOs doing projects, with the funders setting the agenda. In *Ring Ding in a Tight Corner*, Honor Ford-Smith (1989) analyzed the impact on Sistren of dependence on funding agencies which refused to fund administra-tion and institution building; had a project orientation which worked against long-term, strategic planning; and made reporting demands which consumed time and energy and could only be addressed by formally educated members who therefore functioned as brokers between grassroots women and the money they needed.[8]

Internationally, there is a growing literature on NGOs involved in "devel-opment work." One of the more conservative researchers in this area, Alan Fowler (2000: iv), discusses what he calls the "unfair, power-imbalanced and donor-serving framework of aid" in which NGDOs (Non-Governmental

Development Organizations), who are "aid-dependent and vulnerable," operate. Later, Fowler (ibid.: 17) describes the work of NGDOs as follows:

> Delivery of technical, social and increasingly, micro-financial services … still forms the primary weight of NGDO activity. This is a logical outcome of the intentions of most of their funding, be it from official aid, governments … or the general public. There is scant evidence to show that *the bulk* of NGDOs have substantially shifted their operations towards redressing the structural or root causes of poverty and insecurity.

In practice, feminist politics in the Caribbean has de-emphasized the struggle against poverty in favor of analysis, limited advocacy, and projects whose gains for poor women are at best partial, trickle-down and reversible, as are the gains in their access to the labor market. In fact, we should not treat the increased participation of women in waged work as more than a stop-gap, or join in the glorification of "women's survival strategies" and micro- (usually very, very, micro-) enterprise. Honor Ford-Smith (1989: 12) commented that "Women's deteriorating material condition is in contradiction to rising expectations about the job market and their increased potential for organization." She found this ironical; I see it as logical. Low-waged work, like unwaged work, is usually so time- and labor-consuming that it lessens poor women's "potential for organization."

Even in advocacy, there is a lost sense of urgency and combativeness in relation to the economy. For instance, there is less fierce advocacy (still less agitation) around adjustment policies in a context of *increased* adjustment. Of course, the old agitation came in part from the women's arms of political parties which had an adversarial relation to the global capitalist market (Grenada under Bishop; Guyana under Burnham with the opposition People's Progressive Party (PPP) and Working People's Alliance (WPA) holding the same position; Jamaica under Manley with the Workers' Party of Jamaica (WPJ) sharing its position). Now that almost all parties have bought into the policies directed by the global institutions (with the exception of protesting against the loss of preferential markets and the lack of recognition of the special vulnerability of small states), these women's arms are quiet.

What I have come to reject in my own work post-Beijing, is that as the global market and its institutions have become more organized, the market has shown itself more hostile to the interests of poor nations and poor people, beginning with the poorest women; and as the global struggle against the market has risen, I have become less a political activist and more and more a gatekeeper for the development industry, helping to demobilize poor women. Agencies which would never pay me to organize with women, pay me to mainstream gender into institutions which are not designed to serve the interests of poor women or men, and cannot be made to serve their interests. As Sonja Harris once commented in response to a gender mainstreaming proposal I wrote, "Lawd, mih dear. Dih stream too muddy." Or, agencies pay me to design/implement/evaluate sustainable development projects and programs which cannot transform the lives of poor women (their claimed "beneficiaries") when the macro-economy is premised on the increased exploitation of their unwaged and low-waged work. As an unwaged NGO worker, a large part of my work involves projects which provide some poor women with services which governments should be providing and maintaining for all women. Thus, I end up helping to provide services to a few women *instead* of challenging the economic model that prevents governments from providing services to all women. I hear other women say that what we have been doing constitutes a new kind of activism. I do not agree.

I no longer believe, as I used to, what Peggy Antrobus (2000: 27) put far more clearly than I can:

[Feminist politics] starts with an understanding of the way social injustice is embedded in the social relations of gender. It is grounded in a politics informed by that analysis. And ends with a passionate commitment to working for gender justice *as a way of addressing all other issues.* [My emphasis.]

Working for gender justice, like working for gender equality, will not lead to a transformation of all the interacting power relations against which we must organize—if we want to.

THERE IS A RISING GLOBAL MOVEMENT, LED BY WOMEN

Research covering 85 percent of the global population from 91 countries, reported in the *Guardian* on January 18, 2002, shows a massive increase in global inequality between 1988 and 1998, with the world's richest 50 million people earning as much as the poorest 2.7 billion. The richest 1 percent of the world have incomes equivalent to the poorest 57 percent. Four-fifths of the world's population live below what countries in North America and Europe consider the poverty line. Three reasons were suggested: a growing gulf between rural incomes in Africa and Asian countries such as India and Bangladesh and those of the west; steep falls in income in the old "socialist bloc"; and a widening gap between urban and rural incomes in China following its embrace of the market economy (reported in Elliot and Denny 2002).

I cite these only as recent statistics on what we all know: that gaps in power are widening. While it is estimated that US$80 billion would provide for basic needs for all, the United States military budget for 2003 is expected to be US$379 billion, rising to US$451 billion by 2007. Listen to the *Guardian Weekly* editorial of January 31–February 6, 2002:

> In the handful of minutes that it takes you to read this editorial, the United States government will have spent another $2m on defence if President George Bush's hike in the US defence budget is endorsed in Congress. That is $43m an hour, or more than $1bn a day. Meanwhile every day more than 19,000 children die from easily treatable diseases in the developing world. That is 13 children every minute. The first set of figures, the biggest increase in US defence spending in 20 years, was announced by Mr. Bush in Washington at the same time as US officials were discussing the latter figures at the United Nations in New York.

Growing poverty and inequality increase the time and labor that mainly women have to spend in trying to avoid catastrophes for their families, especially for children and elderly people. This is why, globally, the rising movement against an uncaring market is being led by women, in small and large actions.

Much of it is an "immediate" response of women to actions that threaten their families and communities. According to reports, recent examples of this kind of action have been taking place in South Africa, where, as part of the growing "community organization and mobilization … around demands that the ANC government 'deliver,'" evictions and water cut-offs have sparked protests in poor communities; and in the predominantly Indian township of Chatsworth, "the community, led primarily by older women, has successfully confronted gun-toting cops, police dogs and tear gas to prevent people being evicted from their humble council flats" (reported in Dixon 2001).

In Argentina, meanwhile, according to James Petras, "the driving force for the massive mobilization (against the systemic collapse of the IMF-led economy) has its roots in the large-scale, sustained activities of the unemployed movement" in which women, particularly women heads of households, predominate; and there is a high level of participation and militancy among the wives of men thrown out of industrial jobs (Petras 2002).[9]

On January 17, 2002, the Housewives Union in Argentina circulated "A Women's Manifesto," calling on women to meet in their neighborhoods, organizations or wherever else they were active "to express your views, to discuss, to dissent, propose" so that no one's opinions, needs and demands would be excluded. The Manifesto begins by identifying different sectors of grassroots women, knowing that each sector would have specific as well as shared needs and demands: women working outside the home for the lowest wage; women working only in the home; older women and women pensioners; teenagers; migrants from the interior and other countries of Latin America; women discriminated against because of their color or because they are domestic workers or sex workers or because of their sexual preference; women who are victims of violence.

The Manifesto prioritizes the poorest women; prioritizes mothers, and through them, children; draws the inherent connections between the various sectors who are exploited, women and men; demands money; and identifies demands both to answer the present crisis and to answer it by action that points to a society and economy with new priorities.

It makes demands on where resources should be found, including through the suspension of the external debt, and calls for these resources to be used for employment benefits for unemployed heads of households, women and men; for benefits for mothers in acute poverty without any pre-condition that they do more work that would prevent them from caring for their children; for a wage and pension for caring work; for benefits for each child to be paid to the mother to ensure that the children receive the benefit; for the refunding of small savers' deposits; for the suspension of auctions of the land of small farmers who are unable to pay debt. It calls for employment plans to be submitted to women for a "social audit" so that they are not used for political mileage by those who "negotiate with the needs of the poorest." It ends with this declaration:

> Our power is our autonomy, we will not allow anyone to tell us what to think or do. We know what are our needs and those of our families, and therefore we will all together find the ways to build a country and a world which starts from people's needs rather than corporate greed.

Women in other countries are organizing pots and pans protests in support of the women of Argentina. Whatever the outcome of these actions, they remain critically important in what I referred to earlier as the rising global movement, led by women.

On March 8, 2002, the third global strike of women—which last year saw action in 60 countries including Uganda, India, Peru and Guyana—will take place. The demands of the strike are both local and global, and all are understood as among the many ways that money and resources which women are owed can be paid. Some are demands which, in the heyday of both my Marxist and feminist lives, I would have been embarrassed by, such as breastfeeding breaks and other benefits that recognize rather than penalize women's caring work. Others are demands that I used to call "practical" as distinct from "strategic": accessible drinking water; ecologically sound technology for every household; affordable and accessible housing and transportation, all of which I now see as fundamental to reducing the burden of women's unwaged work. One demand is pay equity for all, women and men, *internationally*—which opposes the right to pit female workers against male, those in the North against those in the South, by forcing us to undercut each other's wages. Another is protection against all violence—at home, in the street, in the office, on the farm, in the factory—and the violence of war, linked to a call to stop valuing killing more than caring. Another is the abolition of the Third World debt.

What of women in the Caribbean? In an address to the 3rd Caribbean Media Conference held in Georgetown on May 5, 2000, Prime Minister Arthur of Barbados called this "just about the worst of times" for the region. At the economic level, our relatively high rankings in terms of growth, per capita income and other indicators not only mask the inequalities inside our countries (in particular, the fact that the great majority of Indigenous peoples live in absolute poverty), but also do not take account of the threat to the small, open CARICOM economies being wielded in the name of trade liberalization. The fact that our wages are "high" means that foreign capital which invests here because of our other "comparative advantages" (geographic location; levels of literacy; the fact that many of us speak English), always in search of cheaper labor, is always poised for flight. Capital can move freely, but not labor, except when the developed world needs our skills. The theft of our teachers and nurses is now amounting to a crisis. Public violence (like domestic violence) is escalating, and in one territory after another the response of governments is to increase State violence.

Yet in the face of this, our response is to keep on our narrow path. What I described earlier as the cutting off of gender *in practice* from the other power hierarchies, even among those of us who never intended to be part of this disconnection, has been product and producer of women, too, setting low and narrow limits on what we are fighting for.

We have to think again, all those of us who do not want to build careers. We need, first, to identify the world we want to build, not in the old language of "isms," but in a new language that has clarity and purpose. In sum, my commitment to the global campaign to count women's unwaged work comes from the fact that my goal is a world which values caring labour because, as Selma James has put it, it values caring as the essence of the relationships among people.

What would follow from this is that the campaign must be global; that different sectors with different levels of power must organize autonomously so they can cross their divides on the basis of equality; and that for the campaign to serve the interests of all who are exploited, it must be led and waged in the interests of the poorest women, who bear the greatest burden of unwaged and low-waged caring labour, which is the foundation of all economies.

In closing, I want to thank the Centre for Gender Studies at Mona not only for inviting me to give this year's Lucille Mathurin Mair lecture, but for repeating the invitation after I responded that I preferred not to speak because I could only be critical. This has given me the opportunity not only to contribute to what I see as an essential debate on the future of Caribbean women's organizing, but to do so in honour of Lucille Mathurin Mair.

ACKNOWLEDGEMENTS

This is a slightly edited version of the Lucille Mathurin Mair Lecture for 2002, first published by the Centre for Gender and Development Studies, University of the West Indies, Mona.

NOTES

1. Other evidence comes from Maxwell and Castello's sample of 12 students—ages 20–50—in the Gender Studies program at Mona, 10 of whom (nine females and one male) answered in the affirmative when asked if a feminist movement was still needed.
2. Lest we think those days are over, the following is taken from a letter on the advice page of the Guyana *Sunday Stabroek*, January 27, 2002: "I am a 14-year-old girl. When I was younger, I was light-skinned, but as I grew older my complexion has become darker … I am obsessed with my complexion. I need a fair complexion— at least on my face. Can you suggest something to tone down my complexion? Natasha."
3. The phrase, "the hierarchy of work and wealth," is from Wilmette Brown.
4. In his 2018 review of Bernard Coard's *The Grenada Revolution—What Really Happened* (Vol 1), Rupert Lewis referred to the membership of NJM in September/ October 1983 as "some 500 people."
5. The definition and mission statement were reproduced in *CAFRA News* 9(1) (January–June, 1995).
6. However, what we took with us into women's autonomous organizing was the commitment all WPA Members had to multi-racialism; for several years, the WPA, which worked mainly on the coast, did succeed in building a party with approximately equal numbers of Indo-Guyanese and Afro-Guyanese members.
7. See Selma James, *Women, the Unions and Work* (1976). Here and throughout the text, the argument on hierarchies is shaped by James's *Sex, Race and Class* (1986).
8. Sistren Theatre Collective, formed in 1977, is a Jamaican women's organization.
9. Petras works with the unemployment movement in Argentina and is the author of several books on Latin America, the most recent, with Henry Veltmeyer, being *Globalization Unmasked: Imperialism in the 21st Century* (Petras and Veltmeyer 2001).

REFERENCES

Andaiye. 2000. "The Red Thread Story." In *Spitting in the Wind: Lessons in Empowerment from the Caribbean*, Ed. Suzanne Francis Brown. Kingston: Ian Randle Publishers.

Antrobus, Peggy. 2000. *The Rise and Fall of Feminist Politics in the Caribbean Women's Movement 1975–1995*. The 2000 Lucille Mathurin Mair Lecture. Mona: Centre for Gender and Development Studies, University of the West Indies.

Dixon, Norm. 2001. "Grassroots Struggles Revive." *Green Left Weekly*, June 9.

Elliot, Larry and Charlotte Denny. 2002. "Top 1 Per Cent Earn as Much as the Poorest 57 Per Cent." *The Guardian*, January 18.

Ford-Smith, Honor. 1989. *Ring Ding in a Tight Corner: A Case Study of Funding and Organizational Democracy in Sistren, 1977–1988*. Toronto: The Women's Program, International Council for Adult Education.

Fowler, Alan. 2000. "Civil Society, NGDOs and Social Development: Changing the Rules of the Game." United Nations Research Institute for Social Development, Occasional Paper 1, January.

Hosein, Gabrielle. 2001. "What Does Feminism Mean to Young Women?" Paper presented at the Roundtable on Feminism in the Caribbean. Caribbean Studies Association 26th Annual Conference, Puerto Rico.

James, Selma. 1976. *Women, the Unions and Work*. Bristol: Falling Wall Press.

———. 1986. *Sex, Race and Class*. London: Housewives in Dialogue.

Marable, Manning. 1987. *African and Caribbean Politics: From Kwame Nkrumah to Maurice Bishop*. London: Verso.

Massiah, Joycelin. 1998. *On the Brink of the New Millenium: Are Caribbean Women Prepared?* The 1998 Lucille Mathurin Mair Lecture. Mona: Centre for Gender and Development Studies, University of the West Indies.

Maxwell, Shakira and June Castello. Undated. "What Our Students Think About Feminism Today." Mimeo.

Mills, Charles. Undated. "Out of the Cave: Tensions between Democracy and Elitism in Marx's Theory of Cognitive Liberation." Mimeo.

Mohamed, Patricia. 1998. *Stories in Caribbean Feminism: Reflections on the Twentieth Century*. St. Augustine: Centre for Gender and Development Studies, University of the West Indies.

Petras, James. 2002. "You Have to Take Action from Below." *Socialist Worker*, January 11.

Petras, James and Henry Veltmeyer. 2001. *Globalization Unmasked: Imperialism in the 21st Century*. London: Zed Books.

Reddock, Rhoda. 1995. "Women and Poverty in Trinidad and Tobago." WAND Occasional Paper 10/95.

The Historic Centrality of Mr. Slime:
George Lamming's Pursuit of Class Betrayal in Novels and Speeches
[2003]

ENTRY POINT: ON THE MURDER OF RODNEY

On June 13, 1980, Walter Rodney was assassinated in Georgetown, Guyana. Ten days later, Lamming delivered the first of his 1980–1983 speeches at the memorial service held in Georgetown.[1] In the Foreword to *Conversations: George Lamming*, which I wrote in 1990/1991, I recorded what I thought about the speech:

> June 21, 1980: Although the date had been announced, the authorities had not released the body. The mood in the church was bleak, bleakest among those of us who had worked with Walter in the WPA.[2] WPA youth were all, it seemed, at the back of the church, in the church at all only out of respect for the wishes of Pat, Walter's wife, but unable to enter more fully into what felt so weak a response to atrocity.
>
> The eulogies made before George spoke could not meet the need. The need was for revenge; what was happening was a funeral service with Walter, as it were, twice absent.
>
> When George began, the youth were suspicious: both appearance and manner were at first alienating. "A white-hair man with a accent," one said later.
>
> But when he ended there was first, from the back a single, sharp handclap, which became, almost in the same instant, perhaps one hundred; until the wave of WPA youth applauding moved forward and spread up through the church; and for the first time in my experience, a eulogy in a Guyanese church provoked a standing ovation.
>
> Afterwards, I asked some of the youth what had happened. They said the ovation was not for George, it was for Walter. George had brought Walter into the church, had made possible a Ceremony of Souls with "[its] drama of redemption, [its] drama of returning, [its] drama of cleansing for a commitment towards the future." (Drayton and Andaiye 1992: 8)

Nearly 23 years after that speech was made, I asked one of those youth, now 45 years old, how long it had lasted. She thought for a few moments, then answered, "Close to one hour. Perhaps a little under" (interview, Karen de Souza, April 12, 2003). In fact, the speech could not have lasted more than fifteen minutes; in printed form, it is three pages long.

Why does its impact remain literally larger than life so many years later? I understand that better now than I did in 1990/1991. Once you place the speech in Lamming's whole work and you see his pursuit of betrayal all through that work, you see that what the audience was feeling—or as he explains the function of his speeches ("A Visit to Carriacou"), what he was making the collective mind of the crowd feel—was the size of his and their outrage and sorrow at the loss of a man who was the antithesis of Mr. Slime, a man with whom they were as familiar as he was, from their lives. Part 1 was the outrage:

> Today we meet in a dangerous land, and at the most dangerous of times. The danger may be that supreme authority, the supervising conscience of the nation, has ceased to be answerable to any moral law, has ceased to recognize or respect any minimum requirement of ordinary human decency ... ("On the Murder of Rodney," Drayton and Andaiye 1992: 184).

In Part 2 the tone changed: since Rodney was the antithesis of Mr. Slime, a tribute to him that expressed who he truly was had to be in language that was the antithesis of the inflated language of Caribbean (and other) eulogies. So he said that Rodney was a man who was "serious," who was "not smart," "not bright," who "did not seek to score points for the sake of argument." Who, instead, was "an intellectual worker among those who had been deprived of his advantages," who "had a rare gift of intellect to which he felt a special duty ... [as] a tool, a reservoir of power which could only justify itself if it were put into service, and on behalf of social need" (Drayton and Andaiye 1992: 184). He ended his tribute with the poem Martin Carter had written for Rodney, "Assassins of Conversation," whose very name was an acknowledgement of the Rodney who used to sit before a handful of working people under a bottom-house, or stand before thousands at a street corner, telling them what they made happen.[3]

Although I would say now that my entry point into Lamming's pursuit of betrayal was not the novels but the 1980–1983 speeches (the word "betrayal" is not mentioned once in the foreword to *Conversations*), at that time I did not see that betrayal was central to the speeches. I cannot explain this inability or refusal to see what is now so clear by claiming that I was distant from the politics in and about which the speeches were made. In the period between 1980 when Rodney was assassinated and 1983 when Maurice Bishop, Jacqueline Creft and their colleagues were assassinated, I was an Executive member of the WPA, was centrally engaged in the political struggle in Guyana, and for more than two of those years, involved in meetings of Caribbean left organizations in Grenada. Now that I have seen that Mr. Slime is everywhere in the speeches, I believe that I was unable or unwilling to see this until I had come out of what Lamming calls "the political Left"—because seeing it would raise doubts about my politics that I was not prepared to face, still less, to act upon. And yet the experience of the left in the English-speaking Caribbean—not only elsewhere—shows that the interpretation of the world which begins (and usually ends) with the so-called "point of production" is really about a belief in the management and control of people, and not about the revolutionizing of human relations—including the relations of production.

Admitting that Lamming was pursuing betrayal in the speeches led me directly back to the novels, and in particular to *In the Castle of my Skin*, the novel that launched his pursuit, and *Season of Adventure*, the novel that underlined the deadly serious implications of what was being pursued.

While betrayal is by definition a blow from an unexpected place ("Something startles where I thought I was safest"—the epigraph to *Castle*), the betrayal Lamming is concerned with is of course betrayal of a class, rather than as a purely personal act. In *Castle*, betrayal comes from someone—Mr. Slime—who has deserted his roots in the working class for what Lamming calls in *Season* "a derivative middle-class" (Lamming 2010: 362)—someone who is the enemy of what Trumper knows he and his boyhood community must now live by: "… this world is a world o' camps, an' you got to find out which camp you're in. And above everything else keep that camp clean" (Lamming 2010: 280).

IN THE CASTLE OF MY SKIN: IN SLIME IS THE FURY OF THE CLASS

We know that *Castle* broke new ground by making the community, the village, the "hero." But what precisely does that determine?

The function of the hero/heroine in most novels is to make an experience and change through it. Succeed or fail, there is an individual transformation, a new self-consciousness; the heroine or hero finally understands what is going on in her/his life and/or her/his society. The situation and characters may move on and change, but none besides the main character transforms themselves or us.

It is fundamentally an elitist framework. Though the novel's content may be anti-elitist, the fact is that only one or two people learn the hidden truth and teach us or bring others to it. But if the village is the hero, the reader is invited to appreciate the contribution to laying out the truth of every unique individual usually hidden behind the "ordinary" non-hero or heroine. Then the progress of each is dependent on the collective wisdom and progress of all. G is all the things that Ma and Pa and his long-suffering mother and his experience of Empire Day have taught all of them, all the boys trying to figure out what it is they are living through. It is a collective enterprise and learning and revelation.

That is a very typical working class process, an important part of how the movement moves, of which academics who "think" are rarely aware. Working class people collectively compare and digest experience, debate their meaning and reach collective decisions about what action should and should not be taken. Change is individual but it is also collective. The whole community makes its points of reference, which in turn incite other individuals who give direction to the making of history. This direction, as given in *Castle* by G, has been shaped by the collective. The collectivity ensures that we are less likely to get stuck by taking a moment of time as a fixed reality (what Hegel calls a fixed category), which leads us to actions that suit an earlier moment. It is always the danger with individuals, but the collectivity pulls us all into our future, the next historical stage. At the end of *Castle*, this is where we—villager as well as reader—know we have reached.

Acts of rebellion in a novel based on an "individual hero" are uniquely individual, rarely a manifestation of the general will. But what G learns he brings back to those same mutually-craving-for-understanding boys, now young men, who hear him.

So that treating the village as the hero gives a chance to reveal all the collective history and torment for *every* individual that goes into the novel's time span. No one is less an individual; everyone has more dimensions, and her/his individuality is not an end in itself—quite different from the Freudian century that made every social trauma an individual's responsibility to right individually.

In this sense *Castle* is a novel which in structure and intention is describing a working class process.[4] Given this, it is not surprising that it tackles the fundamental political question of class betrayal. "Well there's something that I want to know / If this council business bound to be so," sang Sparrow in "No, Doctor, No," one of his earliest calypsos, after the first election victory of the People's National Movement. Are politicians bound to sell out? While Lamming does not address exactly this question in *Castle*, he is already claiming that the leadership of the movement to independence is corrupt and available to the colonial power before they get into government, at the beginning of the movement rather than at its apex. In this very early case, it was the promise of power, rather than power itself, that was enough to corrupt. The betrayal is signaled long before it is committed: the character and the name Slime enter the novel early (chapter 3).

And here in Mr. Slime is the fury of the class not only against the colonial power but even more, against the traitors within the working class. The name Slime is a poetic evocation of the filth of betrayal (compare Trumper's "keep that camp clean"). When the villagers are reading the bill which the overseer has posted on the lamp-post to announce that the land has been sold and that information should be sought from Mr. Slime, they don't know yet that they have been betrayed, but the stench of betrayal comes up from the way the words echo in their minds: "It say we got to see Mr. Slime. See Mr. Slime. Mr. Slime. Mr. Slime. Mr. Slime" (Lamming 2010: 239). It is also a signal for us to take note that a fundamental political reality is being penetrated and exposed.

It is not only early in the novel. It is the first in the English-speaking anti-imperialist body of creative work where the enemy within the movement is fingered. Five years after Mr. Slime saw the light of day, Chinua Achebe told us that *Things Fall Apart*,[5] not because of "a foreign conscience called imperialist" but because those we nurture and sacrifice into power help not us, but our enemies.

SEASON OF ADVENTURE: "I ALSO AM MR. SLIME"

In *Season*, as we know, the pursuit of betrayal turns (partly) inward and goes for its roots. The central statement on betrayal in the novel is the Author's Note, which Lamming has called "a shock tactic of intervention" offering a "definition of failure with full recognition of the responsibility involved" ("The West Indian People: A View from 1965," Drayton and Andaiye 1992: 261–262).

This use of the author's voice in a work of fiction was probably unprecedented at the time. It is not that Lamming took himself as author into the fiction. What he did was to take a character in a novel, Powell, and bring him out of the fiction as his half-brother:

> Believe it or not: Powell was my brother; my half-brother by a different mother. Until the age of ten Powell and I had lived together, equal in the affection of two mothers. Powell had made my dreams; and I had lived his passions. Identical in years, and stage by stage, Powell and I were taught in the same primary school.
> And then the division came. (Drayton and Andaiye 1992: 331–332)

The corruption begins early, with the scholarship to secondary school. Lamming explained the purpose of the author's note in a recent interview in *Small Axe*:

> The Author's Note came naturally as part of the narrative ... I felt now that I wanted to personalize that total statement, to say that it is me also that I am talking about, not me as any author but me as a man called "Lamming" who is caught up in that ambivalence about directions, and who daily has to question himself about the value of his relationships. (Scott 2002: 160)

I—middle class by virtue of the privilege of education—am Mr. Slime.

If the device of the Author's Note was *probably* unprecedented, the use to which Lamming puts it was undoubtedly so. It was an acknowledgement of personal responsibility for the desperation that betrayal imposed:

> I believe deep in my bones that the mad impulse that drove Powell to his criminal defeat was largely my doing. I will not have this explained away

by talk about the environment; nor can I allow my own moral infirmity to be transferred to a foreign conscience called imperialist. I shall go beyond my grave in the knowledge that I am responsible for what happened to my brother. (Drayton and Andaiye 1992: 332)

Underscoring that the betrayal was his, the novel refuses to locate it in Chiki, to whom Powell says as Chiki leaves the Forest Reserve to go to high school, "… it ain't you alone what goin' up, is all the boys who have no scholarship, Chick … Remember all the Boys waitin' to hear" (Lamming 1979: 229). And Chiki returns, as he says, "not only to live, but to be where I belong" (ibid.: 237).

Nor does the fact that the "foreign conscience called imperialist" creates the conditions in which he, Lamming, was trained—educated—into betrayal, absolve him of responsibility for scabbing.

PURSUING BETRAYAL IN THE SPEECHES: "THE HONOURABLE MEMBER"

When creative writing is sustained through an umbilical cord to the movement, it can suffer withdrawal symptoms from that movement's decline. In the English-speaking Caribbean this happened in the '60s after the death of Federation, when politicians gave the macho (and disastrous) brag that they were "going it alone." Lamming's history after the movement's decline tells us how political *Castle* was: how much the impulse for it had come from the movement.

When Lamming said "I didn't write that book; I couldn't write that book; that book wrote itself," (private conversation with Selma James, April 2003) he was conveying that it was the movement that had energized and empowered his imagination and liberated his own perceptions to write that rarity, a great novel. But when the movement was betrayed and defeated, his ability to write fiction was undermined. Instead, he made himself into a superb non-party-political commentator. This is how he explains the shift:

> At some stage I had come to feel that if I had anything of relevance and value to say that could be immediately effective in however minimal a way, it would be more effectively done by that statement, by that lecture-form, than by the novel-form … whenever I am asked to give a public address on some major occasion, I am also doing it with a view that it would play the role the fiction would have played if they were able to read the fiction, or if the fiction were made available to them. (Scott 2002: 198)

He ascribes different functions to the novels and speeches: the speeches "making the collective mind of the crowd feel," the novels "making the feeling think" ("A Visit to Carriacou," Drayton and Andaiye 1992: 28–29). Yet as we've seen, whatever the difference in their function, novels and speeches are part of the same project: recording the painful but also life-affirming history of the Caribbean, beginning with the working class, and therefore, addressing the fundamental issue of the whole period from the 1930s to the 1980s, class betrayal leading to defeat.

As statements which translate the themes of his novels, the speeches quote often from the novels. Lamming explains this in *Small Axe*:

> Now as to statement/fiction/lecture/novel, what quite often I am doing—and if you look through *Conversations*, the extracts from the novels are used quite a lot—is spelling out in the lectures the themes raised in the fiction … when I give a lecture about the honourable member, and trace the history of this parliamentarian, from the great-grandfather in the canefield, right through to the schoolmaster whose son is now a lawyer, that is very clear. They're [union members] hearing that very clear. But I am telling them what *Season* and *Of Age and Innocence* is (*sic*) about. (Scott 2002: 197)

He is saying that "The Honourable Member" (which, as we shall see, is all about betrayal by the political elite), is what *Season of Adventure, Of Age and Innocence*—and first, I would add, *In the Castle of my Skin*—are about.

While *Castle* and *Season* deal with betrayal as novels can—"The novel does not only depict aspects of social reality. It explodes it. It ploughs it up" ("A Visit to Carriacou," Drayton and Andaiye 1992: 29)—"The Honourable Member" deals with betrayal stripped of its complexity. This is an address Lamming gave to the fortieth Annual Conference of the Barbados Workers' Union, which describes a 40-year-old lawyer/politician trained at university abroad, returning to work as a lawyer before entering politics. Today he is rich: "His known assets are estimated to be in the region of a figure, not under three quarters of a million" (Drayton and Andaiye 1992: 217). His house is pretentious. His taste is suspect: "The walls, on all sides, are disfigured by juvenile souvenirs of illuminated nights in New York, eating out along the Bay of San Francisco, racially mixed couples at play around a kidney-shaped swimming pool in Miami." He appears not to read, except for magazines: "There are no books anywhere" (ibid.: 218).

The Honourable Member is not unique; he is of the class whose members had "a privilege of schooling" (Drayton and Andaiye 1992: 218). It is a class whose members "now embrace as the most desirable reward of their efforts in this life: social power and material wealth" (ibid.: 219), and which, "putting its own self-interest above and beyond social incentives, is so eager to separate itself, by life-style and the hunger for status, from the working class from which it derived" (ibid.: 221).

The process of social evolution which has brought the Honourable Member to this criterion of success began with a great-grandfather who was a laborer on the estate from age nine, died at 40 (the Honourable Member's age) and continues through a grandfather who was an independent artisan of great skill, whose view of education "as the only possible means of rescuing his offspring from the humiliations his ancestors had endured" (Drayton and Andaiye 1992: 220) made him push for his son, the Honourable Member's father, to become a teacher. The Honourable Member's children have carried the social distance from their roots still further: he has "a girl who went to St. Winifred's from a junior school called "St Gabriel's and a son who, after problems at home, was placed in a minor public school in the South of England" (ibid.: 218). Neither child can remember traveling by bus in Barbados. While the Honourable Member's great-grandfather was a man who, himself exploited, was attracted to stories he had heard in his childhood of workers who had risen up against the merchant/planter class, he himself belongs to the category of men whose major appeal "in what is thought to be an honest election" is that struggle against exploitation is the work of communist agitators.

The audience for this speech would have included women and men who had never read *Castle*, and others who, on reading it, would have pretended not to see themselves in Mr. Slime. The speech is therefore of value for two reasons: it introduced a new audience among waged workers to Lamming's indictment of the political elite, and it brought the indictment unambiguously to their bosses.

"I CAN SMELL THE MIDDLE CLASS EVERYWHERE"

Lamming's 1980–1983 speeches should be analyzed in two groups—those, like "The Honourable Member," which he made between 1980 and mid-1982, and the three he made from late 1982 to the end of 1983. To remind ourselves of the events and feeling of the first of these periods: in 1980, in spite of Rodney's assassination in June of that year, there was strong optimism that the region was in a new stage of rebellion. This had started in March 1979 when Gairy was overthrown in Grenada. Four months later, in July, Somoza was overthrown in Nicaragua. The removal of Gairy from power fed into the multi-racial rebellion against the Burnham regime in Guyana, led by Rodney and the WPA. Overnight, posters appeared on the walls of the capital proclaiming "De Shah [of Iran] gone! Gairy gone! Who next?" Inside Grenada, women, men, children were energized by their belief that the "revo" was theirs and could therefore transform their lives.[6] West Indian people from across the English-speaking Caribbean were working inside Grenada to support the revolution. Cultural workers were organized in its defense.

Grenada was also a pole around which the left in CARICOM gathered strength. Adding to existing left parties, there was a growth in the number and militancy of small, left groups. Meetings of left parties and trade unions were frequent. Closer ties were being created with Cuba and to lesser degree,

Nicaragua.[7] As Lamming has said, "the *region* was in a moment of resistance in Grenada" (Scott 2002: 188).

Of course, this resistance was only part of what was happening in the region. The "loss" of Grenada and Nicaragua meant that the United States was on the attack, actively supported by many CARICOM governments. The "war against communism" continued to have Cuba as a main target, along with Nicaragua and Grenada, but pro-US CARICOM governments demonstrated a particular hysteria towards Grenada. They feared it like a virus which would spread till it infected them. Thus, between 1980 and mid-1982, Lamming was in part responding to what he identified as the betrayal of the Grenadian people by these Caribbean governments, similar to the betrayal of the Guyanese people in 1953 by the same strata.[8]

But where was he smelling betrayal in late 1982 when he made the speech "A Visit to Carriacou"? This speech, addressed to members of the NJM, teachers and other working people on that island, is more informal than any other in the period, and reads like a response to something in the immediate environment that the reader does not know about:

> I have spent a lot of my life in association with Marxists of a variety of colours. But I have never in my life met a Marxist baby. Never. Never … When a man tells me he is a Marxist … I want to know how he got there. I want to know, what was the particular journey that led him from wherever he was to that point of perception and conviction and redemption which he calls Marxist. It is that journey … that allows me to see his connection with what he is calling himself. (Drayton and Andaiye 1992: 24)

What man calling himself a Marxist is he speaking to and about? At the moment of listening or reading, we only know that he is contrasting where he came from with where an unnamed man who calls himself a Marxist, comes from.[9] In other words, we know that the middle-class person he is smelling is part of the Caribbean left:

> when I hear people discussing class, I did not discover that from Marx. I lived with class … I did not discover how class society deforms human relations from Marx. I lived it. And so I developed an extraordinary nose. I can smell middle class people everywhere. (Drayton and Andaiye 1992: 26)

Also in 1982, for the first time he clearly identifies the leadership of the trade union movement as suspect, a group the working class must be on guard against:

> The problem for us here is that these tendencies we identify in what is called the middle class emerge in the leadership of organized labour. And that is

what the rank and file of the working people have got to keep their eyes on: the compromise, the ambivalence of leadership throughout the trade unions of this region. ("Nationalism and Nation," Drayton and Andaiye 1992: 230).

It is true that by 1982 divisions in the left had widened, as those who defined themselves as Marxist–Leninists pushed for an ever-narrowing concentration of power in the NJM, and in those members of the party imbued with "the science" presumably of revolution, in the name of "securing the revolution." But these were not divisions that Lamming would have known about from the inside. The cultural workers Lamming coordinated to work in and for Grenada were not universally welcomed in Grenada. While for Lamming culture could never be "decoration of daily life"—or, in the crude sense, a tool—for the Grenada government the job of these workers was simply to mobilize support for the revolution; and for the orthodox Marxist–Leninists inside the party, Lamming was simply a "social democrat."[10]

He could not know what was happening on the inside; and yet, this small incident in Carriacou in which men of the left shut out working class people, carried him immediately to the pursuit of betrayal.

"THE TRAGEDY OF A WHOLE REGION"

Situating Mr. Slime in the left is never explicit until after Bishop's murder, following which he indicts the political elite of both right and left.

"The Plantation Mongrel" targets the right. Delivered at the Guild of Undergraduates, UWI, Cave Hill, one month after Bishop's death, it is a speech of uncontrolled rage. We recall the environment—the witch-hunting of critics of the US invasion of Grenada and the complicity of Caribbean governments in it. Prominent among these critics was Rickey Singh, a Guyanese journalist based in Barbados, which threatened to deport him. Here was Lamming's answer:

> In recent times, we have heard one notable Black voice, which represents a tradition of the plantation mongrel, howling for the deportation of aliens who infest this island. It is you who are also his target ...
>
> So let us ask our plantation mongrel this question: "How many Barbadians infest Guyana?" "How many Barbadians infest St. Lucia?" "How many Barbadians infest Trinidad and Tobago?" (Drayton and Andaiye 1992: 244–245)

At the close of the speech he tells the students that they have a choice between the two traditions: "You may take the road through Garvey and James to Fanon and Rodney and Bishop. Or you may choose the other tradition which leads you down the defeated tracks of the Black plantation mongrel" (ibid.: 250).

In "The Tragedy of a Whole Region," the tribute delivered at the memorial service for Bishop in Trinidad and Tobago in December 1983, he indicts politicians across their claimed ideological differences as equally colonized: "The colonial legacy is deep and pervasive; *and it has afflicted the political Left, no less than the Right*, with a psychology of dependence which has crippled the imagination and makes it inoperative in moments of crisis" (Drayton and Andaiye 1992: 247; my emphasis).

Here again, he pairs Rodney and Bishop, describing them as men of the same generation with the same "privilege of education" who could have had access to "that minority kingdom" and carry out the function of their class "to reinforce and stabilize [the] ... social division of labour and status" (Drayton and Andaiye 1992: 239):

> But Rodney and Bishop gave the word "ambition" a new virtue, by making the central ambition of their lives a commitment to break, in a decisive way, with the tradition which had trained them to approve and supervise over the intellectual enslavement of their own people. They broke away; and they became subversive traitors to that tradition which could so easily have bestowed on them the blessings of those who proudly identify themselves as affluent consumers. It was this betrayal which ultimately cost them their lives. (Drayton and Andaiye 1992: 239–40)

Honoring Bishop on his own, he chooses words that draw the sharpest possible contrast between him and those who had opposed him, speaking of him as a man "who required no textbook, no sterile list of abstract principles, to recognize where his duty lay. His head found a home in the hearts of his people at mass level; and he tried to move forward from the concrete experience of the reality" (Drayton and Andaiye 1992: 238–239).

The colonized left, on the other hand, required textbooks. Following the US invasion copies of NJM Central Committee minutes were "discovered" in which members are recorded as analyzing the Grenada situation via the most abstract use of Lenin textbooks: they were virtual caricatures of what Lamming said in the *Small Axe* interview about the left:

> even in the better types ... I always saw ... [the leaders of the left] in the role of people who had the text ... and on whom had been conferred the privilege to interpret and explain this text for the others, but who really had no organic connection or direct connection with the daily lives of that other. (Scott 2002: 176)

THE HISTORIC CENTRALITY OF MR. SLIME

Lamming is not a political activist; he need not meet, nor does he meet, the standards we set ourselves. No quantity of speeches of quality changes his novelist status. When he ventures into politics, as he occasionally does in some of the speeches, the step is not always as imaginative and deeply truthful as in his "real" work. For example, when he locates the leadership of the movement in organized labor he is retreating from his own recognition of the unwaged caring labor of women. In "The Tragedy of a Whole Region" he finds the continuing struggle for a "human world" in Trinidad and Tobago not only "on sugar estates, [and] in the oilfields, but also "among the most determined workers in the public and *domestic* services of the land" (Drayton and Andaiye 1992: 238; my emphasis), while in "The Honourable Member" he indicts the politician for his betrayal not only of his male ancestors, but of "the women who fathered many a household, nursed man and child without a wage and have remained to this day the last surviving example of legalized slave-labour" (ibid.: 220). They do the work but they will not lead since they are not part of organized, waged labor. *Castle* has a more truthful foundation. Ma and Pa, for example, are hardly excluded from leadership!

As we have seen, Lamming's achievement is that in *Castle*, *Season*, and "A Visit to Carriacou," he is pursuing betrayal when no one else is. Here is his later explanation of the appearance of Mr. Slime in *Castle*:

> I think there is planted in the change, and what seemed the inevitability of the change, also the question of great doubt about where this will go. In some way I am already very sceptical of the authenticity of what would be the leadership in the form of Mr. Slime ... I am in some way conscious of the kinds of compromise in which this leadership will be involved ... I am going to see '37 and '38 in fact *kidnapped* ... by a leadership that had little or nothing to do with the makings of it. And by leaders who are very decent but saw themselves as the natural heirs to the departing imperial power. Not necessarily the natural leaders of the people who become their constituency ... they chose themselves as the leaders, by virtue of education, by virtue also of the mythology which the school has played in shaping our social relations. (Scott 2002: 112–113)

The novel itself is clearer than this quote suggests when it speaks of "leaders who are very decent." It is true that G says in *Castle* that when Mr. Slime taught him "he seemed perfectly decent" (Lamming 2010: 279), but Lamming did not choose the name Slime as a metaphor for decent men. Later in the same interview, he underscores this when he speaks of Grantley Adams ensuring that working class men with great organizing skill "would be erased in some way" (Scott 2002: 113). He may be referring here to rumors of murders of strugglers by those ambitious for the movement to choose them over more worthy and more working class points of reference.

In *Season of Adventure* "the great doubt" is about where independence will go. Early in the novel Crim and Powell are talking about how education has "wiped out" everything from middle class memory except what they've learned:

> "I was thinkin'," he (Crim) said, "how the Independence would change all that wipin' out, change everything that confuse."
>
> Powell's pride had been aroused. His voice came loud and fretful.
>
> "Change my arse," he shouted, "is independence what it is? One day in July you say you want to be that there thing, an' one day in a next July the law say, all right, from now you's what you askin' for. What change that can change?" (Lamming 1979: 17)

In "Politics and Culture," Lamming says that the warnings against betrayal that he makes to the graduates at the UWI graduation ceremony where he is to receive an honorary doctorate "have their origin in my novel, *Season of Adventure*, in which I offered the prediction that the new independence arrangements would inevitably, fail" (Drayton and Andaiye 1992: 79).

The explanation for his ability to sense betrayal before anyone else lies in the experience of childhood which he says made him able to "smell the middle class everywhere"; this experience "is penetrating, moving through me all the time," he explains, and "is in *Season of Adventure*":

> I was in a situation in which I lived in two worlds. This high school was intended for people to go into the Civil Service, the professional classes and so on. But I was alright there: I was a good cricketer, I redeemed myself in that way; my football was very good. But, and this is the one that hit the vein, if I left that school at ten after three in the afternoon, and that laboratory of democracy was still going on, and we were walking down the main street and without warning I saw my mother coming towards me—that was very serious—should I acknowledge her or not? And in those situations she just caught my eye and I caught hers and as we come nearer to each other we are both thinking about the same thing because I am not too sure that I want to be identified there. And in a curious kind of way she does not mind if I don't because of who I am with now—Dr. Somebody's son. (Drayton and Andaiye 1992: 26)

He finds different varieties of traitor, in different places, but most have their roots in colonial education. For G, High School was "the instrument that tore and kept us (G from Trumper, Boy Blue and Bob) apart" (Lamming 2010: 208). In *Season*, Lamming's betrayal of Powell had its origins in his "migration into another world" after a scholarship to secondary school: "And then the division came" (Lamming 1979: 332). In "Politics and Culture," he asks the graduates what they will do with their education: "Whom does your labour serve? And towards what vision of mankind?" (Drayton and Andaiye 1992: 81). "Where shall you stand in relation to that system which will offer you a market-place for the highest bidder for your skills?" (ibid.: 79). These are questions which are at once a warning to the graduates and an indictment of those faculty in the audience who have used their education to achieve social distance from their community:

> You are a minority; and you are a minority because education is scarce; and was intended to be a scarcity so that it might serve as an instrument of a continuing social stratification, an index of privilege and status, a deformed habit of material self- improvement. (Drayton and Andaiye 1992: 80)

In "The Imperial Encirclement" he makes the point that the problem is not only that a man's education gives him a claim to leadership cut off from the class he claims to lead, but that this separation makes him at best useless to the class:

> By virtue of its uniqueness, that is as a minority, by virtue of its training and skill, which in certain areas were superior to those of the masses of the population, it (the educated minority) assumed as a right the status of leadership. It would have seen itself as the head of the society, unaware that a head cannot move without its belly, for it is the belly which feeds the head ... And it is the ancient neglect of the belly that has made for the continuing impoverishment of the head. ("The Imperial Encirclement," Drayton and Andaiye 1992: 207).

In *Season*, the point is sharpened by Crim in the exchange with Powell referred to earlier: "You can call it forget," said Crim, "was a complete wipin' out from his memory. Is like how education wipe out everythin' San Cristobal got except the ceremony an' the bands. To teacher an' all who well-to-do it happen. Everythin' wipe out, leavin' only what they learn." Powell's answer tells us that this "wipin' out" does not only impoverish the educated; it brings danger to the rest of us: "Is bad that wipin' out," he [Powell] said, his voice grown feeble with contrition. "Is murder an' confusion when it happen. It kill everything. Now an' then an' all what is to come it confuse" (Lamming 1979: 17).

In "The Tragedy of a Whole Region" Lamming ascribes Bishop's murder to our collective failure "to make a decisive break with that old colonial legacy which left us tenants of the very ground which the hands of our ancestors have humanized and made fruitful for hostile strangers; and which, out of habit, we call home" (Drayton and Andaiye 1992: 239). I am certain that, then or now, betrayal does not breed only in the colonial legacy. But it is true that the

Caribbean left did little to help the Grenadian people defend themselves against their internal or external enemies; it could not. In fact, I believe that those of us who would have defined ourselves then as part of that left betrayed the Grenadian people and the region, at least by silence and inaction. We were part of the problem and assumed we were part of the solution. Worse: many of us thought we were the solution.

Since then, although the region's survival (or at least, the survival of some of its territories, and I include the 21st century revolution in Venezuela) is threatened, there is no visible movement fighting back and only isolated pockets form part of the growing global movement against war, against debt, against the international finance institutions, against globalization, against internecine tribalism—that is, racism. In all our territories there is a great deal of violence, and all of that violence is turned inward.

"He [Powell] has not been found in the book," Lamming says in "A Visit to Carriacou," "and I suspect he is still alive" (Drayton and Andaiye 1992: 16). Class betrayal is still the fundamental issue of our time. And part of the reason we do not know that is because we have not acknowledged who Mr. Slime is; we have not examined with all our learning and research all the places he does his betraying; and therefore we have not explored how the education most if not all of us here have received, has in some measure betrayed the movement we often claim to be part of and even speak for. That is what happens when novels are taken to be fiction and fictitious politics are taken to be reality. Mr. Slime lives, but so does brother Powell. He is in our movement, with his mother and his sister, and we know every day better, the many faces of the enemy.

ACKNOWLEDGEMENT

This essay was originally a presentation made at "The Sovereignty of the Imagination: The Writings and Thought of George Lamming," University of the West Indies Mona Campus, Kingston, Jamaica, June 5–7, 2003, later published in *The George Lamming Reader: The Aesthetics of Decolonisation*, Ed. Anthony Bogues, Kingston: Ian Randle Publishers, 2011. Errors have been corrected.

NOTES

1. The 1980–1983 speeches are, in chronological order, "On the Murder of Rodney" (June 1980); "Politics and Culture" (1980; month unknown); "The Honourable Member" (August 1981); "Builders of our Caribbean House" (July 1981); "The Imperial Encirclement" (December 1981); "Nationalism and Nation" (1982, month unknown); "A Visit to Carriacou" (November 1982); "The Plantation Mongrel" (November 1983); and "The Tragedy of a Whole Region" (December 1983). They form part of *Conversations—George Lamming: Essays, Addresses and Interviews, 1953-1990*, edited by Richard Drayton and Andaiye (1992).

2. Working People's Alliance, the political party in Guyana of which Rodney was a founding member.

3. Houses in Guyana were typically built on stilts and the space underneath (the bottom-house) used for a variety of purposes: cooking, washing, lying in hammocks, entertaining visitors, holding meetings. The term "what they made happen" is adapted from something that Powell says in *Season* which is very different: "...ever I give you freedom, Crim, then all your future is mine, 'cause whatever you do in freedom is what I make happen" (Lamming 1979: 18).

4. Working class is not used in this paper with the rigidity that led some participants in a regional left meeting in the early 80s to conclude that one Caribbean island had only about 6–8 members of the working class (or some such number).

5. Title of Achebe's famous book.

6. This view is based on my own observations and discussions in Grenada, and those of several colleagues, including working class members of the WPA. It comes out of the visits made in 1980 and 1981, in particular.

7. There was also clearly a plan involving the WPJ and the NJM to forge a unified left: as one small indicator of this, Lamming reports that at the beginning of his relationship with Grenada, he was approached by Bernard Coard, Deputy Prime Minister of Grenada, to use his presumed influence with the WPA to persuade its leadership to reach an accommodation with the People's Progressive Party (PPP).

8. At the time of the betrayal of then British Guiana these elements were not yet in government.

9. The incident that provoked this is recounted in the *Small Axe* interview. See "The Sovereignty of the Imagination: An Interview with George Lamming" by David Scott.

10. Passage edited for clarification.

REFERENCES

Drayton, Richard and Andaiye. 1992. (Eds.). *Conversations, George Lamming: Essays, Addresses and Interviews, 1956–1986.* London: Karia Press.

Lamming, George. 1979. *Season of Adventure.* London: Allison and Busby.

——. 2010. *In the Castle of My Skin.* New York: Longman Caribbean Writers, Longman Publishers.

Scott, David. 2002. "The Sovereignty of the Imagination: An Interview with George Lamming." *Small Axe* 6(2) (September 1): 72–200.

*The Grenada Revolution, the Caribbean Left, and the Regional
Women's Movement: Preliminary Notes on One Journey*
[2010]

MARCH 13, 1979

I was standing outside the Centre of the Working People's Alliance (WPA) in Tiger Bay in the Guyana capital, Georgetown, sometime during the morning of March 13, 1979 when I saw a man running towards the center, shouting. As he came closer I realized that it was one of the leaders of the pre-party WPA, Sase—the last person I would expect to see running down the street dressed in his well-ironed shirt jac and trousers, briefcase flapping against his leg. Not until he reached almost right up to me did I realize that he was shouting "Maurice overthrow Gairy!" As the news spread, members and supporters poured into the center, euphoric. Soon, posters sprang up all over the city proclaiming "De Shah [of Iran] gone! Gairy gone! Who next?"[1] The answer, of course, was "Burnham," the Guyana President. We knew that getting him out of office would be far harder than removing Gairy in Grenada. The blatant and massive rigging of the Guyanese elections of 1968 and 1973 had demonstrated his absolute determination not to be voted out of office. Key institutions had been brought under his control with the Sophia Declaration of 1974 which promulgated the paramountcy of his party over the state. The level of militarization in Guyana far exceeded that in Grenada. To control workers, the President had state ownership of 80 percent of the economy available for abuse. In 1978, with a rigged referendum, he had ensured himself unprecedented powers under the Constitution.[2] In March 1979, the WPA was still a loosely organized though influential pressure group of just about 50–60 members. But at the beginning of 1979 we made the analysis, carried in the January issue of *Dayclean*, that 1979 would be "the year of the turn," and the victory in Grenada was firing our self-belief as it would fire the self-belief of the people of the whole English-speaking Caribbean. This was the world before Reaganism and Thatcherism and neo-liberalism, a world of rebellion on every continent and sometimes on the islands in between—armed anti-colonial and anti-imperial struggles; youth and student uprisings, including in the United States against the Vietnam war; the civil rights movement; the Black power movement; the rise of the second wave of the women's movement. But Grenada was different: Grenada was one of us showing that we, too, could make revolution.

1979–1982

On July 11, 1979, four months after the New Jewel Movement (NJM) came to power in Grenada, Walter Rodney, Rupert Roopnaraine, and other leaders and friends of the pre-party WPA were arrested on suspicion of involvement in the burning down of the Ministry of National Development and Office of the General Secretary of the People's National Congress (PNC).[3] The twin use of the building symbolized ruling party paramountcy, and the size of the PNC's rage was matched only by the triumphant joy of the people. On July 14, after what came to be called "the arson 3" and two others were released on bail, a spontaneous demonstration in their support ended with the murder of a Catholic priest, Father Bernard Darke, by the House of Israel, a self-described religious group which acted as a paramilitary enforcer for the rulers. From July to November, a civil rebellion erupted on the streets of the city and nearby villages.

On July 27, two weeks after the arson and the arrests, the WPA was launched as a party with a program called "Towards a Revolutionary Socialist Guyana." Guyana now had three parties characterizing themselves as socialist—the WPA, the People's Progressive Party (PPP) led by Cheddi Jagan and the governing People's National Congress (PNC) led by Forbes Burnham.

In the region there was a burgeoning of left groups and parties in the 1970s. Clearly they were not of a single tendency. Since 1969 the PPP in Guyana had declared itself a Marxist–Leninist party following Dr. Jagan's return from a Conference of Communist and Workers Parties in Moscow. With its ties to the Soviet Union and Eastern Europe, it could and did offer support to many of the smaller Marxist–Leninist formations that had emerged. Other parties, groups and individuals had come out of the Black Power and Pan African movements of the 1960s and '70s. Among some, including Tim Hector of Antigua and Walter Rodney of Guyana, C. L. R. James was a large influence.[4] In the WPA, leaders had come out of different experiences but shared views that made them suspect to the orthodox left. For example, we believed that rights they usually dismissed as "bourgeois democratic" were rights that had been won by the working people which a working people's revolution had to expand, not reduce or remove.[5] For the PPP, the WPA was dominated by "revolutionary democrats"—in their minds, a damning criticism.

Before and after it came to power as the People's Revolutionary Government of Grenada (PRG), the NJM had a relationship with both the PPP and the PNC. In fact, before the overthrow of Gairy the PNC had provided the NJM with military training and assistance. No doubt mainly for this reason, post-March 13, although several WPA leaders had had a long personal and/or political relationship with Maurice Bishop,[6] there was initially no very close bond between the PRG and the WPA as parties. The private and public criticisms made by

WPA leaders of a number of actions taken by the PRG, beginning with its closure of the *Torchlight* newspaper in October 1979, would have been further irritants.

I don't know what opened the way to a different relationship between the PRG and the WPA but the break with the PNC that followed the NJM's condemnation of the assassination of Walter Rodney in June 1980 obviously facilitated it. Without proof, I believe that the very fact of Walter Rodney's death might also have made the more orthodox of them readier to deal with the WPA; among regional Marxist–Leninists, more than anyone else in the WPA, Rodney was seen as irredeemably anti-vanguardist and "adventurist."[7]

The real rapprochement started with Rupert Roopnaraine's first visit to Grenada in 1981 when he and I attended the First International Conference in Solidarity with Grenada.[8] Both of us were involved in long talks with the PRG leadership, his lasting well beyond my departure from the meeting place, which I left, saying that they had things to discuss that I wasn't a part of.[9]

No account of Grenada between 1979 and 1983, however critical, can deny the achievements of the four years or the spirit which the process released in the Grenadian people. I was excited and moved to the point that like many others, I was for a long time completely uncritical. On what I remember as my first visit, which was in 1980 or early in 1981, I attended a parish council meeting and a rally alive with energy and visited new housing and schools and, I recall, a newly-built farm run on modern lines. My guide was Phyllis Coard, and I was struck by the enthusiasm she exuded for concrete gains. At the farm she took me through every stage of production, explaining all the details. With and through her I met women who were introduced to me as members and leaders of the National Women's Organization (NWO). My recollection is that I was told at the time that the NWO had more than five thousand members. According to Marable (1987: 238), in early 1982 its membership had reached 6,500 women organized in 155 local units. Far more than any experience I'd had before or have had since, Grenada in those years seemed a living experience of the possibility of transformation and of the reality of region: regional solidarity activists were an ongoing presence; there were regular gatherings of the regional left; and later on, in November 1982, cultural activists collectively added their active support with the First Conference of Intellectual Workers for Regional Sovereignty of the Caribbean.

The left parties met for political training led by the Workers' Party of Jamaica (WPJ), along with the NJM. We also met for political strategizing. I can no longer remember which encounters included which organizations but I remember that many of the unorthodox did not participate in the training. I remember, too, the tensions between the different tendencies. The relationship of some of the left was clearly to Bishop: the Oilfield Workers Trade Union (OWTU) of Trinidad and Tobago, Tim Hector of Antigua and Barbuda,

Bill Riviere of Dominica, Bobby Clarke of Barbados. In one of the training sessions Bishop paid a surprise visit (at least, it was a surprise to many of us), welcomed us, then during his remarks, made the point that work plans were all very well but when all was said and done we had to remember the people out there—not an orthodox view of the importance of political education. Of all the party leaders involved, the one I remember as most openly critical of Marxist–Leninist orthodoxy and of some of the decisions the NJM had taken was Tim Hector of the Antigua Caribbean Liberation Movement (ACLM).[10] Among the most orthodox, I vividly remember Michael Als from the People's Popular Movement (PPM) of Trinidad and Tobago.[11] Representatives of the February 17th movement of Trinidad and Tobago also participated in some of the regional gatherings. Again, I don't recall which.[12]

I also became aware of other tensions. As I've written elsewhere:

> The cultural workers Lamming coordinated to work in and for Grenada were not universally welcomed by the NJM leadership: while for Lamming culture could never be "decoration of daily life"—or, in the crude sense, a tool—for the Grenada government, the job of these workers was simply to mobilize support for the revolution; and for the orthodox Marxist–Leninists inside the party, Lamming was simply a "social democrat." (Essay 2, this volume)

I would amend this now only to say that the impression I got was of Jackie Creft's close involvement with the work of organizing the conference and her embrace of the notion of cultural workers as intrinsic to the revolutionary process; of Maurice Bishop's support for it; and of the orthodox party leaders as at least dismissive of it.

I was uncritical of the revolution but as always, irreverent. And irreverence was my inadequate and irresponsible response to a political education session on party building where the men guiding the training,[13] explained the need for the cadre party to be based on "real" workers who would be trained in the science (of Marxism–Leninism), while others would be in mass organizations. As I was musing on this (the WPA was not a cadre party, had no mass organizations, and had a definition of working people which included housewives in working class households and unemployed people "who have known the discipline of a wage"), the leader of the left party in an island with a rural economy said that this would mean that his party could only have as members the six to eight workers at the single factory-type establishment in his country. I can't quote the answer they gave him but I remember its import: effectively it was that if you have six to eight real workers that is where your cadres will come from. My mind registered the disjuncture between the "science" and the reality. I said nothing.

In Guyana, PPP and PNC mass organizations were directed by the parties. In Grenada, was there hope that in the conditions of revolution they would be more than this? Perhaps they could be, as we were told the parish councils and the zonal councils were, centers of popular power. Later I would see that this was far from the case.

OCTOBER 1983 AND AFTER

The internal conflicts which came to a head in August/September 1983 have been well-documented, including in the minutes of the NJM Political Bureau and Central Committee which the United States seized and gleefully made public after the invasion.[14] These minutes showed that the conflict had begun to deepen at least since 1982. In 1982, too, we would later learn, there were splits in the regional left's solidarity with the NJM. Quest (2007) reports that by that year Tim Hector had broken all relations with "Maurice Bishop's Grenada" and that among his criticisms were the closure of Torchlight, the increasing number of political prisoners, and the failure to curb the "fetish of democratic centralism within the one party state." If the Grenada revolution did not mean independent and elected mass councils and organizations existing side by side with a "provisional executive authority," he is said to have argued, "it would mean nothing."

Among parties which had been close to the NJM, the events beginning with the placing of Maurice Bishop under house arrest and ending with the US invasion forced a rethinking. In the WPA some of the rethinking began at the individual level. The WPA had begun Marxist–Leninist training sometime in 1982,[15] but now the main Field Organizer, Karen de Souza, said that she wanted no part of an ideology that "could do that" to one of the murder accused whom she had particularly liked on her visits to Grenada. Kathy Wills, an older woman whose energy fueled our community-based and street organizing, mourned, "At least Walter was killed by his enemies." There was also collective rethinking. Roopnaraine (2009) reminds us that by 1984 we had abandoned the project of transforming the WPA into a cadre party; dismantled clandestine units; and opted for the electoral path and the return to a mass party.[16] In other words, "the Marxist–Leninist group had to retreat in the face of Grenada" (Rupert Roopnaraine, personal conversation, May 18, 2010).[17] But the WPA survived. Before and after 1984 it continued its political organizing, a high point of which was the food rebellion of 1983 which was led by an alliance we spearheaded, the Sugar and Bauxite Workers Unity Committee (our notion of a "mass org"), and though we did not recognize it at the time, grassroots housewives.

As for other parties, small Marxist–Leninist formations were weakened or collapsed in the wake of the Grenada tragedy, some almost immediately; but as far as I know from the outside, the PPP in Guyana remained untouched, surviving because it was an electoral force and because it had a guaranteed vote based on ethnicity and not on ideology.

The collapse of the left parties—not in itself a bad thing—led not to the effort to build and rebuild movements, but to the NGOization of the region; not only because women and men from left parties formed or joined NGOs, but because they became leaders of a retreat from the project of transformation. Many individual NGOs do useful work—but a proliferation of NGOs, as in Haiti with its estimated fifteen thousand, suggests a plan: pacification not via the military but via the apparently benign activity of NGOs. Haiti also provides us with the clearest example of how we have moved from taking our lead from the working people to taking our lead from the "progressive forces" even where they show their hand by allying with sweatshop owners, armed gangs, drug dealers and mercenaries led by former leaders of the FRAPH death squad and Duvalierists,[18] to carry out the wishes of the United States, as in the February 2004 coup against President Jean Bertrand Aristide.

*   *   *

I want to turn now to look briefly at issues of how women organize.

When the Grenada revolution destroyed itself (albeit under massive pressure from the United States) I was curious about what—if any—role the NWO had played vis-à-vis the internal crisis in the party.

The answer was, it seems, none. First, perhaps, because its decline paralleled that of the party itself. It was smaller in number. Marable says that by mid-1983 it was rapidly losing members. But the decline in numbers was not the only reason for its inaction. The inaction was rooted in the very structure of the cadre party/"mass org" relation.

At an NJM Central Committee meeting in July 1983 which discussed the general crisis, Phyllis Coard blamed the problems on petit bourgeois traits. Yet she herself had led a delegation to a Central Committee meeting on Wednesday September 22, 1982 which included Maurice Bishop and Bernard Coard, to discuss the problems of women party members as put forward in their document to the Political Bureau. They described their concerns as the tremendous overwork and tiredness of women party members; financial problems of women party members who were single mothers; and the non-comprehension of party men of the problems facing women. And so it proved. In response the CC made some specific suggestions, for example, "study must also look at family education (men and women)," and the proposal of the Women's Committee that "there should be somebody at the Secretariat level, that comrades can check on their personal problems." But all too many of the answers it gave were dismissive and sexist. For example, "financial problems are also experienced by men"; or, the lack of concern and support shown by men for the women they have a relationship with "is not to excuse women for wat [sic] they do to earn disrespect"; or "There is an attitude among women members of laziness, mask for excuses, ill discipline." And then there was the following—to me—disturbing readiness to respond to grave, concrete problems with meaningless abstraction: "we must see the woman question," the Central Committee said, "as one of the contradictions within the society and must see the problems of women globally."

It must be clear by now that the place from which I struggled to understand the meaning of Grenada was via the women, and I want to make one last reference to the NWO leader. The Minutes of the Extraordinary Meeting of the Central Committee of the NJM, September 14–16, 1983, record that following a brief narrative analysis of the state of affairs she made at that meeting, Phyllis Coard added "we [word illegible] recognize that the situation is very serious. *The mood of the party members can be graded as (1) or lower. The mood of the masses can be graded as 1.5*" (my emphasis). This description of where party members and the people had reached, rendered in terms of a number out of ten, made me think of Martin Carter, the Guyanese poet, who in his despair over Guyana was often heard saying that Third World Marxist–Leninists had read only the little booklets published by Progress Publishers just for them, and never read Lenin themselves—to which I would add that they had never read, for example, where he said "History as a whole is always richer in content, more varied, more multiform, more lively and more ingenious than is imagined by *even* [my emphasis] the best of parties (Lenin in "Left Wing Communism" cited in Marable 1987: 270). This is not an understanding that can be expressed in "The mood of the masses can be graded as 1.5."

As the WPA woman with the closest relationship to Grenada I had particular problems coming to terms with all this. Even if I had known the precipitous fall in the size and activism of the NWO, I would still have been struck to the core by the realization that it did not have even the minimum capacity for self-direction to bring a human voice into the party crisis as it developed. I want to be fair. This is not something I have discussed with any woman then in Grenada except for one Guyanese who had never been politically engaged before she went there and joined the NJM. She told me that she agonized after the events of October 1983 that she had voted with the majority, angered by Bishop's rejection of the joint leadership proposal because, she said, it was he who had drawn her into the party and he who spoke to her about issues like taking study more seriously, and she felt that he was betraying what he had stood for. The agony was that, as someone later commented, she "had allowed herself to betray her gut and her common sense" (Karen de Souza, private conversation, May 18, 2010).

The story of the NJM women as I saw it, was a large part of the catalyst to my joining CAFRA and helping to form Red Thread, which in the initial years was an NGO whose founders were all members or supporters of the WPA but which did not report to the WPA. This was in the mid-1980s.

I want to close the discussion on women with a very brief note on how I believe Grenada helped shape the regional feminist movement. Again without proof (though based on numerous conversations), I believe that when CAFRA was founded in 1985, the presence of a few key women who had been members or supporters of Marxist–Leninist and other left parties close to the NJM in the period leading up to October 1983, was at least one large reason for its endless search for a style of leadership that was "feminist"—meaning "democratic"—and able to see all sides in a way that the left parties could not; and its insistence on what I used to call "let a thousand flowers bloom," meaning, let all tendencies be part of CAFRA. I don't want to develop the criticism I've made of this here but just mention that the lack of attention to the different levels of power among women meant that far from achieving this "non-hierarchical" form of leadership, what we had was the exercise of what Honor Ford-Smith called in *Ring Ding in a Tight Corner* informal power by those sectors with the most power.

In turn, this meant that our agenda was not shaped by and for women with the least—and this led inevitably to the tendency to isolate gender from its interconnections with class, race and other power relations, and to put technocratic "solutions" in place of transformative solutions, allowing us (as I have done) to commit betrayals such as mainstream gender into neo-liberal plans and policies and to do what I have called elsewhere, genderize imperialism.

In very summary conclusion: whether we are talking about regional women or any other sector of what are still referred to as the "progressive forces" of the Caribbean, in the end the Grenada whose influence lasted was the Grenada of October 1983, not the Grenada that achieved so much in a few years. Clearly that is not the total explanation for the low level of struggle in the English-speaking part of the region. The collapse of Soviet style socialism and the rise of neo-liberalism are the global context in which the movement for transformation worldwide weakened. But it is rising elsewhere; and the absence of any upsurge of regional action against the onslaught of violence of which women, children and poor men are the major victims (even as men are the main perpetrators), and the blatant economic aggression of the Economic Partnership Agreement and the Structural Adjustment Programmes that so many regional governments are again adopting—to choose just two examples—is a reflection of the drastically diminished sense of our possibilities that has grown in the region post-October 1983. It is time we get over it.

ACKNOWLEDGEMENTS

This essay was prepared for a panel, "The Grenada Revolution: Regional Perspectives," Wednesday May 26, 2010, Caribbean Studies Association Annual Conference, May 24–28, 2010, Barbados.

NOTES

1. In his presentation on April 5, 2009 at the University of Pittsburgh Rupert Roopnaraine placed the March *Dayclean* which had the same headline first.
2. The measures Burnham introduced—e.g. nationalization—were often good in principle; it was his use of them that was destructive and anti-working class.
3. Others arrested included Karen de Souza (who joined the WPA out of this experience) and Bonita Harris (who was held briefly)—both of whom were later two of the founders of Red Thread.
4. Eusi Kwayana called Hector "a political pioneer of the Jamesian Left." See his afterword, "Tim Hector, Political Values and National Reconstruction," in Bhule (2006: 219).
5. The pioneering work on this was by C. Y. Thomas.
6. This includes Walter Rodney, Clive Thomas, as well as Eusi Kwayana who had worked closely with Bishop in the preparations for the 6th Pan-African Congress. Bishop had also been one of the members of the defense team for Arnold Rampersaud, an Indo-Guyanese PPP member who was being framed for the murder of an African-Guyanese policeman. Rodney played an active part in the successful agitation for him to be found not guilty.
7. This in spite of the fact that key WPA founders—Eusi Kwayana, Clive Thomas, Moses Bhagwan—were just as strongly anti-vanguardist. It was also true that since the late 1960s, before and after he was banned from Jamaica, Rodney had been characterized as adventurist not only by the Jamaican government and the CIA but some of the left (see West 2008).
8. Prior to this there had been a ban on Roopnaraine's travel.
9. What I meant was that I wasn't in the WPA's clandestine unit. It was also true that at the time I was visibly in bad physical and emotional shape. An aside on the rapprochement: the behavior of two women from a Marxist–Leninist party made me suspicious that our exclusion from and subsequent welcome by the Marxist–Leninists in the grouping were both formal decisions. After treating me with demonstrable coldness pre-1981, in late 1981 they literally embraced me.
10. Later, the ACLM became a member of the United Progressive Party led by Baldwin Spencer and Tim Hector was appointed a senator by the UPP. He was dismissed by the UPP after attending an international conference as an adviser to Bird against their instructions. His former ACLM colleagues were very critical of what was seen as his "softening" towards Bird.
11. Karen de Souza also remembers him from her visits to Grenada, finding him "scathing about the WPA's lack of ideological purity."
12. All this is based both on my own recollections and those of Rupert Roopnaraine, with whom I spoke by phone on May 20, 2010.
13. By this time and in this process the PPP was clearly not the senior left party.
14. I use these because I have not heard or read anywhere that they are falsifications.
15. A draft Constitution for the WPA as a cadre party had been ready since 1979 but had never been implemented.
16. The party had never fully transformed itself into a cadre party. It had members that were not Marxists at all, and many who were not Marxist–Leninist.
17. Nigel Westmass, in an email of May 15, 2010, has reminded me of the tensions in the WPA over the direction the party should take, and Roopnaraine, in the May 18

conversation, of C. Y. Thomas's vehement objections to a proposal that a WPA Code of Conduct should include the vetting of members' writing before publication.

18. "Caribbean Women Denounce the US-Backed Coup in Haiti," statement by Caribbean women, March 2004.

REFERENCES

Bhule, Paul. 2006. *Tim Hector: A Caribbean Radical's Story*. Jackson, MS: University Press of Mississippi.

Ford-Smith, Honor. 1989. *Ring Ding in a Tight Corner: A Case Study of Funding and Organizational Democracy in Sistren, 1977–1988*. Toronto: The Women's Program, ICAE.

Marable, Manning. 1987. "Maurice Bishop and the Grenada Revolution." In *African and Caribbean Politics from Kwame Nkrumah to Maurice Bishop*. London: Verso.

Quest, Matthew. 2007. "Legislating the Caribbean General Will: The Later Thoughts of Tim Hector, 1979-2002." In *CLR James Journal* (special issue on Antigua) 13(1): 211–32.

Roopnaraine, Rupert. 2009. "Resonances of Revolution: Grenada, Suriname, Guyana." Presented to the colloquium "Remembering the Future: The Legacies of Radical Politics in the Caribbean." University of Pittsburgh, April 5, 2009.

US State Department. 1984. "Grenada Documents: An Overview and Selection." Released by the Department of State and the Department of Defense, USA, September. Washington, DC.

West, Michael O. 2008. "Seeing Darkly: Guyana, Black Power and Walter Rodney's Expulsion from Jamaica." *Small Axe* 25 (February): 93–104.

Conversations about Organizing: Revised Excerpts from an Interview with Andaiye by David Scott
[2004]

INSIDE THE WORKING PEOPLE'S ALLIANCE

DS: So let's talk a little bit about the WPA in its shift from a pre-party formation to a party formation. You return on the eve of its becoming formally a political party. What's going on in Guyana, and what is going on inside debates among those who are involved in the pre-party structure that is propelling it in the direction of becoming a formal political party?

A: You know, things moved much more slowly than that—and then leapt. So January '78 is far from being the "eve" of the WPA becoming a party. And maybe "pre-party" is a misnomer because it suggests that we were always thinking of becoming a party, which is not so.

Before I came back [to Guyana], they had done all kinds of work. Walter, Eusi, Clive,[1] and others were doing bottom-house classes with bauxite workers and sugar workers. They had done that extraordinary organizing around Arnold Rampersaud, extraordinary for Guyana because what it meant was that a group of largely Afro-Guyanese people rose to the defense of an Indo-Guyanese PPP man.[2] [They rose up] not only against the Afro-Guyanese government but against the Afro-Guyanese police. They were here and they were active, but they still thought of themselves as a pressure group, and as a group, if you like, working to change … I hate people who talk about changing consciousness, so I'll withdraw that. I think what they were trying to build was the possibility of multiracialness, particularly among workers—hence the concentration on bauxite workers and sugar workers.

They had an executive; that was the structure. The WPA itself met every two weeks, the whole fifty-something people, somewhat shifting. A huge core of people came all the time, but [its size was] shifting otherwise. That [executive] was their only structure, to which Rupert[3] and I got elected at the first meeting. The WPA was taken up a lot in '78 with the struggle against the referendum, which was really a struggle to stop (Forbes) Burnham enlarging his powers. It was really very exciting in those days. I remember one Sunday Kwayana summoned us all out of the holes where we were just liming and enjoying ourselves to say, "Read this thing [the Official Gazette]." So we looked and we didn't get it. Only Kwayana got it. If Clive and the rest of them say they got it,

I will have to concede. But my frank view is that none of us got it: that what Burnham meant was that this referendum was to end all referenda.

Somewhere within that year, talk developed of a party. But the pressure group WPA is still going on. For example, workers at a restaurant go on strike, the WPA would summon out the whole fifty-something or seventy-something (whatever we had become by then), and what you would do is to go to support that strike for whatever number of days it took. I think it was the summer of 1978 that Rupert and Clive were going to be in New York for some purpose and together had the job of drafting a party program. They were the original drafters of *Towards a Revolutionary Socialist Guyana*. The discussions really began to crystallize around the discussion of the draft they wrote. For me, that was the point at which you could say that all of us became engaged in thinking and talking about becoming a political party, and about having a program for transformation beyond what we had been doing all the time.

Many people then in the WPA had come because they were opposed to Burnham but nobody there, I think, in the beginning saw ourselves as an alternative to Burnham; or as doing more than trying to change the society so that the society might in turn change the regime.

DS: What was the response of the Burnham regime to this incipient organizational emergence, the WPA?

A: Well, obviously the very refusal to give Walter the job [at UG] was in the hope that he wouldn't come back.[4] And they could not have liked from the very beginning what he began to encourage. People like Clive Thomas and Eusi Kwayana had their own independent roads to the WPA, but I think it's always true that somebody like a Walter may suddenly act as the catalyst for the coming together and movement forward of people who were walking somewhat differently. I think Walter was that. I think, from that point of view, he was always feared. Much, much later, I had a friend who used to be near the top ranks of the PNC, and she told me that Burnham used to inveigh against what he saw as a pack of middle-class, urban people, who basically were opposed to the revolutionary things that the PNC was doing. She said that was the angle from which people like her saw people like us, and therefore would accept us being dealt with in the way that we were.

DS: Let me ask you something about the perception of Walter. He was offered the job, and he comes back expecting to take the post; then he is denied the job. And in the Burnham regime there is not only a decision to be vindictive but a real concern that Walter might become the center of something. What's that based on? Walter has not been in Guyana for a long time. He had some role in pre-'68 Jamaica, but then he is prevented from entry, and is now away. He has become somewhat well known through *How Europe Underdeveloped Africa*.[5]

He is involved in various East African struggles. But what is it that makes him such a seeming threat?

A: I always thought that he had captured people's imaginations before he came back. Think of how we heard of him.

DS: That's what I want to get at.

A: How we heard of him was by radio and newspaper and word-of-mouth— that he was thrown out of Jamaica. You had this sense, even me who had known him since childhood—and certainly a lot of people I knew who were younger had this sense too—of him as a person who acted in ways that made governments afraid. These are not people who began by reading *How Europe Underdeveloped Africa*. These are people who first heard of Walter Rodney via, say, mutual friends who were in Jamaica. There was this extraordinary relation between him and Rasta in Jamaica which Rasta here [in Guyana] would hear about—this Black university man that a Black government throw out, this Black university man that goes through the region and is thrown out of this place [and that place]. He captured your imagination. So much so that I remember these huge demonstrations for this man that they didn't know. It was a response to this person that you knew had to be—there was a word that we used to use in those days—a forwarder.

One of the rallies, which ASCRIA organized and invited the PPP and others to join, was savagely broken up by House of Israel boy soldiers with revolvers.[6] *The term "boy soldiers with revolvers" should be more precise. To clarify, House of Israel assailants, many of whom were teenagers, typically carried weapons including sticks, bottles and bricks, and sometimes small handguns [Added].*[7] There was a handbill attacking Eusi in particular. Tacuma Ogunseye, who was chairing, was injured. Cheddi Jagan was physically hurt—the attack had begun when he attempted to speak. At the first rally, they had tried to drown Eusi out because they were enraged that he was appearing with Jagan.

DS: This question is about the imagined Walter. Because there is a curious way in which the idea that Walter might be a catalyst of something, that there was some energy in Walter, was a matter of concern to the official regimes in the Caribbean, in the region, but also a matter of concern to at least some parts of the emerging left. The WPJ [Workers' Party of Jamaica] ...

A: Couldn't stand him.

DS: Exactly. And therefore there was a curious way in which there was a repu- tation or an image in circulation of a maverick of a certain sort that was to be feared or at least people were to be cautious about. But you're saying that that sense of Walter was in circulation in Guyana among people who might not have read what he was saying.

A: But people would have read *Groundings with my Brothers*.[8] That was another way he entered people's imaginations.

DS: In 1978 you are elected to the executive of the WPA. From that point on, how does the WPA begin to transform itself and solidify itself into a functioning political party?

A: I'll tell you what I know and then I'll tell you what I think. I know, for example, that it was Rupert who was instrumental in getting us a center. All of the rest of us would have been too scared financially. We had no money. Rupert is the kind of person who could have no money and feel he must go and rent a place. And he did. He and Jocelyn Dow.[9] It made a big difference. You were not just this group that met every two weeks in somebody else's place. You now had a place where you could go every day. And that made a huge difference. I suspect that Rupert would have had a hand in the movement towards the party program, because he is far more oriented towards structure. Clive might have been [like that], I don't know that, but I know that's what Rupert is like. So the center is very important in terms of solidifying the group. At that stage [also], you also now have to have a coordinator, and that was me. From 1978 to when Walter was killed, I was party coordinator (a job that often included unblocking blocked toilets, by hand) and party editor for *Dayclean* and all other publications. I also had another job—to be available to listen to personal problems in my house at any hour of the night; Walter coined the name Mrs. Packer (Personal Affairs Committee) for me.

So sometime in 1978 things begin to become more structured. You have a center from which you're going to produce this [political work], where you're going to meet. And then, of course, you begin to have regular discussions (I think it was at the end of that summer) around the draft program that Clive and Rupert have brought back [from New York].

DS: What in those early years, in 1978, '79 (to the extent that you could gauge it), was the popular response to the WPA?

A: Which year? When?

DS: Nineteen seventy-eight, '79; as it is solidifying and as you are moving towards party formation. Is there a sense that it is warranted, not only because of the worrisome official political conjuncture that you are arriving at (Burnham's moves to lock out political opposition) but a sense that Guyanese people are ready for a new formation?

A: I would say that until July 27, 1979, there were two responses to the WPA. On the one hand, a lot of people were attracted to the call for multiracial politics. A lot of people were very attracted to what came across, I thought, as the courage of saying out loud what needed to be said about Burnham, in a context where the rest of the society was afraid. At the same time that that was true, it seemed to me that most people also assumed that there was no space for anything other than a group that did education and wrote and demonstrated. People really thought the political party space was closed out by the PPP and the PNC. I never got the impression in that period that anybody was responding to us as a potential third force. I really never felt it. I thought that they found us significant at the level of ideas, and perhaps changing ideas. And then the building burned down.[10]

DS: That's what captures the popular imagination.

A: Yes, yes.

DS: So as the WPA is solidifying into a party, the project as you all are discussing it, has as its objective the overthrow of Burnham. That's the talk then. That what is required is the revolutionary overthrow of the Burnham regime.

A: Yes. … The reason for the hesitation is because it was couched in the language of "Burnham must go and he must go by any means necessary." But the WPA functioned a lot, not only pre-party but afterwards, as these things do, very much on a need-to-know basis. And therefore there would not be general talk inside WPA about "overthrow."

DS: Right, I can understand that. But what is becoming central to the WPA—this is my question—is less pressure group opposition, even though that might still have been what was going on in practical terms, but the question of the extent to which state power could be captured. The question of state power has by then become part of the discussion.

A: Yes. For me there was always a built-in contradiction in the WPA. Because I don't personally know anybody in the WPA who wanted to run the state, who saw themselves as the [prime minister], you understand? It really came to a head one day when we were supposed to put up names for the national government we had proposed. We had made some very precise proposals for how many people from each party and group should be in the government. Our position was that since we had not had any free and fair elections, we should not deal with party size; each party or group should have nine representatives. For some reason, somebody outside of the WPA was looking for a discussion in which you knew the names of your nine representatives.

DS: You didn't.

A: We didn't. There was no such thing. The discussion inside the WPA went around the room, and it was just as if people had taken time off from their real lives—Rupert from film, Walter [from history] and so on—in order to do this necessary political work but had never expected himself or herself to have to carry it beyond that. *This is not well explained. What I mean is that we saw our leadership of the struggle as temporary, and didn't relate to ourselves as a government in waiting. Relatedly, the nature of our politics meant that what we expected was that the process of struggle would throw up leaders, as it had already started to do. However, while no one that I know of wanted personal power in the way many people in politics seem to do, I am not suggesting that each of us was going to walk away from the next stage of politics in Guyana. [Added]*

DS: That's very interesting. I remember Rupert Lewis saying something similar about the difference between the WPA as a whole and some members of the WPJ.[11] So I want now to come to a couple of questions around this relation. This is 1978, 1979, and there is already a Marxist party in the region, the WPJ,[12] which sees itself as …

A: … the leader of all men. You could put that in the magazine.

DS: Yes I will. What is the WPA's sense of the WPJ and what it represented?

A: First of all, we would have to break it up more than that. Rupert [Roopna-raine] would be the person subsequently who, although not totally like them, would have been far more Leninist than any of the other major male figures in the WPA in terms of the notion of party structure, democratic centralism, those things. Walter and Clive and Eusi and Moses and Josh and other men like Tacuma Ogunseye and Sase Omo completely rejected notions like bourgeois democracy. They felt and some wrote that in our part of the world (other people could speak for themselves)—those rights having been fought for and won by the working class, they were not rights that we were willing to turn our backs on on the grounds that they were "bourgeois democratic rights." That whole language that certain parts of the orthodox left used was just totally outside of any WPA discussion. Inside WPA, Walter was not a maverick. People were more like him than they were like Trevor Munroe.[13]

DS: Inside the WPA, people were more like Walter than like Rupert?

A: Yes. There are several reasons for that, one being where you have learned your politics. A lot of them had learned their politics [in the context of Burnham]. Rupert's politics were not created in a response to Burnham. If your politics are created in response to Burnham, then you're not going to be attracted by the notion that certain rights are bourgeois democratic rights which it is revolutionary to do away with, because those are the rights that are being taken away from you.

DS: But would you say that Walter's politics are formed in relation to Burnham? After all, Walter is not in Guyana from the early 1960s.

A: I did not say that his politics were formed in relation to Burnham; I said that it's not an accident to me that people would find much that he is saying, and that Clive is saying, and that Eusi is saying, attractive, because what they were saying so closely matched the reality that people were living here [in Guyana]. Walter's politics were formed by growing up here and then going to Jamaica, by his work with C. L. R. James and Selma James, by his studies, by the left in

England, by Jamaica again and Tanzania and Cuba—he wrote to Selma about Cuba "Man is in charge here"—meaning, human beings—not the inhumanity of capital. You had a government in Guyana that said it was socialist, that said that these rights were just being manipulated by the bourgeoisie. All of those things came across as being false abstractions in relation to people's daily experience. Not to mention, of course, that Rupert came back relatively late. Nonetheless, there's a whole role that Rupert played in terms of the period in which we did begin to solidify, to structure ourselves as a party. That was very much Rupert.

DS: So there is no discussion between the WPJ and you inside the WPA as it is emerging as a political party.

A: As far as I know the WPJ treated us with total contempt in the early years. I have no doubt that they would have spoken to an individual when they came across him; him, not her. Our relationship with the WPJ started post-Grenada (at the start of the revolution), and it was part of an emerging relationship in the left, and it was very clear ... I mean, look, outside of Rupert, I am the person who was closest to that scene and became closest to elements in the WPJ and to NJM [New Jewel Movement]. And even though I was very willing to be swept along in that, I was never so stupid that I could not see that somewhere there had been a discussion and a decision, that in relation to Guyana, what they would do is go with the WPA. This was after Walter was assassinated. That they had decided as well who in the WPA [they would talk to].

They had decided what it is they wanted, because they moved overnight from behaving as if we did not exist to this sudden embrace. And as usual, who gives the game away is women. There were women in the WPJ who had never dealt with me at all, even when we were in the same place, who suddenly now have been sent to embrace me.

DS: Was there a sense, then, in which the emerging left movement in Guyana was isolated. I'm remembering some of your remarks yesterday that Guyana's isolation in the region is not new. Is there a similar sense that you were isolated by other leftists in the region who felt themselves more advanced, and that you all were minding your own business and carrying on with what you had to do here in Guyana?

A: I don't remember talking about it, to tell you the truth. Remember that you are talking about days when the WPA in Guyana is huge. Nineteen seventy-nine? Huge. I don't remember anybody in the WPA feeling weakened or demoralized by any sense that we are held in contempt by the WPJ. That's just true. These are my words. I don't remember anybody ever saying that.

What we knew was that we were surrounded by orthodoxy which found us ... well, all the various words that they would use. That was very explicit and led by the WPJ. But there were all kinds of much smaller formations, in Trinidad and so on, that were part of that. And in Guyana, that was the PPP's view. That we were—what were the various things? I don't remember now—adventurists? But remember there were also left regional parties and trade unions which were no part of the orthodox left. We had relations with those parties and unions.

DS: Let me ask you a question from the other side. Was there a sense, as the WPA is emerging, that one crucial element ought to be the emergence of a regional left, not merely a national left?

A: I don't know. Let me try to describe something for you. I can't answer for all the levels of discussion that took place, although I was on the executive, the Political Bureau. But after we formed, the way that our lives went here was having to discuss everyday immediate things: both the immediate politics of what we were doing, and the immediate questions of security, of safety, and so on. I honestly do not remember conversations of that kind [about the left in the region].

DS: As I am listening to myself ask the questions and listening to you answer them, I am aware that there's a certain, perhaps, Jamaica-centricity to them. Let me tell you what I mean. Listening to you—and I had a similar sense listening to Eusi when I asked him about it—that quite apart from the arrogance of the WPJ, there was a sense among people involved in the emerging WPA that what had to be dealt with on a day-to-day basis was a crisis of a size and shape that certainly did not exist anywhere else in the region—not in Jamaica, nor in Trinidad. And therefore the space for posturing did not exist in the Guyana situation in the way that it existed in Jamaica. Is that true?

A: That is true. That's true. I think it's also true, to be fair, that there are things that are not posturing that needed to be talked about that we probably did not have time for because our lives were largely overtaken by the political crisis and by the ways in which the political crisis defined your daily life. You're talking about a whole heap of people already out of jobs, another set who lose their jobs; you're talking about a time in which it would be routine to have your meetings broken up, and to be hit if not beaten. Routine to have your home searched. Routine to be arrested, held, some charged, some not. It was like that.

DS: It was like that. What was the role, 1978, 1979, of intellectual discussion of the sort that's not immediately connected to whether we should demonstrate tomorrow, or what our position should be in relation to this strike? Was there intellectual discussion of a more general nature about, say, class, its relation to race, the question of gender? Were there intellectual discussions of that sort inside the WPA? Were there intellectual cells that met to read and so on?

A: After July 27, 1979, when we were launched, there was a point at which Rupert—with my assistance a lot—was doing something called party education.

And you know what party education is, so you know that it's a very preliminary, conventional, low-level kind of thing. That would happen; the thing that you are talking about, no.

DS: So there wasn't a self-consciousness inside the party that, quite apart from educating the masses, there was a kind of intellectual work that the party needed to do internally?

A: I don't think there was. I wouldn't say that there was any lack of consciousness of the need for that. But in my perception, that [popular] response was so huge, and so unanticipated, that it overtook us. *To clarify, the popular response was not unanticipated; its enormous size was. [Added]*

I do not even know what the size of the membership of the WPA was in August 1979.

DS: It leapt forward.

A: Shortly after launching the party we went to the Corentyne—several of us, I know Walter was there, and I think Rupert was there. We're going to stay in … maybe it was a school, one of those buildings. And in the morning there was this noise. So we got up to see what the noise was. People! Indo-Guyanese, Afro-Guyanese, mixed. We asked them what they came for. They'd come to join. As far as the eye could see: people. Nobody knew that was going to happen. So, in fact, part of what you would have to be talking about is what to do with that; because although we were accused by various persons of never being concerned about safety, that wasn't true. But now you had to discuss what your obligation is to your own security versus that [large mass of popular enthusiasm]. And now you are struggling to come to terms with things that seemed abstractions before: like [the idea of a] cadre party. Because one of the things about a cadre party is not just the arrogance of the handful; it has also to do with safety.

DS: Andaiye, you spoke earlier [off-tape] about the use of a ridiculing ditty in the wake of Rodney's assassination. Can you say more about that?

A: There were some leaflets left on the bridge of his house either the night of his assassination or the morning after.[14] And they began, "Hickory Dickory Dock," and then created a ditty alleging that he'd had a bomb which exploded. I personally felt (and a lot of other people felt the same) that this was not a touch that seemed Burnham-esque. In spite of the fact that one knew that Walter had really offended Burnham, enraged him with the Midas touch story (that everything he touches turns to shit), Burnham was—even when enraged—a very clever man, and a man who would know that in our kind of culture you speak well of the dead. He wouldn't want to speak well of Walter, but it would seem to me that he would know that, whether or not they supported Walter, people would find the use of a ditty to mock a man who has just been blown up, offensive—as indeed people did. And that was just one of the pieces of purely circumstantial evidence that led me for one, and several other people, to think that Walter's assassination was not the direct responsibility of Forbes Burnham.

DS: But was whose?

A: A less clever person.

DS: So, nevertheless, it was the work of the [Burnham] regime.

A: Yes; or work from *within* the regime. *This is not intended to mean that I don't hold Burnham ultimately responsible; I do. [Added]*

DS: I've heard it said that there is a sense in which Burnham and Rodney were rival egos, that there was a very powerful rivalry between them.

A: I've heard it too. I didn't feel that from Walter's side. I never felt that that's what he was doing. To say that is to demean what Walter was trying to do, and what he did succeed in doing. We didn't follow an ego, but someone who was committed to opposing what Burnham was murdering in all of us. I saw him, we saw him, make a very deliberate decision and he tried to write about it in popular form, in *People's Power, No Dictator*, which, incidentally, I didn't at the time understand the importance of until he expressed to me his disappointment that we only had funds to produce maybe a couple thousand. Then I understood that he had meant this to be in written form what he was attempting to do orally from the platform. One aspect of that—not the total thing—was that he felt that given the fact that what people felt about Burnham was awe and fear, what one had to do was cut him down to size. And in that sense, yes, he was pitting himself against Burnham, as the one who cut him down to size. Somebody must do it. And he was in a sense saying, "Yes, I'll do it." But I never felt as though it was in a competition of ego. And this is not to pretend that I thought Walter was a humble person, because I didn't think he was. I'm not saying that he was without ego, but [that] I didn't think that's what was fueling what he was doing.

ACKNOWLEDGEMENTS

This essay is excerpted from "Counting Women's Caring Work: An Interview with Andaiye," *Small Axe* 15 (Vol 8, No. 1), March 2004, 123–217, by David Scott, starting on page 174.

NOTES

1. Walter Rodney, Eusi Kwayana, and Clive Thomas.
2. Arnold Rampersaud was an activist with the People's Progressive Party (PPP), then in opposition, who was alleged to have shot and killed a police constable, James Henry, at a toll station on the Corentyne in 1974. Along with PPP members, Walter

Rodney and Eusi Kwayana were part of a defense committee that contended that Rampersaud was being framed by the ruling People's National Congress (PNC) government. He was acquitted of the charges after three trials, the first in 1976, and the second and third in 1977 (source: Nagamootoo 1978).

3. Rupert Roopnaraine.

4. Rodney's appointment to teach at the University of Guyana was rescinded at the insistence of the People's National Congress government led by Forbes Burnham before he came back from Tanzania to take it up. He came back anyway.

5. Walter Rodney's path-breaking book, *How Europe Underdeveloped Africa*, was first brought out simultaneously in 1972 by Bogle-L'Ouverture Publications (established by Jessica and Eric Huntley in London) and Tanzania Publishing House in Dar es Salaam.

6. The House of Israel was an organization established by David Hill, a fugitive from the United States, who was given protection by the Burnham regime. He assumed the title Rabbi Edward Emmanuel Washington and preached a doctrine based on the idea that Black people were the true children of Israel. Often associated with the PNC's dirty work, a House of Israel member, for example, stabbed and killed Father Bernard Darke in July 1979 outside the Magistrate's Court where Rodney, Roopnaraine, and Omawale were being brought up on charges of arson (see endnote 10). See Spinner (1984: 171–172).

7. I have added a few amendments for the purpose of clarification. These are italicized in the text and identified as *[Added]*.

8. Rodney (1969).

9. A budding businesswoman who was perhaps the most active supporter of the WPA, although she never became an official member.

10. The building on Camp Street, Georgetown, housing the offices of the Ministry of National Development and the General Secretary of the People's National Congress was burned down on 11 July 1979. Walter Rodney, Rupert Roopnaraine, and Omawale were arrested and charged with arson.

11. See Scott (2001): 137.

12. Workers' Party of Jamaica (WPJ), a Marxist–Leninist party.

13. Trevor Munroe was general secretary of the WPJ from its emergence in 1978 until its disintegration in 1992.

14. Rodney was assassinated on June 13, 1980.

REFERENCES

Nagamootoo, Moses. 1978. *The Three Trials of Arnold Rampersaud*. Georgetown: New Guyana Company.

Rodney, Walter. 1969. *Groundings with my Brothers*. London: Bogle-L'Ouverture Publications.

Scott, David. 2001. "The Dialectic of Defeat: An Interview with Rupert Lewis." *Small Axe* 10 (September): 137.

Spinner, Thomas J. 1984. *A Political and Social History of Guyana, 1945–1983*. Boulder, CO: Westview Press.

NOTES ON THE GUYANA INDIAN/AFRICAN RACE DIVIDE, AND ON ORGANIZING WITHIN AND AGAINST IT

To establish a context for the discussion on organizing within and across race divides that follows in Essay 6, we begin by recording how we believe those divides deepened to the point where they have proved resistant to healing. While most commentary on the issue emphasizes what are called the ethnic security dilemmas of the two groups, we focus on feeling—what we've called the rupture of neighborliness.

ESSAY 5

1964: The Rupture of Neighborliness and its Legacy for Indian/African Relations
With D. Alissa Trotz
[2008; 2018]

BACKGROUND

There is nothing unique to Guyana about the existence of two or more race groups set up in competition with each other, or to there being religious and cultural, occupational, residential and other separations between or among them. In the context of the Caribbean, one factor that differentiates Guyana is geography. It is a landspace of approximately 215,000 square kilometers inhabited by only about 750,000 people, where even today there is increased movement around the country. Africans and Indians live mainly on the narrow coastal strip bordering the Atlantic, and the Indigenous peoples in often small, scattered settlements in vast interior regions bordering Venezuela and Brazil. This geographic divide between coast and interior helped entrench the marginalization of Indigenous peoples from the "national" economy and political life. Thus, when we speak of racial conflict among the working people of Guyana, we are really speaking about the conflict between Indians and Africans.

The second significantly different factor in the Guyana situation is that since the leadership of the People's Progressive Party (PPP) which spearheaded the anti-colonial movement was avowedly Marxist, the nature and duration of imperial intervention in colonial Guyana and the impact of that intervention were large enough to break the national movement. In 1953 the two most prominent leaders of the PPP were Cheddi Jagan (Indian-Guyanese) and Forbes Burnham (African-Guyanese). The first split in the party, in 1955, saw the departure of Burnham; while in the second, in 1956, a group of African and mixed race members who had remained with the PPP after 1955 but who developed strong political disagreements with Dr. Jagan also left, leading to an almost complete break along racial lines.[1]

While there were clear ideological differences between Jagan and Burnham— differences that ensured that the British and Americans backed Burnham over Jagan—and while it is beyond question that outside forces manipulated the divisions in Guyana in their own interests, it is impossible to understand the Guyana of the early 1960s unless we understand that by the late 1950s the main rival political parties had become bases for racial self-defense.

Between 1961 and 1964, Guyana experienced a period of violence between African- and Indian-Guyanese of which one researcher has written that its size, unexpectedness and brutality marked it as "the introduction of something indelible ... in its imagery and in its consequential impact" (Mars 1994: 2). This analysis of the violence begins with an example of the contending narratives which it produced, and which were central to its legacy.

CONTENDING NARRATIVES OF THE VIOLENCE

Contending narratives of the 1964 violence developed not only at the popular level but in the writing of prominent leaders; for example, in published accounts by Cheddi Jagan, former president of Guyana and David Granger, former chief of staff in the Guyana Defence Force under the Burnham presidency, and since mid-2015, himself president.[2]

The violence which is perhaps most etched in the separate collective memories of Indian- and African- Guyanese was perpetrated in the bauxite belt on May 25 and July 6, 1964. According to the report of the Commission of Enquiry which was established to examine the events of the first day, May 25 (the terms of reference read, "to investigate the causes of the racial violence on 25 May 1964 by Africans against the minority East Indian population residing in Wismar, Christianburg and MacKenzie"), the immediate back-ground was a strike in the sugar industry called by the Guiana Agricultural Workers Union (GAWU),[3] a PPP-affiliated union, to demand recognition. Beginning in February, it was originally peaceful, but later saw clashes between the striking workers, who were Indian, and the mainly Africans employed to break the strike. "When two non-strikers were killed by a bomb blast at Tain on the Corentyne Coast, and a GAWU supporter squatting at the entrance of Leonora Sugar Factory was crushed to death by an estate tractor, both sides claimed their martyrs," the report added (Wismar Report 1965: chapter 2, §I, "Background").

In recounting these incidents, both Jagan and Granger begin with a decision by the PPP to oppose the imposition by the colonial government of the proportional representation electoral system but immediately, the accounts diverge. What Jagan, with the PPP, calls a "'hurricane of protest' campaign" (Jagan 1972: 305), Granger calls "[A] campaign of domestic terrorism, called the 'Hurricane of Protest'" (Granger 2003: 5). According to Jagan, clashes developed out of an inter-union dispute in the sugar industry between GAWU and the Man-Power Citizens' Association, which the planters continued to favor (Jagan 1972: 305). For his part, Granger writes that the "Hurricane of Protest" was "mounted under the guise of the GAWU strike" (Granger 2003: 5).

These differing perspectives in turn shape their accounts of the violence that erupted and quickly took a racial form. "When GAWU struck," Jagan continues, "the planters employed scabs ... who were mostly Africans from Georgetown," many of whom "acted as 'vigilantes,' terrorizing the Indian workers who had started a passive resistance campaign" (Jagan 1972: 306). The first death that he mentions is that of a GAWU supporter and striking sugar worker at Leonora, Kowsilla, an (Indian) woman killed by a tractor driven by a (probably African) "non-striker." Only after he recounts this tragedy does he mention that two days before, in Tain, a bomb was thrown at a bus carrying "scabs" to Plantation Albion and "two men, Monroe (an African) and Gunraj (an Indian) died" (ibid.). Granger, on the other hand, writes that "[W]hen the Indian and African sugar workers outside GAWU continued to work they "became the victims of violence and significantly, the first person to be killed was Edgar Monroe, an African," adding, "Later, as a result of the same incident, Ramraj Gunraj ... an Indian, also died" (Granger 2003: 5).

The hierarchy of deaths is at once racially and ideologically inscribed.

Developing the background to the violence in the bauxite region, the Commission report recorded that between the incidents outlined above and the more brutal events of May 25, "violence was intensified over the greater part of the East and West Coast of Demerara. Many people were murdered and there were numerous cases of arson and bombings." It continued:

> The murder of a negro couple at Buxton on Thursday 21st May had its repercussions in attacks on East Indians and their property in the streets of Georgetown on the afternoon of Friday 22nd May ... Three days later, on Monday 25th May, the violence which had until then been confined to the coastal strip was extended to the Wismar-Mackenzie Christianburg area resulting in widespread disturbances which it has been our task to investigate. (Wismar Report 1965: chapter 2, §I, "Background")

The report provided figures on the violence on or just after May 25 as well as on the violence of July 6. There were three Indian and two African deaths on or about May 25 (an editor's note says the two Africans killed on May 25 and 27 respectively were involved in looting); 215 houses and businesses of Indians were destroyed; and 744 families (1,249 adults, 2,150 children) were displaced and resettled elsewhere. More than 30 Indians were admitted to hospital with serious injuries. Six women and girls were raped, with some being successively raped by several men.

On July 6, the report also recorded, after an explosion on a boat going to Wismar called the *Son Chapman*,[4] the bodies of 35 persons were taken to Mackenzie while 12 others were missing or unidentified, all African; and on the same day, following the explosion, five Indians were murdered and seven injured at Wismar (Wismar Report 1965: chapter 4).

Jagan characterized the violence against Indians as a massacre, writing that "The strike culminated on May 24 in the massacre of Indians at Wismar":

> The whole Indian population ... was uprooted and their property set on fire. Over 200 houses and business places were destroyed and about 1,800 were made homeless. A large number were beaten, some of them to death; others had to flee for their lives. Women and even children were raped and otherwise savagely maltreated. (Jagan 1972: 308–309)

However, in relation to the *Son Chapman*, like the Commission itself, he referred to the explosion only as a precursor to further anti-Indian violence:

> The *Son Chapman*, a launch transporting passengers from Georgetown to Wismar, then sank after an explosion; more than 2 dozen persons, mainly African workers and their families at Mackenzie, were drowned. This led to immediate reprisals against Indians; 2 of a small number of Indians who had returned to Mackenzie were murdered. (Jagan 1972: 310)

In stark contrast, Granger's account singled out the explosion on the *Son Chapman* and deemed it the worst of the violence. "The most alarming slaughter of the 'Disturbances'" he wrote, "was that of 40 Africans on 6 July at Hurudaia in the Demerara river as they traveled in a motor launch to Mackenzie" (Granger 2003: 5).

In the narratives passed down from generation to generation, to this day people shift numbers and dates and causes and effects. Often, they tell only the story of atrocities against their own race. The rapes of Indian-Guyanese women and girls in Wismar seem to have been wiped clean from the memories of African-Guyanese, while in the memories of Indians they remain stark as an unforgiveable assault on the whole community. It is the unshakeable belief of African-Guyanese that Africans in the *Son Chapman* were murdered by bombing; Indian-Guyanese often dismiss the event as the accidental blowing up of explosives that the PNC was smuggling up to the region.

African- and Indian-Guyanese recount the stories they have learned about the 1961–1964 violence, unconscious or unconcerned that theirs contrast sharply with the stories told by the "other" race about the same incidents. In our 2008 interviews (Red Thread 2008), respondents would represent their group predominantly as victims, and the opposing group as aggressors. Their responses are reproduced below in Creolese and standard English:[5]

> *Blak piipl. Na da taim Blak man a mek chrobl, kil piipl, shuut piipl?* [Black people. Isn't it during that time that Black people made trouble, killed people, shot people?] (Shanti, Indian, age 79)

> *Di fos ting de duu, di Indiyan staat kilin di blak piipl wen de go to wok in di farmz.* [The first thing the Indians did was to start killing black people when they went to work on their farms.] (David, African, age 79)

Where a group's own hostility was acknowledged, it was cast as self-defense:

> *Palitiks kaaz dis ting yes. Wi had apan jat: kulii fo kulii, blakman fo blakman. So dem a go ... Yu a tingk fo yu ... fu yu rees. Blak piipl a tingk fi dem rees.* [Politics caused this thing, yes. We had Apaan Jaat. Indian for Indian, African for African. That's the way it went. You stood up for your ... your race. African people stood up for their race.] (Arti, Indian woman, age 75)

> *Yu een had chais. Yu had to duu wa yu had don.* [There was no choice. You had to do what you did.] (David, African, age 79)

WOMEN'S FEAR, ISOLATION AND DRIVE TO PROTECT THEIR CHILDREN FROM THE VIOLENCE

In fundamental ways, the recounted experience of Indian and African women was similar. For example, isolation was a recurring theme among the women we interviewed. While men only talked about being fearful in one or two of the interviews (this is not to say they were not, but rather that for men of both races, admissions might be contrary to accepted understandings of masculinity), or about staying indoors, in contrast, fear was a common emotion expressed by the women, and shutting oneself indoors a logical response:

> *Ai didn yuuz to go noo wee. Ai de in mi hous. Ai een waakin tu moch aloon. An yu noo it tek mi taim bifoor ai waak in di Indiyan eeriiya. Ai doz tel myself,*

wen yu pasin, de gooin to ron out an chap yu an nobadi wud sii … so it tuk mi meni yeerz biifoor ai go chruu. [I never went anywhere. I stayed in my house. I wouldn't walk out too much alone. And you know, it was sometime before I walked in the Indian area. I told myself, when you're passing there, they will run out and chop you and nobody would see. So, it was many years before I went through there.] (Jean, African, age 72)

Mi na chravl pon di rood. Mi go an lak dong in mi lil plees, get mi beebii an mi de de a gud tai, til evriting kom bak narmal an mi sii piipl start to go arong an muuv arong an ting an taak, an mi sii tingz ronin op an dong … mi na go noo wee. Mi kyaahn heer notn; mi na kom out a hous. Wen mi de in de mi na kom out. [I didn't use the road. I locked myself up in my little place, got my baby and stayed there a good time until everything became normal again and I saw people start to move around and talk to each other and that sort of thing, and I saw things running up and down … I didn't go anywhere. I couldn't hear anything. I did not come out of my house. When I was in there, I did not come out.] (Nadira, Indian, age 79)

A related similarity between the accounts of the women interviewees across race related to the safety of their children. Without exception, it was women of both races who talked consistently about, and provided specific examples of the lengths to which they went to keep their families, particularly their children, safe. If for men the emphasis was on maintaining an income, or organizing to move house from one village to another (an activity that women participated in fully), it was women's labor which was specifically directed towards the care of children and it followed that it was on them that the burden of protection would predominantly fall—one woman dating the start of the violence in her community to the day her child was born; others taking their children at night to sleep with neighbors; one woman sending her children away to stay with relatives; another recalling the beams on her house breaking when the bulldozer began moving it to a squatting area adjoining the village she was forced to flee, and having to spend the night in the middle of the street with her children in an area that many felt had become suddenly hostile to Indians:

Wans muuvin, mi hous breek at di midl striit an lef deer ovanait, an mi stee hool nait an wanda if enibadi go kom insaid … wid tuu children. [Once when we were moving my house broke in the middle of the street and had to be left there overnight, and I stayed in it all night and wondered if anybody would come inside … with two children.] (Indira, Indian, age 65)

The following examples highlight vividly the lengths to which women would go and had to go during the disturbances. The first case describes the night when Mary (African, now 72), then pregnant and with two infants, realized she would have to move as several people she knew had been killed or had had their houses burned down:

Mary: *Ai begin to get afreed nou an fraikn de kil mii tuu, yu noo? Biikaaz ... de ronin ... bai di reelwee an swingin de kotlaas an yu heerin di naiz. Seeyin, "blak man, kom out!" So, so, so, so. So, wii diisaid to go chruu di bak. An wen wi opn di door to go chruu di bak, de did ronin at di bak tu so wii had to lai dong in di gyardn di nait.* [I began to feel afraid that they would kill me too, you know? Because they were running near the railway and swinging their cutlasses and you could hear the noise. They were saying, "Black man, come out!" So, so, so, so. So, we decided to go through the back. And when we opened the door to go through the back, they were running at the back also, so we had to lie down in the garden that night.]

Interviewer: So you came out of the house.

Mary: *Yes, an go arong di bak, an wi jos sidong wiself in di yard.* [Yes, and went around to the back, and we just sat there in the yard.]

Interviewer: With the children? How old were they then?

Mary: *Yes, wan waz tuu, wan waz wan ... an ai kova deer mout an tel dem kiip kwaiyet.* [Yes, one was two and the other was one. And I covered their mouths and told them to keep quiet.]

Interviewer: If they caught you ...

Mary: *Noo, Noo. Evribadi wuda dai. Evribadi de wud kil. Evribadi ... orlii neks marnin ... wi had to ron awee. Di tuu smaal wan ron in front av mii an di wan in di beli, an wi had to ron an kom from Enmore. Street to Golden Grove.* [No, No! Everyone would have died. They would have killed everyone. Everybody ... early the next morning, we had to run away. The two small ones ran in front of me and the one in the belly, and we had to run from Enmore. Straight to Golden Grove.]

In the second example, the story of Meena, an Indian woman now 68 years old, is remarkable in its resemblance to Mary's:

Meena: *Dem ron mi hosban out, an aal awi na si hii bak a hool wiik. Wi had to muuv out. ... Wi go awi neeba dem at di bak an wi stee de ... mi lef mi oon hous, mi kyaahn stee de, kaaz somtaim dem fain out dat mi liv de, an mi hosban na de hoom ... naitaim wi doz slip in di bush ... mi tek dem chiren den mi go chruu di bak a mi neeba an sidong.* [They ran my husband out, and we never saw him again for a whole week. We had to move out ... We stayed with our neighbours at the back ... I left my own house; I couldn't stay there in case they found out that I lived there, and my husband was not at home. At night, we slept in the bush ... I took the children and then went through the back and sat down with my neighbors.]

Interviewer: At night your neighbor also sleep in the bush?

Meena: *Ye! A de bak hous. Aal a wi doz kom out an de in a di bosh.* [Yes! At the house at the back. All of us come out and stay in the bush.]

Interviewer: How did the children make out? Were they crying or scared?

Meena: *Dem lil ... na, dem na krai, dem beli na ful? Awi na fiid dem? Bot dem lil; dem na noo wa a go lang. A awi dis gat fo noo. Den, afta kopl dee, awi de de about chrii ar foor dee; den wi kaal dis baai neem Green. An waz a blak baai, bot awi wel nooin wid ii, an ii gat a kyar. Ii biin jraiv a kyar, an ii kyari wi out to Better Hope/Beta Hoop.* [They were young. No, they did not cry. Weren't their bellies full? Didn't we feed them? Both of them were young; they didn't understand what was going on. We had to know. Then, after about three or four days, we called this boy named Green. He was a black boy, but we were well acquainted and he had a car. He drove a car and he took us out to Better Hope.]

THE BETRAYAL OF NEIGHBORLINESS, THE LOSS OF NEIGHBOR AND NEIGHBORHOOD

These experiences, at once shared, separate, and separating, altered life as people had known it. All the interviewees' recollections were divided into a "before" (which in the case of the older interviewees extended long before the 1950s) and "after" the violence and the tensions leading up to it. This dividing line might be not so much a faithful representation of past realities as it is a way of demarcating, or bracketing, the awful events of 1961–1964, of characterizing the violence as completely out of step with a country in which peaceful mixing had been the order of the day. It is possible that both Indians and Africans we interviewed romanticized the relations they enjoyed prior to the violence, but we were struck by how each spoke of the other as their neighbors, and their earlier relationship as one of neighborliness. They sometimes came at this from different angles. An African woman whose brother was killed in the violence, wept as she recounted the story more than 40 years after, then added without prompting, "*Bot waznt wii kuli dat duu it. Waz dee kuli*"—meaning, "It was not our neighbors. Not the Indians we knew and lived with. It was Indians who were sent." Meanwhile, comments by Indians from the bauxite mining community where the brutal gang rapes of 1964 occurred were filled with distress that this violence had been committed by their neighbors.

[It was] *piipl dat yu noo. Yu doohn noo aal, bot piipl dat yu noo. Piipl dat taak tu yu evri dee. Piipl dat kom to yu stan an bai. Piipl dat doohn hav moni an doz kom (dee doz kaal mi moda "Aanti"). Aanti yu kud giv mi a jrink de? Mi na gat moni; ar a puuri ar somting? Piipl laik dat.* [It was people that you knew. You didn't know everybody but it was people you knew. People that talked to you every day. People that came to your stand to buy. People that didn't have money and would come (they called my mother "Aunty"). Aunty, could you give me a drink? I don't have money. Or a puri or something? People like that.] (Indra, Indian, age 52)

Across communities where we conducted interviews, interviewees described attending each other's ceremonies before the violence, and noted the ease of inter-racial mixing at school and socially:

Evribadi go to skuul togeda—laik frenz. Evriting iz Nigro an Indiyan. De neva had noo prablem reeli. Wen skuul waz out an so, yu neva yuuz to reeli go out av Linden. Halidee yu wud stee an spen in Linden, wid yor frenz an so wi yuuz to go to parti, yu noo, aal dem Indiyan giyorlz ... Wi yuuz to go to skuul dansis an so, an waz sheer niigrooz wi dans wid. Wi yuuz to miks a lot. It waz reel nais. [Everybody went to school together—like friends. Everything was about Negroes and Indians. They never had problems with each other. When school was out, you never really left Linden. You would spend your holidays in Linden with your friends and so we used to party, you know. All of those Indian girls used to go to school dances and so, and we danced with mainly/only Negroes. We used to mix a lot. It was real nice.] (Indra, Indian, age 52)

Ai mis di lov, yu noo? Wii aal liv gud togeda, an [di Indiyanz] wud kom dong ... an mek kori. De get di Indiyan weding an aal awi go. [I miss the love, you know. We all got along well together, and the Indians would come down ... and make curry. They would hold Indian weddings and all of us would go.] (Sarah, African, age unrecorded)

In several instances where Indians and Africans farmed at the back of the villages (known as the backdam, a topography described by Walter Rodney in the first chapter of *History of the Guyanese Working People*), we were told that they would support and look out for each other:

Wi yuuz to plaant an faarmin gyardn an rais, main yu kyatl, main ship ... Di Blak piipl an wi jos liv nais. Dem a kaal a yu; yu kyan paas an go kaal a dem, yu noo, yu de de at di bakdaam an yu paas an kaal fo dem. Dem wud aalweez ansa yu an so. [We used to plant rice and keep gardens. Mind cattle, mind sheep ... The Black people and we just lived nice. They would say hello to you, and you can go over and say hello to them, you know, when everybody was on the backdam. They would always answer.] (Arti, Indian, age 75)

Some of the interviewees volunteered occupational integration as an instance of crossing the racial divide, as for example at Enmore, the largest sugar estate on the East Coast of Demerara and the scene of African expulsion in 1964, where both groups in the community were employed by the estate, and where women tended to work in the weeding gangs.

For the most part, residential neighborhoods were described as fairly tightly integrated, with *"Blak den a Indiyan, den anada Blak, den anada Indiyan"* [Black, then an Indian, then another Black, then another Indian] living side by side. And even where interviewees said that there were "more Blacks" or "more Indians" living in a community, to them this did not make it an African or Indian village, largely, we would submit, because the dominant memory was one of connection across race/ethnic and other divides.

Although several of the men recalled having close inter-racial friendships as children, in general the men tended to offer general comments about living good together with your neighbors, and their remarks also stressed interactions in what we have come to understand as the public domain—the street, the shops—as in this comment:

Prior to dose times [1964], people in the community would meet for discussions and never had dis grouse or racial tings dat would bring about a division in the society ... people used to be on the streets day and night, dose who imbibed would find themselves maybe lying on the road, brace up on a lamp post and still wake up with everything intact, money, clothes shoes ... dat was how it was." (John, African, age 65)

Da taim yu na freed raba, tiif. Yu lef yu door, yu windoo waid oopn, Yu na freed eniting. Yu wun tiif eniting from nobadi. Wi een had elekchrisitii. No waata, no rood. An dat iz hou di piipl yuuz to liv hee. An dem a liv, weda iz Niigroo, Indiyan. De had som Porchuugiiz, aal a dem laik a broda an sista liv hee. Da iz hou de yuuz to liv. De din aidentifai demself akardin to kola an rees. If somting rang wid wan, aal ronin. If de had wedin, evribadi kom. If de had fineral, evribadi kom kiip week. Siknis, everibadi kom an sii wa de kud duu. Da iz hou de yuuz to liv. [That time you were not afraid of robbers and thieves. You would leave your door and window wide open. You were not afraid of anything. You wouldn't steal anything from anybody. We didn't have any electricity. No water, no road. And that is how the people used to live here. And they lived so whether they were Negro, Indian. There were some Portuguese. All of them lived as brothers and sisters here. That is how they used to live. They didn't identify themselves according to color and race. If something was wrong with one, all came running. When there was a wedding, everyone came. If there was a funeral, everyone came to the wake.

During sickness, everybody came to see what they could do. That is how they used to live.] (Deo, Indian, age 62)

In contrast, the women's recollections of inter-racial mixing primarily revolved around the household, or emphasized support by women for women in the carrying out of their household and maternal responsibilities:

> *Mi children dem, mi lef dem an go wok in Victoria bakdaam ... Mi yuuz to lef mi children dem wid Blak piipl ... an de jos luk afta di hous til mi kom bak an luk dem children.* [I used to leave my children and go to work in Victoria backdam ... I used to leave them with Black people ... and they would look after the house until I returned to look after my children.] (Sumintra, Indian, age 74)

Indeed, what stood out in these testimonies was the abundance of examples in which interviewees offered their personal experiences (in contrast to the men) of gestures of support, friendship and empathy, both as children and then later, as mothers.

SEXUAL ASSAULTS THE INDELIBLE MARKERS OF RACE HUMILIATION

Where the experience of Indian and African women diverged in 1964 was in relation to sexual violence as it was inflicted on May 25, 1964 in the mining community of Wismar. Rape was apparently not widespread as a weapon of the race violence, but we have clear descriptions of the six Indian women and girls, recorded in the Commission of Enquiry Report as gang-raped on that day, being victimized as symbols of group identity. "Men were beaten ... it happened to both sex, male and female, but then the women were raped in addition to the beating" (Wayne, mixed, age 65). The following testimony is from a woman who witnessed the assaults:

> *So de jraagin diiz Indiyan giyorlz bai di heer, an de reepin dem ... out on di schriit. If yu si de kech wan Indiyan giyorl, iz about 20 av dem rong shi. Ai noo wan giyorl, ai kyaahnt riimemba hor neem, an Indiyan giyorl. Wi in di seem skuul. Shi came running out an de skrambl shi.* [They would drag the Indian girls by their hair and rape them ... out on the street. If they caught an Indian girl, about 20 of them would overpower her. I know a girl, I can't remember her name, an Indian girl. We went to the same school. She came running out and they overpowered her.] (Indra, Indian, age 52)

A man who identified himself as mixed and who grew up in the community, in describing the incidents of rape said, "I am talking about being violent to persons of another race, stealing from dem, burning down … setting their house on fire, raping of the girls and women, not just raping, but gang raping."

Outside of Wismar, in a few other interviews, women stated that they had heard of occasional cases of rape in other places ("No. No raping in our place. Raping passed other ways, what I hear about, but not here"), as in the case of an African woman, referring to incidents on both the West and East Coasts of Demerara in which sexual assaults were committed by both Indian and African men:

Di Indiyanz dem ova di Wes Koos de teroraiz di blak piipl bai setin faiya to yu hous, an wen yu jomp out de boor yu wit pichfark an I was very very much afraid … Wan leedi shi dehd nou to; shi livin ova di Wes Koos … shi se di kuli men dem, shi waz begin dem not to kil shi; shi se de prapa handl shi … shi se shi had to tek it wit a smail … shi had to get awee out av di eeriya. Shi se de prapa handl shi. Wen shi duu get a chans, shi kom bak to shi hoomland Shi kom bak (pon di Eiis Koos) … An som Indiyan … wud tel yu dat baaiz handl dem to, reep dem … [wen de] hoslin to go de wee, dem blak baai kech dem an handl dem. [The Indians from the West Coast terrorized Black people by setting fire to our houses. And when you jumped out they would stab you with pitchforks and I was very very much afraid. There was this lady—she is dead now—who lived on the West Coast … she said that she begged the Coolie men not to kill her. She said that they raped her very violently indeed. She had to take it with a smile. She had to get away from the area. She said they were really violent to her. When she did get a chance, she returned to her homeland, she returned (to the East Coast). And some Indians … would tell you that boys used them violently also when they were hurrying along their way, the black boys would catch them and brutalize them.] (Jean, African, age 76)

Accounts of sexual assault and mutilation served as a kind of symbolic marker of what the African or Indian community had suffered.

For Africans, the murder of the Sealeys, an elderly couple whose bodies were found on the plot of land they farmed in the backdam behind a village called Buxton, was recounted by almost every African Guyanese we interviewed, and in several instances we were told that Mr. Sealey's penis was found in his mouth. In fact, this image of the (literal) emasculation of the man (and by extension, the African community) was also repeated as something that had happened to other African men. In one case we were told it had happened to a man whose murder was reported in the newspapers. This was however not mentioned either by the newspapers, or by any of his immediate family members whom we interviewed at length.

No one we interviewed said that Mrs. Sealey had been sexually assaulted, but this version of the violence against the Sealeys—the murder of a defenseless elderly couple working their land and the symbolic emasculation of Mr. Sealey—fueled the sense of outrage among Africans at the time.[6]

Among Indians, it is Wismar that stands for Indian humiliation and victimization. Unlike the Sealey murders, victims are not identified by name, but like the circulation of the story of that elderly couple among Africans in Guyana, Wismar was known and mentioned by almost all of the Indian respondents. The expulsion of the community and the beatings were mentioned, but it was the sexual assault of women and girls that was most significant in our conversations, and that was singled out as emblematic of the depths of suffering and degradation of Indians at the hands of Africans.

Just as memories serve to perpetuate the violence—becoming in that sense a cause of further violence—so do silences. Out of shame, Indo-Guyanese women have for the most part been silent about the sexual violence they suffered. To a lesser degree, the same may be true of Afro-Guyanese women—i.e., it is suggested that they may have suffered more sexual violence during 1961–1964 than they reported (although no one claims that it was at the same level or of the same brutality as the sexual violence against Indo-Guyanese women in 1964). Out of shame and/or fear and/or defense of their race, Afro-Guyanese women have also been silent about the sexual violence against Indo-Guyanese women on May 25, 1964. Our research did not find any woman from either race whose narrative differed in any respect from the narrative of her race group.

While if we look at these events through the lens of race we find two contending silences and memories—one Indian, the other African. The women and girls who were raped were also silenced by being made representative not of themselves as women and girls, but purely of the race.

There were also one or two other circulating accounts that referred to the condition of women who had been beaten or killed (not sexually assaulted) as young and pregnant. For example, there was one description of a pregnant Indian woman who died from burns after the car she was traveling in on the East Coast road was stopped and set on fire; and a story of a pregnant African woman who went down with the *Son Chapman* launch. Very rarely were the ages or marital status or otherwise of men mentioned, suggesting how violence against women and children is used to index a more wanton disregard for human life, or elicits a heightened sense of horror and revulsion.

THE SEPARATE MEMORIALIZING OF SEPARATE GRIEF

Public discussions of 1964—when they do occur—are framed as a reflection of the contending narratives. During our time in the field, we were able to observe a ceremony for the victims of the *Son Chapman*, which takes place annually at a cleared space on the banks of the Demerara River at Hurudaia. Small launches and speedboats had been hired or had donated their services to transport Linden, Wismar and other residents to the site, where efforts were then afoot to build a memorial and plaque with all of the names of the victims. Much of the clearing work was spearheaded by women. Members of the regional government office in Linden were present, and speakers on the program included senior members of the People's National Congress (PNC), including the then party leader, that was at the time in opposition.

Not only were all of the attendees African-Guyanese (at least one hundred), but many, particularly young people, had been mobilized to come, by the youth arm of the PNC which plays a central role in organizing the event. We were told that invitations are extended each year to the ruling PPP government and party, but these are never acknowledged. There was also much public criticism of the fact that there is no official recognition from "the other side" of *Son Chapman*.

The event that we attended was highly politicized, with speakers going over the events of 1964 that led to the explosion, discounting PPP narratives that suggest responsibility for the bombing lay with the PNC, and linking 1964 to current African-Guyanese marginalization and the need for resistance. One speaker criticized the narrow-mindedness of the current (PPP) administration's tendency to selectively remember martyrs, apparently unselfconscious that the Hurudaia event had itself done precisely what it spoke out against. In particular, the violence that Indian-Guyanese had been subjected to in Wismar/Linden in May and July 1964 was conspicuously absent from the public pronouncements, referred to once, and then only to justify the July assaults as retaliatory outbursts from grief-stricken African-Guyanese in the aftermath of the sinking of the ferry.

Commemorative practices on both sides become occasions to rally political support, leaving little space for participants beyond these sharply drawn political lines, and foreclosing the possibility for alternative memories to provide an opportunity to reach across zero-sum divisions.

LEGACY

Respondents were unequivocal that party politics was to blame for the disturbances (and the state of the country today), and cognizant of the class tensions that get muted in the construction of monolithic notions of African-ness and Indian-ness, in ways that obscured various kinds of relations across both communities. For them, at the end of the day it was poor people who ended up being drawn into what one respondent called a war against each other, and who benefited the least:

Jagan an Burnham go miks op an jrink an ting, wen mi an yuu a dischrai wan anada … de hool yu an sool yu an wen di chrobl kom … a mi an yu de in chrobl. [Jagan and Burnham would socialize together. While you and I would destroy one another. They would entrap you and sell you out and when the trouble comes, it is you and I in trouble.] (Clarice, African, age 74)

Palitishanz kaaz dis ting, yes … wi had apan jat. Kuli fo kuli, blak man fo blak man. So dem a go … yu a tingk fo yu, fu yu rees, blak piipl a tingk fo dem rees. [Politicians caused this thing, yes. We had Appan Jhaat. Coolie for Coolie; Black man for Black man. So it went. You were loyal to your race. Black people were loyal to their race.] (Arti, Indian, age 75)

But if women and men were unanimously clear on the dangers of what one man called "politricks," it was far more difficult for them to think about or make sense of the betrayal between and within communities that occurred more than 40 years ago, without also recapitulating the very language of separateness and division. The intensity of recognizing that one's life, and the life of one's loved ones are in danger, has lasting repercussions:

Yu tingk iz jook fo noo yuu an yu lov wanz week op dis maanin, an in a mata ov ouwaz de get kil? An du waz total kilin. [You think it amusing to know that you and your loved ones could wake up this morning and in a matter of hours get killed? And that was total killing.] (David, African, age 79)

The loss of trust was most strongly articulated by those who had either witnessed or directly experienced violence. As an Indian couple said, echoing each other:

Tingz kyaahn kom bak, kyaahn kom bak at aal. No moor. Neva kyan kom bak. Neva. Neva kyan kom bak! [Things can't come back, can't come back at all. No more. Never can come back. Never. Never can come back!] (Mr. Narine, Indian, 82; Mrs Narine, Indian, age 74)

Rose, an African woman whose brother was murdered and her family evicted from the community they had called home said:

Ai doohn want to heet anibadi. Bot ai wil oonli fuul myself if ai se dat dat schriik av heechred doznt paas chruu mii. I love Indians but there are times when … you know what it is to see your brother walk out of a home and the next time you see him in a coffin, is without a face? [I don't want to hate anyone. But I would only be fooling myself if I said that that streak of hatred does not pass through me. I love Indians, but there are times when … Do you know what it is to see your brother walk out of a home and the next time you see him he is in a coffin, without a face?]

The lasting effect of this break cannot be underestimated. While in many cases respondents (significantly far more women than men) said they maintained friendships in their old communities, or even began to visit again once the situation had calmed down, there were also several who had never returned. What each side has chosen to remember is significant. It parallels the contending narratives found in the scholarship and the popular press, which render the other side's suffering invisible and only their aggression visible.

These contending narratives have been perpetuated by the development of the racially homogeneous communities which people forced out of their homes created—separate spaces, each with its own collective memory and its own silence handed down orally, generation to generation to generation. They have also been passed down in poetry and novels.

After 1964 there was no more visible political violence that took this virulently racial form until 1992, when the PPP won the first free election in Guyana in 24 years, and each election since then has been followed by violence, because each has confirmed to Afro-Guyanese that in the context of race-based voting, they are permanently excluded from government. In turn, the violence has confirmed to Indo-Guyanese that while they can win elections, their victory will never be accepted.

The next major race violence started when, in February 2002, a group of men broke out of jail and in April of the same year announced themselves as an armed African resistance.[7] The immediate trigger was the murder of a young man in the Afro-Guyanese village of Buxton by the "Black Clothes" (the popular name for the Target Special Squad), which, like its predecessor under the previous government, had been carrying out numerous extra-judicial killings of young Afro-Guyanese men. Now, however, with an Indo-Guyanese-led government in power, in what Eusi Kwayana calls "war propaganda," the killings were described as an attempt to wipe out young Afro-Guyanese men.

Basing themselves in Buxton, the "armed African resistance" began a prolonged attack on mostly Indo-Guyanese civilians. One estimate is that by September 2002, 35 Indo-Guyanese had been killed, 69 had been seriously injured, 44 Indo-Guyanese businesses had been robbed, and 29 vehicles belonging to Indo-Guyanese had been hijacked. There were 21 predominantly African-Guyanese policemen killed and scores of police left the force.

Eusi Kwayana called the "armed African resistance" a criminal political movement in part because of the overlap in aims and personnel between politics and drugs. Buxton itself became increasingly militarized. The security forces were based in the community. In the backdams, the "resistance" had set up a training camp. Inside the village itself men and boys with guns walked openly through the streets. According to Kwayana:

> Armed persons from the village began to carry out several robberies using motor transport, cell phones and bullet proof vests. They soon began to distribute part of the stolen money to villagers to make themselves popular. They gave money to many poor people and held parties after a successful robbery.
>
> The gunmen ... soon became the main enforcers in the village. What they allowed was allowed. What they opposed could not be done. They burned out a family accused by them of being informers. They were ... a state within a state. For a long season the gunmen did all the policing, imposing all the punishment up to execution. Many of them raped females and impregnated many. They gang-raped several. Mothers invited them to discipline their wayward children. They took over many homes with their guns. They kidnapped citizens and held them in the village for ransom. Some were found dead in the village. (Kwayana 2005: 45–46)

African-Guyanese women have been no less silent about the sexual violence by the gunmen against African-Guyanese women in 2002–2006, than they have been about sexual violence against Indo-Guyanese women.

The more recent carnage which ushered in 2008—particularly the murder of five children, three women and three men in Lusignan, a village with a predominantly Indian Guyanese population, followed three weeks later by the slaughter of 12 men of different races in a riverine community, Bartica—has led to perhaps the most explicit references to the civil disturbances of 1964 and entreaties to Guyanese to ensure that it is not repeated.

Once again, statements named one side as victim and the other side as aggressor in what is described as a racial war. Almost as a reflex gesture, the two narratives continue to provide a conceptual lens through which the current crisis in Guyana can be interpreted.[8]

In the end the "resistance" was defeated not by the security forces but by the operations of the Phantom Squad, a paramilitary organization headed by an Indo-Guyanese drug lord, Roger Khan, who the United States had captured and charged, and who it is alleged has killed some two hundred people in Guyana.[9] In a media statement, Khan said he had carried out the killings in collaboration with the crime-fighting section of the Guyana police force. There were also allegations of the involvement of government ministers.

The focus on women and children in this essay and its title is not intended to suggest that men were not victims of the violence; many were. Or that women did not commit any acts of brutality; they did. Nor are we unaware that there was more at work in the violence of the early 2000s than the legacy of the violence of the early 1960s. However, our purpose here has been to examine what we believe are the very real connections between the two. We argue that something other than what Perry Mars calls the size, unexpectedness and brutality of the 1960s violence, explains why its impact has been so long-lived. We have heard visitors to Guyana from deeply divided countries like apartheid-era South Africa remark that race division is not apparent to them in Guyana. In our view, the depth and longevity of our division—however invisible to the stranger—come from the fact that the violence of 1961–1964 was a violence between neighbors, breaking the sense of safety with each other which they had retained even as Indian/African relations fractured at the national political level, and that the rupture was as deep as it was and persists to this day in large part because of how those acts of violence that involved women and children were experienced, silenced and remembered.

ACKNOWLEDGEMENTS

This essay was expanded from an excerpt from a report of a research project carried out by Red Thread in 2008; the report drew on interviews conducted in 2006 and 2007 with 44 African and Indian women and men from several communities which had directly experienced the violence of 1964. Since one of the direct consequences of the violence was the dislocation of households, most of the interviewees had in fact relocated from where they had been living in 1964. Thus for instance, on the East Coast of Demerara, the Indian women we found in Enmore were originally from villages like Golden Grove and Victoria, those in Better Hope were from Plaisance, and those in Annandale from Buxton, while the village of Haslington seemed to be populated almost entirely by Africans forced out of Enmore.

NOTES

1. Eusi Kwayana, a leading member of the 1953 PPP, remained with Jagan after the Burnham-led 1955 split but left with the "ultra-leftists" in 1957. Later he joined the PNC and became its General Secretary. See the following essay in this volume.
2. Cheddi Jagan's account is in his well-known book *The West on Trial* (1972), and David Granger's briefer account is in a paper entitled "Civil Violence, Domestic Terrorism and Internal Security in Guyana, 1953–2003" (Granger 2003).
3. After Independence, GAWU became the Guyana Agricultural and General Workers' Union.
4. While the spelling used on some documents is Sun Chapman, we use the spelling Son Chapman throughout.
5. The essay is the only one in the anthology to use Creolese orthography, because it allows us to render without bias all the forms of Creolese differentiated by race, place and level of formal education. Where a speaker used the structures of Standard English, albeit with a Guyanese intonation, that has been left unchanged. Our thanks to Charlene Wilkinson, Coordinator, Guyanese Languages Unit, Department of

Language and Cultural Studies, Faculty of Education and Humanities, University of Guyana for doing this work.

6. In a personal communication with Nigel Westmaas on this issue (March 2, 2018), Eusi Kwayana said that "there had been three separate riots, and Buxton was not involved in the two previous riots of 62 and 63. The Sealey incident brought Buxton into the riots of 64 and indeed the '60s riots.' Many Buxtonians lived in Linden [this was the mining community that in 1964 was known as Wismar-McKenzie-Christianburg]. What incensed Buxton in the main was the fact that the Sealeys were old and the woman had also been violated. Also the fact that they had to find the bodies. Nothing happened until after the funeral when Indians who lived in Buxton were attacked and their homes destroyed. The Wismar incidents then overshadowed and clouded the Sealey atrocity."

7. The paragraphs on 2002 are excerpted from notes prepared for Friedrich Ebert Stiftung/United Nations Development Fund for Women workshop on Women, Memory, Politics and Violence in the Caribbean: "Is All Violence Gender-Based Violence? Perspectives of Women's Movements," CSA Annual Conference, May 24–28, 2010, Barbados.

8. If the violence in Lusignan (a predominantly Indian community on the East Coast of Demerara, which tends to be seen as a PPP community) made it fairly easy for the general public to reach for racial explanations for the violence, the murders at Bartica (located on the Essequibo river) three weeks later made this a difficult argument to sustain (the victims, all men, were from across the racial spectrum, and the community tends to vote for the PNC in the elections), but the suspicion and distrust across these sharply drawn lines has made it just as hard to kickstart a genuine national conversation on violence.

9. The number cited is sometimes as high as four hundred.

REFERENCES

Garner, Steve. 2008. *Ethnicity, Class and Gender: Guyana 1838–1985*. Kingston: Ian Randle Publishers.

Granger, David A. 2003. "Civil Violence, Domestic Terrorism and Internal Security in Guyana, 1953–2003." Threats to Caribbean Security panel, Center for Hemispheric Defense Studies, REDES 2003, Research and Education in Defense and Security Studies, October 28–30, Santiago, Chile. Photocopy.

Jagan, Cheddi. 1972. *The West on Trial: The Fight for Guyana's Freedom*. Berlin: Seven Seas Publishers.

Kwayana, Eusi. 2000. *Buxton Friendship: In Print and Memory*. Georgetown: Red Thread.

——. 2005. *The Morning After*. Georgetown: Caribbean Politics Publications.

Mars, Perry. 1994. "The Significance of the Disturbances, 1962–1964." *History Gazette* 70: 2–11.

Red Thread. 2008. *The Memories Would Always Be There: Thinking About Gender, Race and Political Conflict During the 1964 Disturbances in Guyana*. Georgetown: Red Thread.

Rodney, Walter. 1981. *History of the Guyanese Working People, 1881–1905*. Baltimore, MD: Johns Hopkins University Press.

Wismar Report. 1965. "Report of the Wismar, Christianburg and Mackenzie Commission (1965)." Commissioned by the Governor of British Guiana, Sir Richard Luyt, September 1964.

Organizing within and against Race Divides: Lessons from Guyana's
African Society for Cultural Relations with Independent Africa, Indian
Political Revolutionary Associates, and the Early Working People's Alliance
[2008; 2017/2018]

INTRODUCTION

In 1974, the African Society for Cultural Relations with Independent Africa (ASCRIA) joined with three other groups in Guyana—the Indian Political Revolutionary Associates (IPRA), the Working People's Vanguard Party (WPVP) and the University of Guyana-based Ratoon, to launch the multiracial Working People's Alliance (WPA).[1] Ten years earlier, ASCRIA had been formed as an organization whose aims, in broad terms, were the defense of Africans globally, the restoration of their cultural pride, and their economic and social transformation. In other words, its express purpose was the pursuit of African interests as it defined them at that time. In its first phase 1964–1972, therefore, it prioritized race over class, though always with a focus on the working people of the race; while in its second phase, it increasingly worked to build alliances across race among the working people. This essay's main focus is what we can learn from a small number of key statements by ASCRIA and its chief spokesman, Eusi Kwayana, about the why and how of these two phases. Because of the relationship which developed between ASCRIA and IPRA after the latter was launched in the early 1970s, and because of the role that IPRA played in the formation and growth of the WPA, it also draws on the few IPRA documents that are available and personal exchanges with IPRA's founder, Moses Bhagwan.[2]

Relying largely on statements by ASCRIA and Kwayana has obvious limitations: as one main example, the relationship between ASCRIA and the People's National Congress (PNC) is viewed only from ASCRIA's perspective.[3] Strong criticisms of ASCRIA by members of the national and regional left are omitted. Although I recognize this, I have chosen this approach because it is the self-reflections, glimpses into internal debates, and self-criticisms in the statements by ASCRIA and Kwayana that raise the critical questions about building racial unity which I want to record and comment on, questions that still remain to be addressed in Guyana today.

*   *   *

In one of his groundings in Jamaica in the 1960s, Walter Rodney argued that Black Power in the Caribbean had to be understood as including both the Indian and African working people. Rodney's starting point was that they shared a common relationship to capital, and for him, the Black Power movement was a challenge to that relationship. Thus, "black" was not simply a racial category. Rather, he said:

> we can talk of the mass of the West Indian population as being black—either African or Indian. There seems to have been some doubts on the last point, and some fear that black power is aimed against the Indian. This would be a flagrant denial of both the historical experience of the West Indies and the reality of the contemporary scene ... the underlying reality is that poverty resides among Africans and Indians in the West Indies and power is denied them. (Rodney 2014: 17)[4]

As the only two West Indian countries with large African and Indian populations, Guyana and Trinidad and Tobago would have been the main (though not the only) places Rodney was thinking of when he made his case. In Guyana, it was a position shared by Ratoon which according to Paul Tennassee, "gave expression to Black Power in Guyana" and which, in the late '60s or early '70s, having invited Stokeley Carmichael (later Kwame Ture) to Guyana, explained to him that in the context of Guyana, Black Power "meant non–white and embraced oppressed people of various ethnic backgrounds." Tennassee went on to recount that when, in spite of this, Carmichael (Ture) proclaimed at a public forum that Black Power was only for African people and that Indian people should find "an appropriate and corresponding slogan and ideology," Ratoon disassociated itself from this view (Tennassee 1982: 22).[5]

The possibilities inherent in the definition of Black Power as including both Indians and Africans were confirmed by the experience of the 1970 Trinidad and Tobago uprising. Whatever else it was, the Black Power rebellion in Trinidad and Tobago was a moment of class confrontation with the post-colonial state and the economic system the African-led government had left fundamentally unchanged. That is why many Indian sugar workers joined in the protest marches that constituted one of the two main components of the uprising. As Raffique Shah, an Indian army officer who co-led the army mutiny that was its other main component later wrote, "those who argue that Indians were not part of the 1970 revolution either do not know, or they deliberately ignore, the role of the sugar workers" (Shah 2000).

Nothing remotely similar to the events in Trinidad and Tobago happened in Guyana at that time. Here, the key factor in political life from the closing years of the 1950s until the early 1970s was the growing race divide between Africans and Indians. Notwithstanding Kwayana's stated position that "[I]f Black Power means the overthrow of white power by non-whites, by black men and brown men and yellow men on a world scale, we identify ourselves with it completely and without reserve" (Westmaas 2014: 159–178), one of the stated reasons for ASCRIA's founding in 1964 was to defend Africans in Guyana against what it saw as a threat of "Indian domination" (Eusi Kwayana, personal communication, January–February 2008). In 1961 he had co-authored a document calling for joint and equal prime ministership between the leaders of the Indian and the African people; a legally established committee made up of people of all races, especially minorities, to supervise the spending of government funds and the benefits derived by various races; and a socialist system without foreign links. Socialism was defined as inclusive of the religious traditions of the people. The section outlining the proposals was captioned "The Plan for Honour and Peace" (Kwayana 1978). Kwayana's analysis was that:

> [T]hese were important issues in the genesis of the formative nation which at that point threatened to fall apart ... This crude structure would then be used to promote the unity which it was my feeling had never been really cemented. (Kwayana 1988)

The alternative to the proposals, he said, was partition. The rest of the proposal was ignored and it was widely condemned as a proposal for partition. It would have seemed self-evidently impossible for Africans and Indians to unite under any banner at that stage.

ASCRIA 1964–1972: WORKING FOR A REVOLUTION OF ONE RACE

In its first phase, ASCRIA pursued its aims in Guyana by working towards a revolution of one race. While I found no public statement that this was its strategy, Kwayana reports that in the early 1970s, the organization held an internal debate on whether a revolution of one race was possible and concluded it was not, and "ASCRIA's Friday night ideology class took a formal position by resolution denouncing revolution of one race in Guyana" (Eusi Kwayana, personal communication, January–February 2008 and July 29, 2017). In other words, it repudiated a position by which it had hitherto been guided.

Given its 1964 reading of race relations in Guyana, ASCRIA saw African-Guyanese solidarity as critical. Its membership was predominantly African working class but included large numbers of the middle class. ASCRIA was sufficiently allied with the PNC that its formal membership, which an early Organizing Secretary estimated as fluctuating between one thousand and three thousand during his tenure, overlapped with that of the PNC and its youth arm, the Young Socialist Movement (Hinds 1996–1997: 32). Kwayana explained ASCRIA's thinking as follows:

Both leaders, after the split, first Jagan, and afterwards Burnham, consolidated racial bases in the form of political parties and began to conduct the inter-racial rivalry from those bases. Burnham was heavily assisted by ASCRIA, since Africans at first had no perceptible race consciousness after centuries of conditioning with Euro-Christianity through white missionary activities. (Kwayana 1973)[6]

ASCRIA gave the PNC total support in its electoral campaign of 1964 (ASCRIA 1973). As late as the 1968 election whose massive rigging was exhaustively documented, Kwayana spoke on the PNC platform and has said that he was not aware of the rigging machine at the time. It has been suggested that he was deeply suspicious of the widespread national and international expose of the rigging (David Hinds, personal communication, February 2008).

Although, as ASCRIA later acknowledged when it broke with the PNC, prioritizing race solidarity was not in the long-term interests of African-Guyanese working people, both the working people and other sectors of the African population did make certain gains in this phase of ASCRIA's organizing.[7] First, as in other countries where education about African history and culture was widely provided, there was the beginning of a revolution among African-Guyanese in their view of themselves and of their African heritage, reflected in their embrace of previously unknown or despised names, dress, ceremonies and even language. A culture hitherto disparaged as working class and/or rural began to be respected. This, Kwayana said, was the result of a shift in focus: as he put it:

> instead of cultural relations with independent African countries, never realized, ... [ASCRIA's] energies were spent in encouraging a respect for inherited culture which had been driven underground and deprived of all recognition and dignity, and ... [which] was to be found almost exclusively among the most marginalized and low–profiled groups of Africans. (Eusi Kwayana, personal communication, January–February 2008)

Second, the ideological training that ASCRIA provided also bore some fruit. The training included "weekly Friday night classes on ideology at Third Street [the ASCRIA centre] where we argued for a collectivist revolution based on African traditions and the Guyana post-1838 village movement" (ibid.), as well as mass political education on the need for economic and social revolution, collectivism and *ujaama*, and liberation politics. Putting collectivist theory into practice, members helped build a road to the interior and organized in support of a program the government had initiated to establish cooperative settlements in the interior.

Marudi was "the most significant of these truly cooperative settlements," involving "Marxists, Pan Africanists and *ujaama* socialists ... [who] ... saw themselves as people building a new society." Participants built roads, an airstrip and buildings, and planted several acres of food crops. Further:

> They had a collectivist leadership, classes in political economy, science and Swahili. They worked along with Amerindians and were inviting them to join the cooperative. They made careful plans of everything and discussed them fully. Among them were many skilled, pioneer minded people, bent on building a community without any exploitation and snobbery. (ASCRIA 1973)

It is worth noting that in this first phase of ASCRIA's organizing, at a time when most ASCRIA members were still supportive of the ruling PNC, everyone in the ASCRIA leadership was not closed to collaboration with other forces, including the PPP, in the face of PNC hostility. A key example of this was in 1969 when one of ASCRIA's leaders, Omawale, organized a protest at Parade Ground in Georgetown against Guyanese economist Clive Thomas's expulsion from Jamaica.[8] Omawale organized the event in his capacity as President of the University of Guyana Staff Association, in collaboration with ASCRIA, IPRA, PPP and the Movement against Oppression (MAO). He recounts that before it took place, Prime Minister Burnham told him he should disinvite Cheddi Jagan who was advertised as one of the speakers. The meeting went ahead but was broken up by PNC thugs as soon as the microphone was given to Jagan. He was hit in the chest with the microphone attached to its stand and there was a melee followed by a radio interview, in which Omawale was critical of Burnham. At a meeting organized following a demand by an ASCRIA elder for an explanation of why Omawale had criticized what the elder called "ASCRIA's pride" (Burnham), Kwayana supported Omawale by pointing out that he had joined ASCRIA with the express provision that he was not required to support the PNC or its leadership (Omawale, personal communication, March 9, 2018).

But by 1970 the contradictions between ASCRIA as a collective and the PNC had begun to emerge. April 1970 saw full state repression against a strike of bauxite workers, and against ASCRIA's advice to "listen to the cries of the workers ... [T]he PNC used all the repressive machinery against the strikers: police, troops, tear-smoke, arrest, court, everything" (Omawale, personal communication, March 9, 2018). In November of the same year, ASCRIA took the decision to fight governmental corruption, even while it was still in an alliance with the ruling PNC, warning party leaders about the corruption they had discovered. In January 1971, the PNC government closed down Marudi and other less developed cooperative communities organized by ASCRIA in the interior. Later, in June 1971, ASCRIA attacked the government publicly after they "saw that plans to punish corruption were farcical" (ibid.). The anti-corruption campaign brought matters to a head, as the government's response to it was extreme victimization. The formal break announced in a statement from ASCRIA's Coordinating Council on April 1, 1973, was an indictment of the PNC and what the Council termed its betrayal of the African-Guyanese working people:

> ASCRIA announces today for the benefit of those in doubt that we have come to a definite break with the PNC. In our opinion the PNC has betrayed the wishes and the interests of the African people, and is engaged in a vicious betrayal and exploitation of the manual workers, farmers and brain workers and of all true revolutionary principles. Its foremost leaders are almost without exception corrupt and live a life of personal plunder of public resources. (ASCRIA 1973)

* * *

The fact that ASCRIA saw the clash between the government and itself as a clash of class interests was underlined when its April 1, 1973 release stated that while some of the Government's missteps could have been political mistakes, corruption was not a political mistake. "It is a deliberate choice of a gang of men who are determined to get rich off of public office. *They have thus made themselves into a class and must be attacked as a class*" (ASCRIA 1973; emphasis added).

The class contradictions inside ASCRIA itself also became unsustainable. "When the movement developed its momentum they (the middle class) simply stood aside. As the conflict with the PNC leaders sharpened they closed ranks with the PNC," Kwayana reported (personal communication, January–February 2008).

SELF-CRITICISMS BY ASCRIA AND KWAYANA

ASCRIA's April 1, 1973 statement criticized the organization's failure to take class into account in its embrace of the PNC in the following terms:

> ASCRIA's mistake was to lead the African people to believe that, once the problem of African solidarity was solved, a people's political line would be followed. Again, we, especially our leadership, trusted too much in the platform declarations of the elite and our leadership was slow to believe rumours of corruption among ministers. It did not exercise the vigilance necessary always, and especially when dealing with opportunists. ASCRIA therefore, unwilling to risk a "split," remained silent at the PNC's doings and accepted rather weak excuses for the failures of the Government to develop

a mass line, to inspire the people and give them the right to govern. (Eusi Kwayana, personal communication, January–February 2008)

Kwayana also made at least two separate self-criticisms. Although their direct references are to statements he made in the late 1950s and early 1960s, they, too, are fundamentally about the dangers of not taking differences in class interests into account. The first is from a speech made in 1978 which I quote at length because it is Kwayana's clearest exposition of his political perspective and how he thought he had strayed from it:

My own statements on the racial question dating from the late fifties and especially in 1961, if I may say so self-critically, did not bring out in the way they should have, our basic acceptance of class struggle as the moving force of history. Critics might have read a class position into the sum total of what was said and written, but that does not excuse us of the fault of not saying again and again very clearly that we were trying to clear the way for a class struggle. There were several factors that no doubt tempted us in this imperfect behaviour. One was that the class aspects of the struggle in Guyana were not at that stage the foremost ones. Another was that racial solidarity, or ethnic solidarity, at that stage, was far more advanced among the (East) Indian population, and this for very clear historical reasons, than among the African population …

There was very little said by us that should not have been said. But as revolutionaries of a certain type we should have, in spite of the surrounding circumstances, and in fact because of that, spent some more time on the more long-term aspects of the problem. (Kwayana 1978)

His second self-criticism, while again about class, is more about what he called his "failure" to distinguish among classes as he made criticisms of "Indo-Guyanese responses and claims," and he brings out the feelings which in his view, help explain this failure:

My one important failure in what I wrote in the 1960s was this: My disappointment was so great, that in my criticism of Indo-Guyanese responses and claims I did not make a distinction between the leaders and the led, but treated all as equally responsible. I did not allow for class distinctions among the Indo-Guyanese population. Although the whole of that sister community tended to respond as one, it was important to examine the differences, even to come to similar conclusions. (Kwayana 1988)

Seeking still more clarity I asked him "What exactly were you apologizing for?" and he answered:

> I apologized for the abrasive manner in which I raised the racial issue. The drift to ethnic violence was then very clear to our small group and especially to me who had been close to both ethnic masses. Jagan had said in the Mahaicony district in the 1957 election campaign that his party would take up arms if it lost. Burnham had said in the city that if the PPP won the people could regain their freedom only by a bloody rebellion. I treated the Indian voting population as a herd and tried to make the African into a similar herd. (Eusi Kwayana, personal communication, January–February 2008)

This is a different way of saying that his error (or as he put it, failure) was ignoring class distinctions—and he is critical not only of the content of what he said but of his tone. Here, he refers to the manner in which he discussed race as "abrasive." Elsewhere, in a discussion of the 1961 document on possible solutions to the racial crisis which he co-authored (the same one which has often been mischaracterized as a proposal for partition), he again uses the word "abrasive" to describe the language the authors used in setting out the reasons, as they saw them, for the fears of the African population, strengthening the self-criticism by adding that it was language "reflecting the grossness of the times" (Kwayana 1978).

1972–1974: ASCRIA'S NEW DIRECTION: TOWARDS UNITY OF THE WORKING PEOPLE ACROSS RACE

The conclusion of ASCRIA's internal debate that a revolution of one race was not possible, cleared the way for moving in a new direction, which came dramatically to light in January 1973 with what has been called the land movement or land rebellion of 1973. Kwayana described the internal dynamic in ASCRIA that shaped the movement:

> The land movement took the form it did because there had been a debate that exposed the facts in ASCRIA: whether the enemy of the Africans in Guyana was the European or the Indian presence. It was influenced by both [Rodney's] *Groundings* and CLR James. It is after this that the land resolution was discussed and adopted in 1973. (Eusi Kwayana, personal communication, Oct 9, 2016)[9]

In January 1973, after protesting deals for sales of land by the sugar companies, ASCRIA "called upon African and East Indian workers and peasants to rebel against feudal-capitalism, the system by which Foreign Sugar Companies, notably Bookers, control the best lands of the coast, 200,000 acres, almost exactly as they did during African slavery and Indian indenture." Pointing out that "racial competition between Africans and Indians was the deliberate design of the Sugar Plantations," the organization "demanded that to begin solving this contradiction the African and Indian workers and peasants must make a joint assault on imperialist property, beginning with unused sugar lands." It added that "the campaign aimed at using the historical dialectic to achieve two things: a destruction of feudal capitalism and an honourable basis for unity among the exploited masses" (Kwayana 1973).

According to Kwayana, the response to the call to retake the land was overwhelming:

> People of both races were listening to our dispatches over Radio Demerara, then private. We made the call because it was reasonable, concrete and a serious step and said that the descendants of slaves and indentured Indians deserved a share of the imperialist—I think we said "heritage." They understood that very very well and no questions were asked among the rural masses. (Eusi Kwayana, personal communication, January–February 2008)

IPRA, ASCRIA, WPVP, Ratoon and some PPP individuals joined forces, some people leafletting, others speaking at bottom-house meetings in estates and villages and a rally at Bachelors Adventure of "Redemption Day" as they named it (Eusi Kwayana, personal communication, July 29, 2017). Kwayana explained that in the campaign, "We avoided looking like a political party. The campaign did not depend on speeches. It had a working document titled 'Guidelines,'[10] and speeches were not wide-ranging. I told visitors (that is, people and groups who came in support), 'hold your own meeting,' giving them many copies of 'Guidelines' for discussion" (Eusi Kwayana, personal communication, July 29, 2017).

ASCRIA reported that:

> Indians and Africans in communities on the East Coast of Demerara adjoining the sugar estates occupied the lands and, urged by ASCRIA, formed people's committees in each village to coordinate the campaign. Some 245 acres of land are estimated to have been occupied and about 2,000 people involved in the campaign. (ASCRIA undated)

The land rebellion ended on February 17, 1973, when the people occupying the sugar lands were forcibly removed by the police after refusing a 48 hour ultimatum to stop the occupation. Their shacks were burnt and three of them faced charges for trespass which the courts later dismissed. Having made its point, ASCRIA decided to call off the protest and marked the last day of the campaign, which it designated "Day of Redemption of Sugar Lands," with a series of activities (ibid.).

Commenting on the multi-racial nature of the campaign, the *Guyana Graphic*, the privately–owned daily newspaper, reported in its January 7, 1973 edition: "ASCRIA in general, and Eusi Kwayana in particular, are making a potentially serious approach to national unity in a country where there is so much superficiality and still an uneasy truce between the two races." While the PPP and two Indian cultural organizations, the Hindu Maha Sabha and the Muslim Islamic Anjuman, did not join the campaign, they declared support for it (ASCRIA undated). Kwayana also remarked on the support by the WPVP, and on the PPP's "patriotic contribution" in offering the government its votes in Parliament which would have provided the two-thirds majority needed for the government to take the sugar lands without compensation (Kwayana 1973).

ASCRIA evaluated the land rebellion as important to the growing resistance in four ways (ASCRIA undated):

1. it confirmed the rupture in African solidarity across class;
2. it was the first mass protest in almost two decades;
3. the participation by Indians laid the groundwork for a multiracial movement outside the PPP and PNC; and
4. the government response was a demonstration that it would brook no dissent even if the dissent was not directly against itself.

The land rebellion had won a small victory by forcing the Sugar Producers Association to turn over most of the unused land to the government (ibid.). Its larger victory was that it demonstrated the possibility of Indian- and African-Guyanese working people deciding for themselves to come together— even if only for a short while—to take militant political action in their shared interests.

Subsequent joint actions with other groups were held. A main example was the protest rallies ASCRIA called in 1974, after a decision by the University of Guyana academic board to appoint Walter Rodney as head of the history department was overturned by the PNC-controlled university board. The first rally, which attracted thousands, was described as "like 1953 both in size and multiracial composition." The PNC attempted to prevent later rallies, but according to Kwayana, "Its thugs were unprepared for this public response and had to confine themselves to heckling with racist jibes at the fact that Cheddi Jagan and I had appeared on the same platform after twenty-one years—with the exception of a single protest meeting in 1968, protesting the banning of CY Thomas from Jamaica."[11]

*   *   *

In its announcement of its break with the PNC, ASCRIA had lamented the absence of "an Indian organization with the courage to criticize the PPP leadership as we are doing with the PNC leadership." It continued:

> Many Indians are very ready to take the PNC to pieces, but utter not a word of criticism of the Indian political leadership and the Indian based party. This factor, more than anything else will hinder the movement for real power and authority to the workers and farmers. (ASCRIA 1973)

ASCRIA's wish was met when IPRA was launched in 1973,[12] stating that its founders were Indian-Guyanese who saw a need for an Indian organization of a new type, and who were from a younger generation of Indians who were militants (IPRA undated a). In the words of founder Moses Bhagwan, the IPRA would be a "revolutionary ... departure ... from the conventional politics of the Marxist–Leninist PPP leadership, that really didn't even think of the depth and challenges of ethnicity and laboured only to harvest the ethnic votes" (Moses Bhagwan, personal communication, October 4, 2016). He explained:

> IPRA was not a replica or imitation of ASCRIA (but was influenced by its precedent) within the Indian community. The historical cultural and political contexts were different. IPRA subscribed to the identity factor. However, Indians were not bombarded with western cultural influence as [were] Afro-Guyanese. So IPRA was not oriented towards consolidating Indian cultural practices which were well in place and not officially challenged by the authorities.
>
> But the Indian culture was always in the colonial environment belittled and treated with contempt. There was, in relation to the colonial power and Afro-Guyanese closer to the corridors of power and heavily concentrated in the civil administration, added to the fact of lower educational standards among Indians, a feeling of marginalisation or residing in the shed. (Cheddi controversially called this "a feeling of oppression.") Indo-Guyanese were very uncomfortable in the final analysis. This has to be seen too in the context of shared poverty, colonial control, the plantation system and the exploitation that dominated social existence.
>
> There was a kind of duality. Proud of the richness of their culture and diminished and overpowered within the social system. (Moses Bhagwan, personal communication, October 4, 2016)

IPRA identified two "fundamental questions" which the new generation of Indian-Guyanese had to address. One was opposing race/ethnic marginalization. In its view, "sinister forces in the core of the PNC regime [were] threatening him [the Indian-Guyanese] with a status of permanent inferiority in the multi-racial Guyanese society" (IPRA undated a).[13] The second was the urgency of crossing race divides between the Indian and African working people. IPRA argued that "the Indian-Guyanese deeply desires and must labour for a working co-existence with other races, in particular the African masses" (Moses Bhagwan, personal communication, October 4, 2016). It therefore embarked on teaching history to community groups and students with emphasis on the Indian contribution "hoping to lay a basis for building confidence and being able to relate to elements of the society without fear or sense of inferiority or hostility," and from that base, contributing to initiatives, mainly from ASCRIA, to open up the "relatively taboo subject of race ... and racial identity for legitimate national discourse." IPRA wanted to "redirect focus from an Indian/African confrontation in the struggle for power to a strategy of shared power" (ibid.).

For its part, seeking ways to unite the African and Indian working classes in the struggle against the "common enemy," ASCRIA established contacts with the newly formed IPRA (ASCRIA undated). The alliance between these two groups and the work they set out to do together constituted a qualitative leap in involving African- and Indian-Guyanese in rebuilding relations across their divides.

In a joint statement, ASCRIA and IPRA (1973):

1. committed themselves to uncovering and stating the causes of conflict and division between Indian- and African-Guyanese and to a course of action that would lead to racial dignity and the revolutionary class interests of the two groups of working people;
2. agreed on the need for each group to have its own revolutionary organization and from that base, build understanding between the two groups, rejecting the idea that Guyanese can't be Indian or African and Guyanese at the same time;
3. agreed on the rights of all races to equality, respect for the culture of each, and the right of each to maintain traditions without their being exploited by "empire builders"; and
4. opposed any theory of domination of one race by another.

The two organizations denounced "the policy of collision between Africans and Indians in Guyana" and undertook to "try to replace rivalry with justice in a new social and political system of collectivist or socialist development." Significantly, they also moved to address what had so far been absent from their organizing across race, pledging to "extend fraternal solidarity to the Amerindian masses and invite them to take part in the ending of the old gangster politics."

The most specific decision they announced was the setting up of an unofficial joint commission to make a record of the views of the people on the race problem, discussions to be held in communities with each ethnic group able to say clearly how they think they suffer at the hands of the other community. This commission was established, and persons affiliated to ASCRIA and IPRA, along with a few individuals not in either group, held bottom-house meetings in both Indian and African villages, seeking the people's views on race relations and the possibility of non-race politics. They were encouraged by the response on both sides (Eusi Kwayana, personal communication, January–February 2008). IPRA described the launch of the commission as "an historic, political and cultural event" and reported that it was meeting Indians and Africans throughout the country, hearing their views on racial problems" (IPRA undated b).

In this second phase of its organizing, ASCRIA also set out to develop joint action with groups other than IPRA. For example, in 1974, it decided to treat the denial of employment to Walter Rodney as a multiracial issue, inviting IPRA, the PPP and all other groups to join the protest. It was not the official opposition that took Rodney's case to the streets (Eusi Kwayana, personal communication, October 9, 2016). The other groups included Ratoon and the WPVP, which later joined IPRA and ASCRIA in forming the WPA.[14]

The end-product of this process was the formation of the WPA. A meeting held in Georgetown in November 1974 passed a resolution launching an alliance of ASCRIA, IPRA, Ratoon, and the WPVP. The new alliance's aims, outlined in the announcement of its formation, reflected the conviction that unity between Indian and African working people could be cemented, this time alongside Indigenous people. These aims included the determination:

- To teach and fight to bring about the unity of the working people— workers, employees, farmers, landless peasants, the unemployed, housewives, students, progressive professionals, working producers, small traders, craftsmen, and self-employed toilers;
- To develop, out of the struggle of the people, a political line of the working people based on the theory of their emancipation;
- To stand for the genuine multiracial power of the working people, expressed in organizational forms which guarantee the nature of this power, benefitting from the work being done in this respect by its member organizations;
- To address itself to the contradiction between the Indian and African sections of the population and to the historical exclusion of Amerindians from the political process (Dayclean 1974).

QUESTIONS ON ORGANIZING TO SUSTAIN RACIAL UNITY

Although the formation of an alliance doesn't require the disbanding of its constituent parts, with the launch of the WPA the period of separate organizing by

ASCRIA and IPRA effectively ended.[15] Then or shortly afterwards, both groups were persuaded that separate organizing was no longer necessary. My direct experience of this came when I joined the WPA Executive in January 1978 and noted that it functioned as a body of individuals, although most of its members had originally come on to the Executive as representatives of the organizations that had formed the alliance.

Asked to explain why ASCRIA gave up its individual identity after WPA was formed Kwayana replied:

> WPA was a new political organization. So far as I recall, ASCRIA remained active in the cultural area. Its positions when taken would be in support of those of the WPA. ASCRIA members were free to choose to become WPA members. Some broke away even before WPA's formation, the moment we began to go against the government. In time ASCRIA ... withered away but individuals carried on ceremonies in various places.

He added that at that point he felt that the WPA expressed what they wanted of race relations in Guyana (Eusi Kwayana, personal communication, January–February 2008).

For his part, Bhagwan explained that IPRA ceased functioning since its individual members joined the WPA when it was launched:

> On the formation of the WPA, IPRA was dissolved and its associates became free to choose a political path. As far as I know all chose to become active for the WPA. IPRA did not have a cultural agenda in the same way as ASCRIA. We were for a political reorientation for the Indian community, with loyalties to the working class, recognition of the dignity of all ethnic groups and from the beginning a search for reconciliation. Our principal concerns were fully accommodated in the WPA and in fact this was the kind of collaboration we wanted to be engaged in.
>
> At first we were not fully for the integrated model but yielded quickly to the good sense of the unified structure of the WPA. (Moses Bhagwan, personal communication, December 7, 2016)[16]

In sum, both Kwayana and Bhagwan are saying that the WPA represented the cross-race alliance that ASCRIA and IPRA had been working towards.

In considering their decision it may be instructive to compare the 1974 WPA with the 1953 PPP as cross-race alliances. While internationally, the left has historically emphasized the level of multiracial working class unity in the anti-colonial struggle led by the early PPP, inside the PPP, there were voices, including Kwayana's, arguing that more had to be done to solidify relations between Indians and Africans before risking going into government. Seecharran records that:

> [O]n the eve of the first general elections under adult suffrage, in April 1953, the People's Progressive Party (PPP) … was really a weak alliance of the two main ethnic groups … [and] [T]his fragile condition had prompted Eusi Kwayana (supported by Martin Carter, the poet) to move in the executive committee of the PPP that they should face reality and contest only eight seats in the general elections. If they fielded candidates in all the constituencies, Kwayana argued, they would surely win the elections and therefore have to precipitately face the trauma of being in government. He did not believe that the PPP was ready for office because "it was a kind of coalition … [some] racial unity was there but it was not well-grounded; it was tenuous." (Seecharan 2018)

As it turned out, not only did the PPP field candidates in 24 constituencies and win in 18, but in direct response to its victory the British government suspended the British Guiana constitution after 133 days and invaded the country. Several party leaders were detained or restricted. This set in train a process leading to a shattering of the "tenuous coalition."

The 1974 WPA was a coalition of a different sort. It was a coming together not of Indian and African leaders but of Indian and African organizations. In the second phase of ASCRIA's 10 year organizing and the whole of IPRA's shorter period of organizing, not just the leaders but members of each group committed themselves to crossing the race divide between the Indian and African working people. Each held internal discussions and/or classes and spoke publicly on the need for unity. Led by ASCRIA, they were involved along with other groups in joint actions, including, as described earlier, a land rebellion which involved masses of Africans and Indians acting in their shared interests. ASCRIA and IPRA jointly organized a Race Commission which held discussions with Indians and Africans in their communities on the question of race relations. Finally, the process towards the formation of the WPA, and in the elaboration of its goals, involved all the constituent groups.

The coalition of Indians and Africans in 1974 was therefore much better grounded, much more carefully constructed than the coalition of 1953. But it is also true that the 1974 WPA, unlike the 1953 PPP, had to contend with the legacy of the violence of 1961–1964 (see Essay 5), while the 1953 PPP predated it. It was that legacy which had led Walter Rodney—in spite of his deeply-held position that "[T]he specificity of the early 1960s can scarcely be used to characterize the entire history of Guyana" (Rodney 1981a: 189)—to the view that a period of separate organizing was necessary. Neither he nor ASCRIA and IPRA was being separatist; for all of them, a major aim of separate organizing of Indians and Africans was to build mutual understanding and respect and a shared project (ASCRIA and IPRA 1973), which also included Indigenous peoples. Here is what Rodney said in the early 1970s:

> Over the last decade, Indians and Africans, in Guyana, have been at each other's throats, for a variety of reasons, internal and external, and ... there is a tremendous amount of ill-will and suspicion, on both sides ... Now, some people try to deny this, and talk about racial harmony, but it just is not so. It may be submerged but it is there; it has to be there; the system ensures that. But, what can we do about it? I feel that there are, at least, two levels at which one must try to organize against the prevailing condition of racial antagonism. One must organize within the African community, within the Indian community, too, to build different forms of consciousness, different types of social bases, which will ultimately be the forms of the new State, and, simultaneously, one must begin to find effective revolutionary integrative mechanisms, both organizational and ideological, in terms of people, purely and simply people, you know, as contributors to the new concept of group consciousness, group power. (Salkey 1972: 385–386)

He added that the integrative mechanisms were necessary since "if you organize separately, this may well be construed by each group as something exclusive and hostile." Moreover, there was a need to "act in the kind of fashion and use the kind of language which makes it clear to the other group what the national aims are"; and the integrative mechanisms must be organized to include the Amerindians, "the original inhabitants of the country" (Salkey 1972: 386).

Kwayana reports that when Rodney first returned to Guyana in 1974 he took "soundings," and it is fair to assume that what he was enquiring into was whether working people thought it was now possible to organize across the race divide. Having taken the soundings he joined the WPA. Clearly he had concluded that the time was right for an alliance and that separate organizations were no longer needed. A further clue to his thinking came later, in a statement in his last written call to action before he was killed on June 13, 1980, that "the firmest unity is unity in struggle" (Rodney 1981b: 20). It was the process of struggle that would make the unity that had begun to be restored, solid.

And there was growing race unity inside the core of the WPA and its wider membership, as well as among the masses of people who participated in the civil rebellion of July to November 1979. You could feel it. There were few incidents of racial hostility in or out of the party. At the same time in casual conversations you heard the continued strength of racial stereotyping. Both were there at the same time. Not disharmony, but something that could descend into racial disharmony in the wrong conditions.

If "the firmest unity is unity in struggle," it is equally true that when the struggle ebbs—particularly if it ebbs before it wins victories that are powerful enough to sustain it and even propel it forward in lean times, the stage is set for it to weaken.

In hindsight, then, the question is whether what Rodney called the "tremendous amount of ill will and suspicion, on both sides" had been sufficiently overcome for the level of racial harmony built up to withstand testing.

The 1979 civil rebellion came to an end with the death of the first WPA leading member to be killed, Ohene Koama, in November 1979. Between 1980 and the mid-1980s the struggle for radical social change in Guyana and the rest of the region was derailed by the assassination of Rodney, the implosion of the Grenada revolution, and the defeat of the social democratic experiment in Jamaica (see Scott 2004). Internationally, conditions for transformation were eroded with the rise of neo-liberalism. However in Guyana, while Rodney's assassination was a terrible blow, it is untrue to say, as some people do, that the WPA died with his death. In fact, throughout the 1980s and beyond, it actively organized not only in African and Indian communities on the coast but for the first time, systematically in the Indigenous communities of the interior. The context was now a struggle for power of the multiracial working people via elections.

But in what was the first certifiably free election since the 1960s, the vote in 1992 was effectively split along racial lines between the PPP and the PNC. This result was in large part a rejection of multiracial politics, at least at the electoral level. Rodney was right that the violence of 1961–1964 was not typical of relations between Indian- and African-Guyanese historically. But once the struggle became purely electoral in the 1980s, the working people returned to which race (not which class) could be trusted with power. In 1992, there were clearly many factors other than racial solidarity or racial insecurity that might help explain why the vote was so completely race-based (the death of Rodney, the popularity of Jagan and the feeling that he had long been robbed of power, tactical voting).[17] But in the violence directed by some Africans against Indians after the PPP's victory (and repeated after every electoral win by the PPP from 1997 to 2011), and in the nature of some Indian commentary on that violence ("There is no war, no battlefield. There is one side, Africans, robbing, beating, raping, kidnapping and killing Indians"),[18] the size and weight of the racial mistrust and hostility left behind by 1961–1964 are clear.

In less than a decade there was a new rise in racial tension, and between 2002 and 2008, Guyana experienced periods of race violence that were as brutal or perhaps even more brutal than the violence of the 1960s—with a self-described "armed African resistance" organized around a small number of prison escapees attacking and murdering mainly Indian individuals, families and communities, and a shadowy group called the "phantom squad," allegedly with connections to members of the ruling PPP, executing mainly African men. Inevitably, two opposing narratives of this new generation of violence were created, each side calling up its narrative of the violence of 1961–1964 as evidence of the continuing racist aggression of the other. There was no group which had both the will and the capacity to speak and to be heard from outside of, or across the two camps. By then, the WPA, a much smaller and weaker force, carrying out far less work in communities than before, was seen as purely pro-African. At the same time, given the disbandment of IPRA and ASCRIA there were no ethnic organizations unaffiliated to the party of their "own race," or without overlapping memberships with that party, and whose aims included building unity of the working people across race.

Looking back, I believe that IPRA and ASCRIA should have continued as autonomous organizations inside the WPA because the conditions they had fought to change before the WPA came into being had not irreversibly changed with the formation of the WPA.

In my view, if ASCRIA and IPRA had remained alive as autonomous political organizations within the WPA,[19] they would not only have been positioned to help work against the renewed descent into race violence and the further entrenching of opposing race narratives, but to ensuring that the WPA remained a force in touch with and representing the separate and shared interests of Africans and Indians, well beyond the time it lost that strength. In particular, the continuation of the work that the two groups had started with the Race Commission could have provided an enduring space for people to speak out in their communities about racial marginalization and/or domination as they experienced it, including acts of violence. That could also have been a forum in and through which their grievances could be addressed. Working alongside a similarly autonomous organization of Indigenous peoples could have ensured that their interests were also properly addressed. We should have understood that clearing the way for class struggle, to use Kwayana's words—by which he meant clearing racial insecurity and hostility out of the way of class struggle—was ongoing work.

NOTES

1. The first of these groups of which I was a member was the WPA, although I was briefly associated with Ratoon in its very early days.
2. Both Kwayana and Bhagwan have criticized themselves in communications with me for the references in their statements to "he," "him" and "men." In an email of October 4, 2016, Bhagwan apologized for what he called "the old male gender bias" which he said (and I concur) he grew out of shortly after.
3. Other limitations are that the essay does not cover the critique of ASCRIA from the left, nor from others like Guyanese artist and writer Denis Williams who according to Quinn (2014: 33) "criticized the Africanization elements of ASCRIA's 'cultural

revolution' as limiting and divisive." "Strive as we may to maintain the image of such a relationship," he reportedly said, "we can never again become Indians or Africans or Chinese or Europeans. We are peoples of the New World."

4. This view was generally shared by the more radical groups in the Caribbean Black Power movement.

5. I remember the forum well. As Tennassee records, he and a number of young Indian-Guyanese with him stormed out after Carmichael (Ture) made these remarks, which left many of us in the room with a sense that efforts at crossing divides between Indians and Africans had just suffered a major blow.

6. I would comment here that by "race consciousness" Kwayana must have meant a consciousness of being African. Guyanese of African descent certainly had learned to define themselves as a race different from "the other."

7. The two examples chosen do not touch on ASCRIA's broader achievements, including its key role in establishing a Pan-African Secretariat based in Guyana in 1970, which in turn founded the annual May 25 African Solidarity Day in 1971. See Kwayana (1973). Nor do they mention what ASCRIA described as its ideological influence on the PNC and its role in building relations between the PNC and the Black Power, Pan Africanist and African liberation movements. See ASCRIA (1973).

8. Clive Thomas later helped found Ratoon.

9. Separately (personal communication July 29, 2017), Kwayana has reported that within about a year of its publication, Rodney's book was being used as a text book at Unity High School, a school he founded in Buxton, the village where he lived.

10. In "The GIFT Report: Its Rights and Wrongs," Kwayana explained: "The guidelines said that if an African group and an Indian group should find the same plot, they should discuss and share the plot." (Kwayana 1999: 13).

11. Other accounts put the year at 1969 (see Hinds 2008: 39).

12. While a number of publications say that IPRA supported the January 1973 land rebellion, according to the IPRA publication, "One Year After," IPRA was formed only in September 1973. IPRA was a deliberately loose formation, and I suspect that prior to its being launched, elements who later grouped together under that name were already active in various ways, including in support of ASCRIA initiatives. At an individual level, Bhagwan's collaboration with ASCRIA started much earlier. In a personal communication, he told me that in 1965, shortly after he resigned from the PPP, he participated as Chair in an ASCRIA programme held at its centre, commemorating Ghana's Independence.

13. In a personal communication of October 4, 2016, Bhagwan explained that although "influenced by its precedent, IPRA was not a replica or imitation of ASCRIA ... within the Indian community. The historical cultural and political contexts were different ... Indians were not bombarded with western cultural influence as [were] Afro-Guyanese. So IPRA was not oriented towards consolidating Indian cultural practices which were well in place and not officially challenged by the authorities. But the Indian culture was always in the colonial environment belittled and treated with contempt. There was in relation to the colonial power and Afro-Guyanese closer to the corridors of power and heavily concentrated in the civil administration, added to the fact of lower educational standards among Indians, a feeling of marginalisation ... There was a kind of duality. Proud of the richness of their culture and diminished and overpowered within the social system."

14. It is an insufficiently recognized fact that it was the increasing joint actions by parties and groups, and especially those between ASCRIA and IPRA, that laid the groundwork for Rodney to return home, which he had decided he would do only when he could see the way clear to organizing with Africans and Indians together. This in no way negates the impact of his return on moving the process forward.

15. This section relies largely on Kwayana and Bhagwan because it is they who led the two organizations which had come into being to address the problems of racial insecurity of African- and Indian-Guyanese; and Walter Rodney, who was the first and most influential of the individuals who joined WPA and who has left us an extensive record of how he saw issues of race and class in Guyana. See *Groundings with my Brothers* (Rodney 2014) for his position that Black Power had to include both African and Indians, *A History of the Guyanese Working People* (Rodney 1981) for the chapter "Race as a Contradiction among the Working People," and *In Defence of Arnold Rampersaud* (Rodney 1982), a speech printed after his assassination, and which was a call on African-Guyanese not to allow themselves to be used against an Indian-Guyanese falsely accused of murdering an African-Guyanese policeman.

16. The last IPRA document I've found, "Plight of Indians in Guyana 1975," is dated May 1975.

17. Some WPA and pro-WPA voters admitted voting for the PPP because they feared that a vote for the WPA would help the PNC.

18. Retrieved from www.gina.gov.gy/archive/researchp/statements/sto30613.html on August 7, 2007. [This URL is no longer working—A.T.]

19. I mention only ASCRIA and IPRA because the focus here is only on how autonomous organizations of Indians and Africans might have been able to help stop the descent into racial barbarism between 2002 and 2008 and continue the work of fostering race unity between those groups. I support autonomous organizing of all sectors of the working people including Amerindians, women and youth.

ACKNOWLEDGEMENTS

The origin of this essay was a presentation at a conference on Black Power in the region organized by the Centre for Caribbean Thought at the University of the West Indies, Mona, Jamaica, on February 21, 2008: a work in progress, that presentation was titled "Black Power Organising and the Multiracial Challenge in Guyana: Lessons from ASCRIA" and made the case that while ASCRIA did not organize in the name of Black Power, even in its first phase its aims, relations with Black Power groups in the region, and local and international activities made it a form of Black Power organizing. The paper was later developed based on material and personal communications that I didn't have in 2008, which raised critical questions about organizing within and against race divides.

REFERENCES

ASCRIA. "Statement on the Negative Directions in Guyana." April 1, 1973. Printed handout.

——. Undated. "ASCRIA's Anti-Corruption and Land for the Landless Campaign." Printed handout.

ASCRIA and IPRA. 1973. ASCRIA-IPRA Commission on Race Issue. December 28. Printed handout.

Birbalsingh, Frank. 2007. *The PPP of Guyana: 1950–1992: An Oral History.* London: Hansib Publications.

Dayclean. 1974. "Working People's Alliance Formed." *Dayclean* 1(2): 1.

Hinds, David. 1996–1997. "The African Society for Cultural Relations with Indecent Africa (ASCRIA)." *Emancipation* 4: 32–38.

——. 2008. "Walter Rodney and Political Resistance in Guyana: The 1979–1980 Civil Rebellion." *Wadabagei* 11(1): 36–63.

IPRA. Undated a. "The Stand of IPRA." Printed handout.

——. Undated b. "IPRA, One Year After." Printed handout.

——. 1973. "Race, Class and the Guyana Dictatorship." September 14. Printed handout.

——. 1975. "Plight of Indians in Guyana 1975." May. Printed handout.

Kwayana, Eusi. 1973. "Burnhamism, Jaganism and the People." April 26. Printed handout.

——. 1978. "Racial Insecurity and the Political System." Unpublished.

——. 1988. "Footnotes to the West on Trial." Unpublished.

Quinn, Kate. 2014. "Black Power in Caribbean Context." In *Black Power in the Caribbean,* Ed. Kate Quinn. Gainesville, FL: University Press of Florida, 25–52.

Rodney, Walter. 1981a. *History of the Guyanese Working People, 1881–1905.* Baltimore, MD: Johns Hopkins University Press.

——. 1981b. *People's Power, No Dictator.* New York: Black Liberation Press.

——. 1982. *In Defence of Arnold Rampersaud.* Georgetown: WPA Press.

——. 2014. *The Groundings with my Brothers.* East Point, GA: Walter Rodney Press.

Salkey, Andrew. 1972. "An Interview with Walter Rodney." In Andrew Salkey, *Georgetown Journal: a Caribbean Writer's Journey from London via Port of Spain to Georgetown, Guyana.* London: New Beacon Books, appendix B.

Scott, David. 2004. "Counting Women's Caring Work: An Interview with Andaiye." *Small Axe* 15: 123–217.

Seecharan, Clem. 2018. "Cheddi Jagan, Communism and the African-Guyanese." *Stabroek News*, March 22, Diaspora column.

Seecoomar, Judaman. 2002. *Contributions towards the Resolution of Conflict in Guyana.* Leeds: Peepal Tree Press.

Shah, Raffique. 2000. "Black Power and Indians." June 9. Retrieved from www.trinicenter.com/Raffique/blackpowerandindians.htm.

Tennassee, Paul Nehru.1982. *Guyana—A Nation in Ruins: The Puerto Rican Model Failed.* Toronto: Guyanese Research and Representation Services.

Westmaas, Nigel. 2014. "An Organic Activist: Eusi Kwayana, Guyana and Global Pan-Africanism." In *Black Power in the Caribbean,* Ed. Kate Quinn. Gainesville, FL: University Press of Florida, 159–178.

Three Letters against Race Violence
[2004, 2008]

1. NOT IN MY NAME

Dear Editor,

If we look at the recent killings by police and civilian criminals through the eyes of the children who witnessed them, we ought to be able to see past our usual racial/political party blinders. How can any of us find it acceptable that children should see their parents gunned down?

Guyana—or at least, coastal Guyana—is split straight down the middle. An African-Guyanese is shot down by the Black Clothes police and Indian-Guyanese opinion sees this as a legitimate attack on crimes against them, while African Guyanese see it as more evidence that their (our) lives are worth nothing. Lost in all this is the fact that these killings fuel more rage without doing anything at all to reduce violent crime.

On the other "side," when an Indian-Guyanese is killed, Indian-Guyanese understand this as an assault on their community, while African-Guyanese say it has nothing to do with race, but with drug wars. There are two problems here: one, they don't know that this is true and two, even if it is true, what is the argument? That executing people because of a deal gone sour is legitimate? Isn't this another kind of extra-judicial killing?

I return to where I started. Think of the children who, in two separate killings last week, saw their parents murdered! How can we tolerate this?

Finally, for now. I have not seen the two leaflets distributed by men describing themselves as "freedom fighters," but friends I trust have seen them and tell me it's true that they describe themselves as freedom fighters on behalf of the African Guyanese nation. To this my answer is, as one African Guyanese: "No. Not in my name. I do not know what acts you have committed since you left prison, killing one man and wounding one woman in the process. But at the very least you are driving fear into children, women and men who have done nothing to deserve it, and you cannot do so in my name."

Andaiye

2. BUXTON IS A TERROR CAMP
(with David Hinds and Eusi Kwayana)

Dear Editor,

The willful and malicious setting on fire of a human body is an aggravated crime against humanity. Treating women as a prize of armed conquest, either by rape or attempted rape, is an especially odious crime against the mothers of the human race and against humanity. Both these offences were carried out recently at Non Pareil, East Coast, Demerara. The reports so far are not very clear, but what is already clear is that most of those assaulted were Indian Guyanese.

In the past, each of us has made statements condemning African Guyanese atrocities against Indian Guyanese, and we condemn them even more strongly now, as the violence becomes more brutal.

A similar though less brutal violence has begun to spread to African Guyanese victims. We warned before that in the end, crime and violence know no race. This is coming to pass. In recent weeks the violence has taken on added proportions as African Guyanese are being targeted.

While it is difficult to distinguish naked crime from political violence, we think that there is a political element in all of this.

Today, African families and communities are also becoming victims of the madness that is consuming Guyana. And according to news reports and eye-witnesses, a few Indian Guyanese criminals are operating out of Buxton under the leadership of their African Guyanese counterparts.

Illegal weapons are playing a large part in the upsurge of brutal violence. Only the government of the country can have final and operational responsibility for the presence of illegal weapons among a population. After all is said and done, these weapons have crossed borders or passed through ports to enter Guyana. The government has official custody of these transit centers.

Yet in spite of the progressive increase in gun-related crimes, the statute books remain as they were. There are provisions which are not being invoked. In fact, the public has no evidence that the police know for certain what ammunition or what weapons were used on a particular occasion. If they do, they are silent about these details, which can help the public to make sense of the incidents. This part of the statement focuses on the government, not because those signing it have any doubt of the anti-government direction of the crimes. It has that focus because the government and its agencies can take certain actions:

1. There must be arms control regulations crafted to suit the present situation.
2. An expert voice from the law enforcement agencies must frequently address the offenders in the hearing of the nation. Law enforcers can offer options to those who know they are offenders, including the option of a fair trial under international observation.
3. Through the law and the parliament, if the situation does not improve, the Government should admit that it is out of hand. After meaning-ful consultations with opposition forces and civil society, it should apply

standard coercive regulations necessary to prevent the country from sliding knowingly into the abyss.

These are the short-term actions we recommend.

The PPP has erred badly in the way it has governed since 1992, which has impacted negatively on almost all sectors of the society, but in particular ways, most negatively on the already demoralized African Guyanese community. In relation to the violence perpetrated by the Black Clothes against African Guyanese, its failure to act has fueled the claim of an Indian Guyanese conspiracy against African Guyanese.

We have long called for power sharing as one of the answers to our problems. We still believe this to be essential. But we distance ourselves unequivocally from any scheme aimed at arriving at power sharing as a result of the calculated escalation of violence. There are at least three reasons why we must oppose the view held by some African Guyanese extremists that violence is pushing or will push the PPP away from its obstruction of peaceful constitutional remedies.

First, it is immoral. Why should innocent people have to endure daily terror and rape and young people be turned into child-soldiers and spies in order to bring a government to its senses?

Second, it cannot hold water, since the more the violence, the more the PPP claims that there is no crisis in the country.

Third, the naked violence and inter-ethnic violence have already created a climate in which people are unwilling to trust one another and thus will be unwilling to seriously address sharing of power, which is so essential for human development in Guyana. Because of this we have an additional reason for opposing the present violence. If the situation continues, by the time we get to power sharing there will be no power to share, as political parties would be prisoners of violent extremists, criminals, and drug lords.

Today Buxton is a terror camp in which villagers have become prisoners. The psychological, social and cultural damage being done to that village surpasses anything since slavery, including the dreaded 1960s. Both the PPP and the PNC must take full responsibility for that deterioration, for it is their zero sum political behaviour that paved the way for the boldness of the criminal and other extreme elements who now run things there. We warn that if the situation is not brought under control, more Buxtons will emerge overnight.

The PNC, by not publicly breaking with those who have been pushing Black supremacy and violence and excusing murder, rape, and mayhem as revolution, has contributed in no small way to the crisis.

This is no longer simply about politics and "marginalization," it is about the destruction of the nation in the name of saving the nation or under the guise of seeking power for African Guyanese.

We therefore appeal to all Guyanese who still have the courage to speak out, to do so with one strong voice. We urge the PPP and the PNC to separately and together come off their partisan horses while it is still possible to do so and help to save Guyana. As African Guyanese we urge Black People who are support- ing the violence to stop confusing naked terror with our historical quest for freedom; and we urge Black people who mutter quietly that they oppose the violence to say so in a loud voice, because your public silence is encouraging the perpetrators of the violence and adding insult to the injury caused to the victims of the violence. Any freedom that any group seeks through the rape and murder of its fellow citizens, including some of its own race, can never be real freedom.

Yours faithfully,

Andaiye, David Hinds,[1] Eusi Kwayana[2]

3.   AFTER THE MASSACRE IN LUSIGNAN: THIS HORROR CANNOT BE JUSTIFIED
(with Alissa Trotz)

Dear Editor,

A village was left homeless on Saturday morning. Eleven people were shot in their homes. Shot in their beds. Shot while sleeping. Shot begging for mercy. Shot clutching each other. Shot trying to save loved ones. Shot trying to run from a certain death. Shot trying to hide, in houses too small and too flimsy to protect them from doors being kicked down or from bullets penetrating the walls. Shot not knowing why they were randomly chosen to die. Shot not knowing that to the gunmen it did not matter who would be murdered, only that Lusignan would be turned into a sea of blood that night.

But they do matter. They matter to us all.

Clarence Thomas, Vanessa Thomas, Ron Thomas, Mohandai Gourdat, Seegobind Harrilall, Seegopaul Harrilall, Shazam Mohamed, Shaleem Baksh, Seecharran Rooplall, Dhanrajie Ramsingh, Raywattie Ramsingh.

Behind every name was a life. Behind every name is a story. Behind every name is a family, friends, a community left to grieve. Multiply them again and again, because behind every name is a part of all of us, all Guyanese, that died on Saturday morning.

This horror cannot be justified. It cannot go on. It must stop.

We have heard through the media, and from word on the street that what happened in Lusignan was revenge exacted by a criminal gang for the disap- pearance of Tenisha Morgan, a 19-year-old expectant mother from Buxton, a community that has seen its share of grief and loss, where just recently another mother, Donna Herod, was cut down in front of her young children, whom she had gone to collect from school.

In this war, lines are drawn in the sand. What we see here, so clearly this time, is how those most vulnerable are caught in the middle. In the name of a missing woman, allegedly abducted by the state, other women and children are mercilessly cut down. Always, it is women and children who become the grounds upon which these wars are carried out. In their name, in the name of protecting communities, protecting the defenseless, this violence is repeated, and continues, and increases in atrocity.

Meanwhile the body count grows longer.

Meanwhile a mother in Buxton holds out hope that her teenage daughter, heavily pregnant with twins and missing for over a week, is alive. And in Lusignan eleven people have been gunned down. One woman has lost two children and her husband, and must find the strength to mother her two remaining sons, both hospitalized with gunshot wounds. Next door, a young man has returned from Trinidad to bury his wife and their two young children. Down the road, a woman, her husband and their daughter—an entire family— are dead. Five children were gunned down, ages 12, 11, 11, 10, 4. This war has now been visited, with unimaginable cruelty, upon those who are too young even to understand death. And the surviving children of Lusignan know now, and with terrifying certainty, that not even they are safe anymore, and that the reassurances of parents will never be enough again to protect them.

This is the price of these wars. Those of us old enough to remember the communal, divisive violence of 1964 understand this well. We pay with the destruction of families, with the bodies of women and children. We pay with the blood of the innocent.

We hear, with few exceptions and from the safety of separate camps, big pro-nouncements. We hear calls for calm. We have seen expressions of sorrow and support. But it will not matter, it is cheap talk, all of it, if it does not begin with those who continue to pay the highest price of all. It is time we learn to listen to the anguish of a mother's cries, to recognize that her grief knows no race, no politics, no camp, only unspeakable loss and love. If we fail to recognize and reflect this in our responses as a community, as a people, as a country, then we have lost.

This horror cannot be justified. It cannot go on. It must stop.

Yours sincerely,

Andaiye, Alissa Trotz

ACKNOWLEDGEMENTS

Letter 1 was originally posted at http://guyanacaribbeanpolitics.news/?page_ id=536, September 27, 2004. Letter 2 was originally posted at guyanacaribbean politics.com, October 20, 2004. Letter 3 was originally published under the title "Stop It" in *Stabroek News*, January 28, 2008.

NOTES

1. Dr. David Hinds, a Guyana-born scholar-activist, is an Associate Professor of Caribbean and African Diaspora Studies in the School of Transformation at Arizona State University. He is an executive member of Guyana's Working People's Alliance (WPA).

2. Eusi Kwayana, formerly Sydney King, is a Guyanese politician and cultural activist and co-founder of the Working People's Alliance. Kwayana is the author of several books, including *Next Witness, Scars of Bondage, Guyana: No Guilty Race, Buxton in Print and Memory, Morning After, Genesis of a Nation: The Indo-Guyanese Contribution to Social Change (in Guyana)* and *Walter Rodney: His Last Days and Campaigns* (see Essay 6).

PART TWO

A DIFFERENT PERSPECTIVE:
STARTING WITH THE UNWAGED CARING WORK
OF MAINLY WOMEN WE REACH ALL SECTORS

SECTION I
WHY AND HOW TO COUNT UNWAGED WORK

ESSAY 8

*Valuing Unwaged Work: A Preparatory Brief for CARICOM Ministers
Responsible for Women's Affairs Attending the 4th World Conference
on Women*

[1994]

HISTORY OF THE CAMPAIGN TO VALUE UNWAGED WORK

Since the beginning of the Decade women have been seeking better measurement of their contributions to development. The 1988 UN System of National Accounts (SNA) recommended the inclusion of goods and services not exchanged for money in the concept of economic activity.

But the SNA still excludes goods and services produced in the household "for free," including childcare and housekeeping. In other words, it excluded women's unwaged household work.

Unwaged work has always existed, but it became product and producer of the inequalities between groups only as the dominant economic system became one based on wages, and unwaged work became devalued. For us in the Caribbean, the campaign against unwaged work therefore begins with slavery.

Internationally, the modern history of struggle against unwaged work began with the formation of the International Wages for Housework Campaign (IWFH) in 1972. The starting point of IWFH is the recognition that what women do in the family and community produces and reproduces labor power, and that the invisibility of this work underlies the various forms of discrimination they face in and out of the home.[1]

In 1980, the UN published the well-known statistics: women do two-thirds of the world's work, receive 10 percent of the world's income and own 1 percent of the world's assets. The International Labour Organization (ILO) then estimated that women in fact receive only 5 percent (rather than 10 percent) of the world's income. In 1990, a document of the UN Economic and Social Commission for Asia and the Pacific provided the estimate that about 70 percent of the world's poor are women. There is a deep connection between these statistics and women's unwaged work which needs to be drawn to the surface.

In the years leading up to the Final World Conference on the UN Decade for Women in 1985, IWFH agitated for the counting of women's unwaged work. Highlights of the struggle for this goal from Nairobi in 1985 to this point of the road to Beijing are outlined below.

1985

At Nairobi, paragraph 120 of "Forward Looking Strategies for the Advancement of Women" (FLS), amended by delegates from Sierra Leone, Jordan and Uganda along lines proposed by IWFH, committed governments to the following:

> The remunerated and in particular, the unremunerated contributions of women to all aspects and sectors of development should be recognized, and appropriate efforts should be made to measure and reflect these contributions in national accounts and economic statistics and in the Gross National Product. Concrete steps should be taken to quantify the unremunerated contributions of women to agriculture, food production, reproduction and household activities.

Paragraph 120 of FLS was singled out by many, including the Head of the US delegation to Nairobi, as one of the most important decisions of the Decade, and ratified by the UN General Assembly.

1989

The Counting Women's Unremunerated Work Bill was introduced into the British parliament by Mildred Gordon, MP. The Bill was endorsed by over one hundred MPs and was followed by the Recognition and Remuneration for Carers Bill for people engaged in full-time care of frail, elderly, disabled or very young relatives.

1990

The UN Commission on the Status of Women moved the target date for implementation of Paragraph 120 from the year 2000 to 1995.

1993

An Unremunerated Work Act, first introduced in 1991, was re-introduced in the US House of Representatives by Barbara-Rose Collins. The Bill requires the Bureau of Labor Statistics to conduct time-use surveys of unremunerated work performed in the United States—including household work, work related to childcare and other care services, agricultural work, work related to food production, work related to family businesses, and volunteer work; to calculate the monetary value of this work; and to include the measurement in a comprehensive GNP. Its endorsers included the Congressional Black Caucus (all but one member), the Congressional Caucus for Women's Issues, International Business and Professional Women, the National Organization for Women, and the Committee on the Elimination of Discrimination against Women. The Bill was also endorsed by a woman who is another kind of institution—Rosa Parks, the woman who in 1955 sparked the modern civil rights movement in the United States by refusing the extra work of sitting in the back of a bus in Montgomery. The US bill calls for the counting of the unwaged work of women and men.

The European parliament adopted a report calling on European Union governments to quantify and value women's unwaged work and include it in their GNP.

1994

Trinidad and Tobago Independent Senator Diana Mahabir-Wyatt served notice of her intention to introduce a Bill on counting women's unremunerated work in the parliament.

So now the work of carrying forward the decision of Nairobi, ratified by the UN General Assembly, has come home. It is no accident that it is happening first in Trinidad and Tobago, given the long years of agitation in that country by Clotil Walcott and her associates. Clotil Walcott, a grassroots woman activist and advocate since 1965, is the founder of the National Union of Domestic Employees of Trinidad and Tobago and a member of the International Wages for Housework Campaign and Counting Women's Work Network. A petition to Count Women's Work circulated by Clotil was able to win support from a spectrum of trade unions and women's groups including the Trinidad and Tobago Registered Nurses Association and the Trinidad and Tobago Teachers' Union Women's Auxiliary.

If we are to take the necessary action in the other territories of the sub-region, we need to discuss the why and the how of counting women's unwaged work.

WHY COUNT WOMEN'S UNWAGED WORK?

The pillars of our economy are composed of an invisible workforce of unwaged workers. We reap the fruits of their labour but ignore their every existence. I want them recognized.

—Congresswoman Barbara-Rose Collins, US House of Representatives

As the UN has pointed out, national accounts and labor statistics

> provide the fundamental picture of national economies which govern-
> ments and the public use to monitor and assess national development and
> to prepare and implement economic and related social policies. Failure to
> properly recognize and measure women's role in production leads to gross
> distortions and biases in economic decision-making at both micro (individ-
> ual and household) and macro (national and international) levels.

Unwaged work involves a spectrum of activities—physical, mental and
emotional—which somebody does, without a wage, to keep individuals,
families and communities going. It is, most centrally and most invisibly,
the work of bringing up the future labor force and of daily replenishing the
energies of the present labor force. The value of this work internationally has
been estimated at US$4 trillion; and as far back as 1985, a US Department of
Commerce report put the value in the United States (excluding volunteer work
and work on farms), at US$1,462 billion. For India it has been estimated at 33
percent of the GDP.

The reason that this monumental workload is invisible is that because it is
not exchanged for money, it is not part of the formal system of exchange. When
we were working on the national reports for the English-speaking Caribbean
we began to develop a hypothesis which we believe to have validity for the
wider sub-region: that in the Caribbean, the burden of women's unwaged work
is so heavy that it negates the impact of those favorable changes that have been
achieved in many of our countries, in women's access to education, and in their
legal status.

I want to use the example of Guyana to make the point. The laws governing
the status of women are quite advanced, and females participate in education at
all levels at the same rate, or at a higher rate than males. While the situation for
women in these areas has been steadily improving since 1980, it is not new. Yet
in the 1990s, women still constitute only 17 percent of Members of Parliament,
12 percent of executive managers and 11 percent of registered factory owners.
It is no accident that weaknesses in the law relating to women's rights are all
reflective of a failure to recognize and value their unwaged work (e.g. maternity
laws, the Married Persons Property Act).

At least five factors seem to be interacting to produce the extraordinary
weight of unwaged work in the Caribbean:

1. The high proportion of single parent female headed households as a result
    of slavery and our long and continuing reliance on emigration as a survival
    strategy.

2. The degree of entrenchment of gender stereotypes and the strength with which they continue to be fostered by all the institutions that shape consciousness—home, school, media, popular culture and religion. (The last is not insignificant in our societies, which are so deeply religious).
3. The level of underdevelopment in some countries and regions of countries.
4. Because of the geographic location, small size, ecological fragility and economic dependency of many of our countries, our vulnerability to militarism and war, natural disasters, endemic economic crisis and massive debt, each of which increases the unwaged work of ensuring survival.
5. The lack of social support for reproductive work (especially child and family care), except through arrangements among women.

Since a Structural Adjustment Programme (SAP) has been introduced into most countries of the sub-region, whether through a formal IMF program or not, it is perhaps the best starting point for demonstrating the value of counting unwaged work.

The underlying assumption of macroeconomic planning, reflected in the choice of work to be counted in national statistics, is that labor power is a factor of production that is not itself produced (like Topsy, it just "growed"); or that rather, since it is produced "for love," it has no political or economic cost.

In its present conditionality the SAP builds on this. It shifts activities from the public sector to the household/community sector as though what happens in that sector, being unwaged, carries no cost.

SAPs increase unwaged work because they lead to, or worsen the contraction of services, the deterioration of the infrastructure and the growing gap between prices and incomes. In physical terms, this new burden of unwaged work is largely made up of travelling longer distances (for services, fuel or water) and waiting longer periods (for transport, health care, electricity), and hunting and gathering cheaper foods (which then take longer to cook).

Since for many women SAPs also mean an increase in the need for waged work, there are clear implications for their physical and mental health. And since women's physical and mental energies are not infinitely elastic something often has to give, and often, it is children—children taken out of school to do waged and unwaged work or who become part of the growing army of street children and children heading households.

The impact may not be immediately visible in economic terms, but except for those who believe there is no connection between human resource development and economic development, its underlying economic implications are clear.

If we accept that our economies need some form of structural adjustment, we must also understand that structural adjustment can only be sustainable if it does not deplete non-renewable resources, including human resources.

Counting the unwaged work of producing and reproducing human resources under Structural Adjustment would provide policy makers with the basis for evaluating its true cost and for arriving at a more rational allocation of resources. It would also show that SAPs, under their present conditionalities, work against the achievement of the goals of FLS and the Convention on the Elimination of all Forms of Discrimination against Women.

The invisibility of unwaged work is a discrimination against women which fuels other forms of discrimination against women. I want to expand on this only in relation to some of its effects on women's overall economic status, although it has far wider implications for women's relative lack of social power:

1. Because unwaged work is invisible it brings with it no entitlements: thus, after a lifetime of a double unwaged workday (in subsistence farming and in the household), an elderly rural woman can find herself with no financial "security" except through her husband/partner. Incidentally, in some of our countries the unwaged work of women in food production is on the increase as men migrate internally in search of jobs. One effect of women's continuing invisibility in agriculture is that the introduction of new technology and extension services are still targeted at men.

2. The invisibility of women's unwaged work devalues women's waged work. The fields of study and work into which females still cluster are low-waged first at all, because they are extensions of the unwaged work they do in the home. Waged domestic work, which is the most direct extension of all, is not only among the lowest-waged jobs in any of our countries. In some countries it is not even recognized in labor legislation.

3. The invisibility of women's unwaged work shapes women's participation in waged work and their ability to organize to defend themselves in the workplace. It is behind their choice of home-based production and part-time work. It defines the areas and levels of self-employment in which they engage. It legitimizes bias against their access to credit and other productions resources. It justifies the employer's denial to them of job security, training and promotion on the grounds of their "unreliability."

The relationship between men and women in the waged workplace is established by their relationship within the household. Counting women's unwaged work would provide the basis for establishing equity in pay and entitlements, and for working towards the recognition of childcare as a social responsibility as required by the Convention on the Rights of the Child.

The burden of unwaged work falls particularly hard on certain groups of women—rural women in general and Amerindian women in particular; women with disabilities or who care for dependent relatives with disabilities; elderly women living on their own; and female heads of household caring alone for dependent children. There is an economic (not only a social or political or moral) cost to failing to provide for their needs.

Although I have concentrated on how counting unwaged work would reveal the cost of structural adjustment, it is equally true that it would reveal the cost of coping with militarism and war, natural disasters, massive migrations, intolerable debt, and in the case of Cuba, blockade.

HOW TO COUNT UNWAGED WORK

Methods for counting unwaged work are being developed and tested by a number of groups, including the International Research and Training Institute for the Advancement of Women. Basically, the possibilities envisaged are:

1. *Replacement of services* by measuring:
   a) their *market cost*—how much it would cost to take all the services performed in/around the home into the market place;
   b) their *replacement cost*—how much it would cost to get someone to come in to perform all the household jobs; or
2. *Replacement of the woman* by measuring her *opportunity cost*—how much a woman could earn in a job outside the home if she weren't doing housework full-time.

This last method is unacceptable because a woman's opportunity cost would reflect inequalities in the labor market based on class, race, age and disability.

The basis for counting unwaged work would be time-use studies which measure what people do in the course of a day (or longer) and how their time is distributed among various kinds of activities. According to a 1991 UN document, between 1985 and 1990 time-use studies were carried out or planned by national statistical services in more than 15 countries.

Fear has been expressed that the inclusion of unwaged work in the GNPs of poor countries would provide a false impression of wealth. Pending global acceptance of the need to count unwaged work in the GNP, the proposal is that countries retain their GNPs in their present form, within a "comprehensive" GNP which would show not wealth, but the effect of poverty. In societies where unwaged work is done in conditions of low technology and weakened services and infrastructures, those who work hardest do not produce the most. Counting women's unwaged work in those conditions would therefore measure *both* women's contributions to survival *and* what it costs them and ultimately the whole society for them to make this contribution.

I want now to report on a pilot survey that is being done in Trinidad and Tobago on the unwaged and waged domestic work of women under the sponsorship of CARICOM.

PILOT SURVEY ON THE UNWAGED WORK OF WOMEN

As a step towards sub-regional action on paragraph 120 of FLS, the CARICOM Secretariat undertook the responsibility of obtaining the relevant information in a few countries of the English speaking Caribbean—Trinidad and Tobago, St. Vincent and the Grenadines, Belize and Guyana. However, various factors needed to be considered, the most significant of which were time and cost. After much deliberation, the Secretariat engaged the services of a Research group, Caribbean Researchers, to conduct a pilot study in Trinidad and Tobago.

The survey seeks to identify, quantify and value those activities which constitute women's work in the household undertaken by women who are housewives or engaged in home duties, and women who receive wages in exchange for their labor in households. The survey design therefore comprises two parts to be conducted concurrently:

1. a survey of one hundred randomly selected households on unwaged work of women; and
2. a survey of one hundred domestic workers to be quota sampled.

The results obtained from the two-part survey would allow comparisons to be made between the work involved in women's household labor in unwaged and waged situations.

The methodology involves the use of two questionnaires. For part 1, the survey design is the same as that used by the Central Statistical Office for the Continuous Sample Survey of Population (CSSP). The CSSP, which is a multi-purpose household survey used mainly for collecting national labor force data, was used to identify those persons who stated "Home Duties" as their economic activity in the 4th quarter of 1993. The number of enumeration districts in that 4th quarter was 63, which generated 421 households. A random sample of 1 in 3 was then applied since the aim of the survey (part 1) was to sample approximately one hundred households in order to obtain meaningful information for analysis.

Part 2 of the survey concerns those women who work in households other than their own, and who receive a wage in exchange for their labor. One hundred households were approached in the areas of Arima and Valsayn (St. George East), Diego Martin and Goodwood Park (St. George West), and San Fernando.

In addition, where in part 1, interviewers encountered persons who stated "Domestic Work" as the "type of activity," a part 2 questionnaire was completed, thereby minimizing time/cost for part 2 of the survey.

For the conduct of the survey, six field interviewers (including members of the Domestic Worker's Union) were employed for a two-week period beginning June 8, 1994. The survey was spread throughout Trinidad and Tobago.

It should be noted that although the sample size is small, the significance of the project is that the results could serve as the basis for developing the methodology, design and concepts for subsequent measurements of women's unremunerated work in the wider Caribbean region.

CONCLUSION

In the Caribbean, the voices raised against counting women's work come from within four communities. The first two are governments which fear creating an illusion of wealth would lose our countries' access to aid, and technocrats who believe that there are no appropriate mechanisms for carrying out the count. This paper has already stated that proposals exist for addressing both these "problems."

The other two voices are also easily answered. They are the voices of men who believe that counting women's work is a call to increase the marginalization of Caribbean men; and the voices of Caribbean women who still insist that to count women's unwaged work is to legitimize that work and especially, their role as housewives. The answer is in a long quote from Selma James, founder of the International Wages for Housewives Campaign which in turn initiated the Counting Women Work Campaign:

> The demand that governments count women's unwaged work is the focus of an international movement to achieve the implementations of Paragraph 120, uniting women with more power and women with less, quantifying and making visible the workload of each. The demand makes visible for the first time how much all economies are based on this work. The visibility of women's enormous contributions is a lever of power making an unanswerable case for women's entitlements, from being called "workers" to equal pay and comparable worth; from appropriate technology to land and inheritance rights; from clean, piped water to health care and housing; from the right to safe birth control and safe abortion to the right to refuse sterilization and the criminalization of rape within marriage.

ACKNOWLEDGEMENTS

This essay was originally prepared for presentation to Ministers Responsible for Women's Affairs, Directors of Women's Bureaux and Technical Advisers on Women's Affairs at the Economic Commission for Latin America and the Caribbean/CARICOM/UNIFEM Caribbean Sub-Regional Conference, Preparatory to the 4th World Conference on Women, Curacao, June 28–29, 1994. UN documents and documents of the International Wages for Housework Campaign were used in researching the presentation. Ministers attending agreed to support the demand to count unwaged work and CARICOM played a lead role in advocating for the demand in the government fora at Beijing, while the International Women Count Network carried out a sustained lobby among delegates. The presentation was later published as an Occasional Paper of the Women and Development Unit of the School of Continuing Studies of the University of the West Indies Barbados campus (WAND) Occasional Paper 4/94).

NOTE

1.   This does not mean that the invisibility of unwaged work totally *explains* the various forms of discrimination.

Grassroots Women Learning to Count their Unwaged Work: Summary Report on a 2001–2002 Trial
[2009]

In a two-year process of preparation for the 1995 Beijing Conference on Women, researchers and activists in the English-speaking Caribbean sought to explain, in material terms, why women remain so concentrated at the bottom of the economic ladder in spite of their clear advances in education: girls and women are so far "outperforming" boys and men in secondary and tertiary education that it has fueled the male marginalization thesis. Since 1995 the analysis remains the same, particularly the analysis of the extraordinary and growing burden of women's responsibility for unwaged caring work in the Caribbean. The factors explaining this include the level of poverty and under-development in some countries and areas of countries, which increase the work of ensuring survival.

The findings of a 2001–2002 time-use survey in Guyana by Red Thread, the first of its kind that we know of, confirmed the weight of unwaged work done by grassroots women, showing that in all racial/ethnic groups, the typical working day for the majority of women ranged from 14 to 18 hours, with little help from anyone, often with minimal or unreliable technology, limited access to amenities and with very little leisure or free time for themselves. Several women had longer days—up to 21 hours. The great majority of women were busy by 6:00 a.m., with a significant number of women in all ethnic groups starting earlier, as early as 3:00 or 3.30 a.m. For example, an Indo-Guyanese woman got up at 3:30 a.m. to cook her husband's breakfast and prepare a packed lunch before he left for work as a cane cutter at around 5:30 a.m. while her three small children, under three years old, slept.[1] Many women in all the sectors had no breaks in a day. This was as high as 50 percent among Indigenous women—one of whom lamented it was her day off!

The lack of technology had a major impact on their day. In some Indigenous communities, the absence of electric light forced women to fit their work into daylight hours, while lack of piped water nearby had women going to the creek several times a day to wash clothes, bathe themselves and their children, and get water for drinking and cooking. For many women in any sector, especially those with small children who were by their side all day, a "break" represented not a cessation of work but a reduction in its intensity; that is, they stopped tackling more than one job at a time. For many women in all sectors the only time they could call their own was a few minutes' prayer or devotion at the beginning and end of their day. Illness and pregnancy sometimes slowed women down but clearly did not stop them doing a full day's work, including heavy jobs such as chopping wood. And any working day could unexpectedly be stretched to 24 hours, for example, when a child was ill and needed attention through the night as one mother recorded, which does happen to every mother of a young child (IWCN 2004).

In the process of compiling the time-use diaries, whether they were writing themselves or dictating to a Red Thread woman what to write, the women revealed their work to themselves, and in some cases developed a confidence that this work entitled them to the resources they needed to reduce their burden. That consciousness was the underpinning of Red Thread's organizing with hundreds of grassroots women to demand support following the worst flood in Guyana's history in January/February 2005. At that time, of Guyana's total population of just over three-quarters of a million, three hundred thousand people in 110 villages or nearly 40 percent of the population was affected:

Entire communities lived under stagnant and contaminated water (more than four feet deep in some places), accessible by boat, or the vessels—upturned fridges, boards lashed to oil drums—improvised by residents. The shelters that the government opened offered temporary relief to less than six thousand persons, leading many to decamp to the coastal main road in search of dry land, food and potable water. Households suffered extensive losses that included furniture and personal effects, vegetable gardens, farmlands, poultry, livestock and outdoor equipment. Of the 34 deaths, seven were due to drowning; the rest were the result of flood-related illnesses, with hundreds admitted to hospital. (Trotz 2010)

Red Thread organizer Wintress White recounted how the group responded:

We went into the communities on the coast that were badly hit by the flood. We went there to find out how the people were coping and to see if children and people who had chronic illnesses were sick, and if so who we could approach to get help for them (More precisely our participation in the delivery of flood relief targeted "elderly people, pregnant and breast-feeding mothers, people with disabilities and women with young children"). News soon spread that Red Thread was the place to go to for help and Indo-Guyanese and Afro-Guyanese women—even men—came to see what help they could get. We told them that even if we were in a position to give them food, and we were not, when the food was finished, then what? We told them that they should organize themselves together and make some demands to the government as they were not responsible for the flood. We started to organize meetings so they could prepare ... At one meeting in our small centre there were about 220 women from 14 communities— Indo-Guyanese and Afro-Guyanese. (White 2009)

Women were in the forefront of every activity in their communities after the flood. The Minister of Labour, Human Services and Social Security acknowledged this when she said, "It is the women of Guyana who defended their children from disease and death during the flood" (meeting on March 9, 2005, organized by the Women's Affairs Bureau and women's groups to mark International Women's Day 2005). But the Red Thread organizers wanted more than this acknowledgement. They were determined that the women's defense of their families and communities would be counted as work and that its full spectrum of skills, creativity and dedication to life be seen. Thus the language they used was of "the grassroots women of every race who braved waist-deep and even chest-deep flood waters … to invent ways to feed, clothe, shelter, teach, nurse, worry about and provide safety and a sense of security for their children first of all" (Red Thread 2005).

Counting the work in turn opened the way to demanding that the women were entitled to resources to do the mountain of work of restoring lives and livelihoods. This led Red Thread to the decision to hold a speakout at which the women would speak their minds about their experience and needs and demands to representatives from the media, parliament, trade unions, government units, local NGOs and international donor agencies. The women wrote lists of the household goods and stocks and animals and kitchen gardens they had lost, what extra workload they were carrying, and what their demands were on government and other agencies (Red Thread 2005).

"Grassroots Women Speak Out: Counting our Work for Guyana's Survival from the Flood" was held in Georgetown on March 13, 2005 with representatives from all those institutions and agencies hearing the testimony and the demands of the more than two hundred Indo-Guyanese, Afro-Guyanese, Mixed race and Indigenous women who had gathered. In a written statement later published in the media, the women prefaced these demands by describing themselves in terms of the unwaged, subsistence and low-waged work they usually did and how the products and tools of their labor had been damaged or destroyed:

We are mothers, grandmothers, aunts, daughters and sisters who care for our families full-time without any wage, or who care for our families and also work outside the home for low wages. We are women with disabilities and women looking after children with disabilities.

We are cane farmers who lost our crops and who are unable to replant and unable to pay leases for farmland. We are garment workers, security guards, domestics, newspaper vendors and other women with jobs outside the home who were not able to earn even our usually low wages during the flood.

We are market vendors, fish vendors and vendors of snacks and other goods who lost our stocks to the flood and who cannot restock because we have no money and no one is willing to trust us money. We are farmers, vendors and other small businesswomen who owed installments (*sic*) on loan repayments. We are housewives and caregivers who suffered massive losses of household possessions, kitchen gardens, poultry and small livestock.

We are not asking anyone for handouts; but we do want what we are entitled to – the actions we need all of you to take so we can continue to ensure the survival of our children, families and communities without the impossible burden we have been carrying since the flood started [emphasis added]. (Red Thread 2005)

In material terms, the women's organizing helped win a small amount of compensation, replacement for small livestock and plants lost, and assistance from the ministry of agriculture to villages that it had not visited. But they won much more than that; they won the invaluable experience of mobilizing and organizing to win, and of winning.

ACKNOWLEDGEMENTS

This essay is previously unpublished, and is drawn from a talk prepared for a lecture given at the University of North Carolina in 2009.

NOTE

1. Many women incorporate activities from which they can earn some money from home into an extended workday; for example, one Afro-Guyanese woman was up by 3:00 a.m. to cook a range of snacks before the rest of the household was up and making demands, and in order to start selling at 8:00 a.m.

REFERENCES

IWCN. 2004. "Report on Red Thread Time-Use Survey." November 30. International Women Count Network.

Red Thread. 2005. *Organizing for Survival: Grassroots Women and the Flood.* DVD and transcripts. Georgetown: Red Thread Women's Organisation.

Trotz, D. Alissa. 2010. "Shifting the Ground Beneath Us: Social Reproduction, Grassroots Women's Activism and the 2005 Floods in Guyana." *Interventions: Journal in Postcolonial Studies* 12(1): 112–124.

Wintress White. 2009. "January–March 2005: Grassroots Women in Guyana Organizing to Regain our Lives and Livelihoods after the Worst Floods in Guyana's History." Presented at Floods, Drought, Pollution and Survival: Women from the Global South Speak out about Climate Change, February 5, 2009, London, UK.

ESSAY 10
Looking at the Legalization of Abortion from
the Perspective of Women as Unwaged Carers
[1993]

In supporting the legalization of abortion in Guyana, I'm not going to make the usual pro-choice argument. My problem with that argument is best summed up in the words of a woman, Claire Glasman, speaking on behalf of Winvisible, an organization of disabled women, during a public debate on legalized abortion in the United Kingdom in 1988. Claire said:

> The … argument that women should have "the right to choose" tends to ignore the fact that many women who would like children cannot afford to have them … we need to have the power to have or not have children, which can only come with the economic independence to reduce our work and determine our own lives.

The Convention on the Rights of the Child recognizes the way that the rights of women and the rights of children are linked when it calls for childcare to be embraced as a social responsibility. But as I listen to the debate over legalizing abortion in Guyana, what strikes me is that, if a woman decides to abort a fetus that's everyone's business; if she decides to carry it to term, it's her baby. The problem does not lie only with what happens in the family where few men—whatever their background—are equal partners in raising their children. That's a critical issue; but we have to place it alongside another issue, that is, that the other institutions of society are not organized to support women in childbearing and childrearing, either.

Tell me. If you who are listening to this, man or woman, are interviewing a woman for the position of domestic worker or cleaner, will you employ her if she is six-months pregnant? Or if you employ a woman who then gets pregnant, can she have all the time off she needs to attend clinic? Is it OK that she might no longer be able to stoop to sweep up your dust? Is it OK? Or will you weigh her needs against yours and find in your favor?

Pregnancy and childcare qualify women to be dismissed as "unreliable." Women in Guyana can still be, and are fired from their jobs because they are pregnant. Higher up the ladder, they lose out in the battle for promotion because of the demands of childbearing and childrearing. Small business women applying for bank loans on their own (that is, without the backup of a man) are asked how they will run their business when they get pregnant or children become ill.

It is easy to locate the rise in abortion in Guyana in "promiscuity." The crucial link is the link between the rise in abortions and the distortions in our economy which have made life harder for most women. A few examples:

1. The forced migration across and out of Guyana in search of waged work has often been a migration of individuals, not families, and has led to an increase in de facto single-parent, woman-headed households.
2. In a situation where there is no social security, large numbers of women of childbearing age can find no better way to earn a living than the migratoriness required for trading.
3. Especially in poor families, as more and more women of all ages move into waged work, the extended family, which was the base for childcare, has been all but shattered.

No one is arguing in favor of abortion as contraception. But here, too, there's a problem that has to do with a woman's place. I don't know any studies of contraceptive use in Guyana but in day to day conversation, women complain that men simultaneously leave the arrangements for contraception to them, while reserving the right to say what kinds of contraceptives they find acceptable. Again, it's not just a problem of individual men. Women also complain about contraceptives that don't work because they are not always educated on how to use them effectively, or because doctors don't do a good enough job, or even because they are provided contraceptives which are past their expiry date. This hearsay evidence suggests that, in spite of the work of the clinics and the Responsible Parenthood Association, effective contraception is not widely enough available to low-income women.

In the UK debate over legalized abortion I referred to earlier, a woman MP Mildred Gordon, explained the problem of abortion to the House of Commons in the following way:

The whole question of abortion is closely linked to other campaigns that women have been fighting for many years ... If we were to win these other campaigns ... we would have a more civilised society; there would be few abortions, and late terminations would all but disappear. To achieve that end, we need improved sex education. We need safer childbirth ... we want nursery provision for young children ... we need money ... as of right, for women who are carers of children, the disabled, the sick and the old. If we win those campaigns, women will be able to have their children and we will have a civilised society in which the rearing of children will be the joy it should be.

Mildred Gordon, as I said, was speaking about England. But she could be speaking about Guyana.

Imagine that my name is Sheila. I am a woman of 16, 20, 30, 40; Indo-, Afro-, Amerindian, mixed Guyanese; rural, urban; married, unmarried; religious. I am not pro-abortion; few women ever are. I have had abortions but I have never had an "abortion of convenience"; no abortion is really physically or emotionally convenient. And I would rejoice in a world where abortion becomes less and less necessary because women's basic rights become more and more honored in law and in living.

I believe that is the campaign in which we should be joined.

ACKNOWLEDGEMENTS

This essay was originally a radio viewpoint, Tuesday, June 22, 1993.

BREAKING THE FRONTIER BETWEEN HOME AND STREET, UNWAGED AND WAGED

ESSAY 11
Strike for a Millennium which Values all Women's Work and all Women's Lives: A Call to Action
[2000]

Nan, a Guyana-born, Caribbean-bred friend of mine, published an essay last year on the experience of caring for her father while he had Alzheimer's. What she was writing about was how that caring was both love and labor. Looking after children, looking after ageing parents (and doing what a Rastafarian friend, Keturah, calls "mancare")—all these involve labor, even when they involve love.

That is what the women of the National Council of Ireland are drawing attention to as they call a woman's strike in Ireland for March 8, 2000, the first International Women's Day of the "new millennium," to demand recognition of and support for all the unwaged work which women do in the home. They also want recognition of and support for the unwaged work women do in agriculture, in family business, in the community.

Why? Every woman caring for small children or ageing parents by herself knows why. She knows what that other labor means for her work and income and authority as a vendor, a farmer, a security guard, a member of parliament, a union official. Every new mother who wants to breastfeed her child and keep her paid job knows how hard it is to do both. Across the globe, there is something called "women's work," not so frequently done by men ("Stan' home from me wuk tuh look at sick children? You tek me fuh a 'oman?"). And this work that people call "women's work" is unwaged when we do it with our families and communities, low-waged when we do it for others. The UN has calculated that across the world, women's yearly unwaged contribution—that is, the value of the work we do for no money each year—comes to at least US$11 trillion. Society and the economy would not survive without this work. Yet it is not measured or valued, or even recognized as work. Very little support is offered to those doing it. In fact, women are penalized for doing it, sometimes by other women.

Ever since the Irish women made their strike call outside the United Nations in 1999, women from other parts of the world, rich and poor, have been expressing support for it. Then the International Wages for Housework (IWFH) campaign, which coordinates an international network of women including women from India (working against bonded labor, like the bonded labor into which Amerindian men and women here are sometimes tricked), Africa and the Caribbean, began the work of making the strike global; global in its demands and global in its geographic spread. So far, the leaflet publicizing the strike has been translated from English into Punjabi, Basque, French, and Spanish; and is being translated into Arabic, Bengali, Catalan, Chinese, Finnish, German, Gaelic, Gujarati, Italian, Persian, Portuguese, Swedish, Tigrinya, and Urdu.

The IWFH calls for a global women's strike for "a millennium which values all women's work and all women's lives." A millennium that values life. In Trinidad and Tobago, the legal affairs minister says domestic violence claimed the lives of 80 women, 23 children—girls and boys—and two men, between 1990 and 1995.

I anticipate a number of reasons some people will give against the strike:

1. Women will ask, "What will the strikers do with their children or whatever family each of them has to look after while they strike?"
   The answer is, "What women always do—they make arrangements to ensure that their children don't suffer while they do their waged work or their unwaged work or whatever. They'll work it out." The very fact that women have to work it out underscores how essential family care is to everything else.
2. A strike has to be against an employer. It has to be called by a union—by Organized Labour.
   Not true, as previous, smaller women's strikes have shown. On October 24, 1975, women in Iceland took a day off and demonstrated that "When women stop, everything stops." In 1985 they celebrated their tenth anniversary with another "Day Off," and women in 24 countries took "Time Off for Women." In 1993 women in Switzerland held a national strike.
3. The "global" strike is a rich women's event; poor women in poor countries have too much to do to engage is such "luxuries."
   The answer to that is, it's because poor women in poor countries have more work and less income than everyone else that the strike is their business first. This is why the strike call has been taken up by women in Asia, Africa, Latin America and the Caribbean and by low-income and no-income women in the United States, Canada and Europe. It is why on July 22, 1999, Mexican house-wives went on strike "to draw attention to the fact that housework benefits the entire family and society as a whole." It is said that millions of women took to the streets, and according to a British newspaper, the Telegraph of July 24,

"By Thursday evening, calls of support for the strike had poured in from all over Mexico."

4. The strike will be divisive.

    No. The only division the strike endorses is a division against those who exploit. The organizers of the strike have called on men and boys to support the strike. They point out that whatever gains women and girls make, everyone will benefit.

    The strike seeks the support of the labor movement, and one of the groups that has written IWHC offering such support is a union of teachers in Senegal.

Women everywhere are working out their own strike demands to suit their own conditions. So far, the demands other women have established are:

- Recognition of and support for the work of raising children and caring for others, including wages for caring work, whether in the family or not; paid maternity leave, breast-feeding breaks and other benefits that recognize women's biological work instead of penalizing women for being women.
- Accessible clean drinking water and ecologically sound technology for every household.
- Affordable and accessible housing and transportation.
- Pay equity for all.

Strike organizers have also raised another kind of demand—a demand for action to be taken at a global level which will free resources for the things we need at the national level. *They demand the abolition of the Third World debt. They say, "The work women do—which has increased with every crisis and every 'solution' introduced by the IMF and World Bank—has more than repaid the debt."*

The experience we Guyanese have had with efforts at radical change has not been good. At the end of it we've been left poorer as a country, more racially divided, with more of our families and friends living outside. The words "protest" and "strike" are bad words for many of us—for those of us who have protested and gone on strike and won little or nothing, and those of us who have been unjustly attacked during protests and strikes. Yet that is not our whole history. Part of our history is about people struggling to make real change and succeeding in bringing it about. (OK, I know I'm preaching again.)

The point is, when we hear that the women planning the March strike are demanding abolition of the debt for countries like ours, it sounds fanciful. But is it? The very criticisms Caribbean and other Third World women made 10 and 15 years ago about the economic policies imposed by the IMF and the World Bank are accepted by those institutions today. The call for debt to be reduced has been heard. When enough "ordinary" people demand change it becomes the self-interest of those who have power to accept the need for change. A wise man (Frederick Douglass) once said, "Power concedes nothing without a demand. It never has, and it never will."

In the same spirit, women in many places are demanding "a world which values all women's work and all women's lives," and they are saying that there can be such a world if we refuse to go on accepting the alternative. The global strike called for March 8, 2000 has as its theme, "Stop the world and change it."

We should join it.

ACKNOWLEDGEMENTS

This essay was first published in the Woman's Eye View column in *Stabroek News*, January 30, 2000.

The Impact of the IMF Structural Adjustment Programme
on Women's Unwaged Work and How We Can Resist It
[Date not available; circa mid-1980s]

If you ask economists what structural adjustment is, they would name a whole list of measures that few of us would understand. But it seems to me, in looking at the situation in Guyana, that our list of what structural adjustment does would read like this:

> It freezes wages or cuts wages. It cuts government employment. It devalues. It cuts subsidies. It introduces a series of measures that result in prices going up and wages going down. It cuts health services. It cuts education services.

Behind all this, whatever the economists say, what structural adjustment does is make certain tasks more onerous for women and add other tasks to their already heavy workload. As one example, when it cuts services in health, it throws onto the household and community a greater and greater burden of work in trying to access or find alternatives to those services.

WHO DOES THE WORK IN HOUSEHOLDS AND COMMUNITIES?

First, let us look at communities. I don't know Trinidad and Tobago very well, but I don't believe that you are unique. Certainly, in Guyana, the majority of activist men are activists at the macro level, and the majority of activist women are activists at the micro level. I would suspect that even in Trinidad and Tobago where unlike Guyana, you have an active and visible women's movement which is confronting sexism, the answer to this question would be the same as in Guyana, Jamaica, St. Vincent and the Grenadines, Antigua and Barbuda, or anywhere else.

Who in Trinidad and Tobago organizes jumble sales for the children's school? Who organizes cake sales? Who organizes functions for the elderly, programs for children? Who does all those volunteer jobs in Trinidad and Tobago?

I imagine that here just like everywhere else, the people who do what is called welfare work, are women. That is why the more structural adjustment advances in a country, the more international funding agencies begin to glorify the leadership potential of women in the community; and since they work in alliance with the international policy makers who insist on the necessity of structural adjustment, they put money into the development of various services in communities with the certainty that women will administer them for free.

What they are capitalizing on is that fact that women provide volunteer services anyway. Certainly, again in Guyana, the poorer we have become and the more necessary it has become for us to have services like feeding programs, the more you see women setting up those feeding programs all over the place.

But even if it is not as absolutely true here as it is in Guyana that it is women who do the work at the level of the community, it must be true at the level of the household.

When prices rise and incomes plunge, whose job is it to walk from shop to shop and stall to stall in order to find the cheapest items of food, and then to go home and do the extra cooking that is required to make cheap items of food more edible?

When as in Guyana, all the systems for the provision of safe water fail—Guyana is a country in which international agencies still insist that 90 percent of the Guyanese people have running water, which is such a joke now for Guyanese because not 30 percent of us have running water on a regular basis—who goes to fetch water daily from downstairs, or the next street, or two miles away except women, very often accompanied by their young children?

When as in Guyana, we become prey to water-borne diseases, including those that were supposed to have been eradicated, who has to try to hold the line against the total collapse of the immediate environment of the family, except women? When women fail in this and disease does strike, who has to run up and down to take family members to hospitals which have become ill-equipped because of government cuts?

Structural adjustment has had a particular impact on women because it assumes correctly, that what women will do in the face of the deterioration that it brings, is to increase the unpaid work that we do without even thinking about it, in an attempt to ensure that our families survive.

It is also true that the more structural adjustment eats its way into the country, the more women have to increase the work they do for money in addition to doing all that extra unpaid work. This is in part why we have such an explosion in the size of the informal sector all over the Caribbean with women travelling through the region trading, often working in two, three, four areas of informal sector work at the same time.

Structural adjustment was introduced in Guyana about four years ago. The only thing we have left in Guyana is a sense of humor, so in Guyana it is called the Economic Recovery Programme. (Actually, that's its official name; it's not meant to be funny.)

Now, the terrible situation in which we find ourselves today in Guyana is not totally the result of structural adjustment. Structural adjustment has had a worse effect on Guyana than it has had in many other places, because of the previous economic policies—good and bad—under the government of the People's National Congress (PNC).

In Guyana we had a high level of government ownership of the economy—and since one of the measures that structural adjustment imposed was a cut in government spending, government had to divest itself of part of what it had nationalized. More jobs have been cut in Guyana from government service than would happen in a country in which the government employed fewer people.

When prices began to rise and wages began to fall, it had a harsher effect on Guyanese, because the gap between prices and income was already so big.

Conditions in Guyana today are harsh. Again, without suggesting that it's all due to structural adjustment, I'm going to compare 1985–1986 figures with 1990–1991 figures, two to three years before and two-three years after structural adjustment was introduced.

- *Value of the dollar*: I know other Caribbean people laugh at us in Guyana because the Guyanese dollar is worth almost nothing. But I don't know if you remember that in 1985, which is only seven years ago, US$1 was worth G$4.15. In 1985. Today, US$1 is worth G$125. In 1985, the minimum wage per day in Guyana was equivalent to US$2.78. Today, it is equivalent to 96 cents.
- *Life expectancy* in Guyana is now 65 years. It is the only place I know about in the region, except if Jamaica joins us, where it is falling. Everywhere else, it is at least 70 years.
- *Infant mortality* in Guyana is 50 per 1000. In Jamaica, it's 18 per 1000; Barbados, 11 per 1000. The 50 per 1000 in Guyana is a Ministry of Health figure.
- Or let us take *per capita income*: in Guyana it's the equivalent of US$360 a year, compared to Barbados's US$5,104. In 1965 it was the other way round: per capita income in Guyana was US$653, that's to say, nearly twice what it is now, when in Barbados it was US$437. So Barbados moved from US$437 to US$5,104 and Guyana moved from US$653 to US$360. In 1992, it was estimated that 75 percent of the Guyanese population lived below the poverty line.

How can we resist the pernicious policy of structural adjustment? When Working Women asked me to speak about resisting IMF policies I thought, this is a curious question to pose to a citizen of the country, in the West Indies, which was in the worst possible situation to resist the IMF. By the time we came to 1988, which is when structural adjustment started in Guyana, there was only one political question left: which political party was going to rule. There was no independent, non-party or non-party-aligned political space from which you could fight a policy like structural adjustment. So there was never any sustained protest against it.

That's not where you are in Trinidad, so you are obviously in a better position. When Barbados marched against the introduction of structural adjustment there we were ashamed; because throughout the region we're always saying how conservative Barbados is and there it was: the Barbadian people were marching against structural adjustment when we in Guyana had not. It's true that one Bajan calypsonian sang that trade union leader Trotman had marched the people up to the top of the hill and then marched them down again—meaning that the demonstrations had led nowhere—but they did better than we did; they tried. When I was in Barbados looking at those marches, it occurred to me that Barbadians were protesting because they still had something that Guyanese had lost—they still had a sense of being *entitled* to a good standard of living. They still had a sense that they were entitled to make demands of their government. As I often say, we Guyanese have lost our sense of legitimate entitlement.

Even in parts of the region which are not like Guyana, I don't think we should fool ourselves that the issue is going to be, at this stage, stopping the IMF from coming in. They are everywhere already. So the issue has to be, how can we position ourselves to try to do two things? One is, to try to make sure that they don't impose on us the worst possible conditions. The second one is, to try to position ourselves so that we don't have to go on to the next IMF arrangement, and the next, and the next; so that we don't find ourselves 15, 20 years from now still under the thumb of the IMF.

In Barbados the major resistance to the IMF came from the unions. That's because, as I've said, structural adjustment cuts people's wages, cuts employment and it is therefore a worker issue.

The question I want to pose to you tonight is this: if the fight against the IMF is a fight for the unions, what is to happen to the vast number of workers in the informal sector who are not in unions? Rhoda Reddock said years ago that until the 1930s, people like banana handlers used to be unionized in Trinidad, then the unions decided that they only organize in the factory, in the field and in the office.[1]

But informal sector workers today are not in unions, so if this is made into a fight by unions, they will not be involved.

I also want to ask what is going to happen to the even vaster number of people, women as housewives, on whose backs structural adjustment is being constructed. What happens to housewives if the fight against the IMF is a fight for the unions, because you know that today unions don't organize housewives, though they once did!

I don't believe that if we try to mobilize against the IMF in Trinidad or anywhere else, we will have enough strength for the fight if we leave out all those people who are called not workers. I don't think we can do it. I don't think it is going to work either, if we try to have an alliance between the unions, who are powerful because they organize workers, and women's groups, who are not so powerful because you don't.

I don't think that any attempt to create a resistance to the IMF is going to work except if we find a way to propel all those thousands and thousands of women on whose backs structural adjustment rests, into action.

Now, to close. The problem is that we who call ourselves the Caribbean women's movement don't really believe that women produce anything except if we are doing something non-traditional. You know that's true. We have the most complete contempt, most of us, for anything that is called women's traditional work. In fact we are terrified of it, when we're not contemptuous of it.

So our problem is not that people in the unions don't have any respect for women's work. It is that we ourselves, in the first place, don't have any respect for that work. We've also, I think, bought into the idea that women, at least in their capacity as housewives, don't struggle, can't struggle, can't be organized.

Earlier I mentioned that under PNC rule in Guyana, everybody had begun to stop fighting back in the early 80s, including many trade unions. But there was one case in which there was massive and sustained resistance to the government. It's one which people never count. It was by what are called "ordinary" unorganized people and they were led by "ordinary," unorganized women. It was when the government of Guyana decided overnight to ban several food staples at the beginning of the 1980s. And almost overnight, the same population in Guyana that had been sitting down quiet and taking all these blows, said "no."

Women in their thousands transformed themselves overnight into smugglers, transporters of flour, buyers of flour, sellers of flour, at a time when the government had said that flour was illegal. At a time therefore, when for carrying out all of those actions, they were subject to jail and were sometimes jailed. In spite of that, all these masses of unorganized, ordinary people and in particular, unorganized, ordinary women, carried on that fight until eventually the government gave up.

One of the reasons it always strikes me as curious that nobody ever mentions it, is because it is wrong to underestimate what that refusal to accept the ban on wheat flour did to the government of Guyana. A government of the kind that we had in Guyana is able to function only when it convinces an entire population that its power is absolute. The minute any large section of the population says "no," it begins to be in trouble. I'm not saying it falls; it begins to be in trouble. Post-Rodney (i.e. the assassination of Walter Rodney), the beginning of the resurgence of feeling in the Guyanese population that the government was not absolutely strong, was in that resistance to the ban on wheat flour.

I'm telling that story obviously, in order to say that I have seen housewives who are not organized, do things that organizations in Guyana were not capable of doing.

In the course of the next two days we are going to be in a campaign for the recognition of domestic servants, as they are called, as workers. It is a campaign which Red Thread is doing in association with Clotil Walcott. I believe that if we want to fight back as women against structural adjustment, that we have to begin by locating the key to how it exploits women as women. I've suggested that the key is what we call reproductive work; all that cooking, cleaning, shopping, hunting and gathering that women do.

I think we have to mobilize on that base for three main reasons. The first one is that if people keep on mobilizing ourselves only within the unions, it remains easy for people to play us off against each other. I'm not saying people should leave their unions, but if you fight via unions you're going into battle divided into different sectors.

I think the second reason why we should try to mobilize as women on the basis of our shared work and shared exploitation, is because in the course of trying to link up with each other, we are also going to be able to separate sheep from goat. And goat in this case, is the kind of woman who is very willing to fight against the exploitation of her own labor, while she exploits the labor of the other women.

The last reason why we should try to mobilize as women is that it is the only way we're going to make sure that this fight against the IMF is not simply a fight between what is called organized labor and these forces, but a fight in which unorganized labor, which is made up overwhelmingly of women, comes centrally into the battle.

ACKNOWLEDGEMENTS

This essay was originally presented as an opening night feature address to Working Women, Trinidad and Tobago. I spoke very informally and therefore have edited the speech without changing the views it expressed.

NOTE

1. In relation to the presence of informal sector workers and housewives in trade unions in Trinidad and Tobago, see Reddock (1994), especially chapter 10—"Responsible Trade Unionism and the Woman Worker (1939–62)."

REFERENCE

Reddock, Rhoda. 1994. *Women, Labour and Politics in Trinidad and Tobago: A History*. London: Zed Books.

ESSAY 13
Housewives and Other Carers in the Guyanese Resistance
of the Late 1970s and Early 1980s: Looking Back
[2010]

A NOTE ON REBELLION

When Walter Rodney was completing his last book, *A History of the Guyanese Working People 1881–1905*, he had a furious exchange of correspondence with Elsa Goveia,[1] who had taught him history at the University of the West Indies (UWI), about how he should characterize the events of November–December 1905 when widespread strikes and protests shook the colony of British Guiana. Rodney wanted to class these events as a rebellion or a revolt (I no longer remember the exact word but it was something of that order); Goveia preferred to class them as riots. The chapter is called "The 1905 Riots," but it begins almost exactly as Rodney had planned when he was thinking of revolt or rebellion:

> Riots and disturbances punctuate the history of the British West Indies. Most were minor phenomena with little significance beyond the small circle of lives touched by a brief explosion. *But there are times when the disaffection was more wide-ranging and the scale of violence larger; and when the level of consciousness and organization of the participants carried these elements forward into a moment of challenge to the colonial authority.* In different degrees, these characteristics were present in the riots of November–December 1905 in the county of Demerara. (Rodney 1981: 190; my emphasis)

In other words, they were more than riots.

I don't pretend to be clear about how to characterize different measures of political resistance. Guyanese elder Eusi Kwayana has called the anti-government protests of 1979 in Guyana a civil rebellion (Kwayana 1998: 26). I have less justification for using the word rebellion for the events of 1982–1983 on which this essay will focus; though, to return to Rodney's definition, the disaffection was wide-ranging and the level of consciousness and organization substantial enough to challenge the ruling authority, however briefly. What is more important than definitions is why and how what I am referring to here as rebellions happened; what we in the Working People's Alliance (WPA)—of which I was a member—did right and where we fell short; and what all that tells us about organizing. I intend to focus on the events of 1982–1983, when protests sparked by the government's policy of banning staple foodstuffs ignited broader actions against an increasingly repressive People's National Congress (PNC) regime. Thirteen years ago, I wrote a paper analyzing those events, but without understanding what needed to be learned from them. This article is a start at making visible the self-organized leadership of grassroots women across race in the food rebellion, and at drawing out some of the lessons of a moment of struggle in which the Guyanese working people acted together not only across race, but also across gender.

WALTER RODNEY AND THE GUYANESE RESISTANCE

While this article does not center on Walter Rodney, it is about strengths he brought to the Guyanese resistance, starting in 1974–1975, strengths that outlasted his life. Rodney was killed on June 13, 1980. The period of resistance we're considering lasted from 1974/1975 to 1983. For all of it, Rodney was the point of reference; that is to say, although he was part of a collective, the WPA, he was, in his own person, key to the gradually growing resistance to dictatorial rule in Guyana beginning in 1974–1975, and critical to both the explosion of that resistance in 1979 and its resumption in 1982–1983.

Walter Rodney returned to Guyana when work on crossing the race divide between Guyanese of African and Indian descent was already under way. Two ethnic organizations, the African Society for Cultural Relations with Independent Africa (ASCRIA) and the Indian Political Revolutionary Associates (IPRA), had begun to work together, conducting a well-received Race Commission that held bottom-house meetings,[2] in both Indian- and African-Guyanese villages, seeking the people's views on race relations and the possibility of non-race politics. In January 1973, ASCRIA, supported by IPRA, called on African and Indian Guyanese to seize vacant sugar lands from the sugar companies and to divide them equally, in a form of reparations for the unwaged and low-waged labor of slavery and indenture. The two groups were joined by the university-based Ratoon and a small group, the Working People's Vanguard Party (WPVP).[3] While the approximately two thousand land occupiers were forcibly removed by the police on February 17,[4] less than a week later the government announced that the Sugar Producers Association, the group that represented the sugar companies, had agreed to turn over most of the unused lands to them. Perhaps more important was what the privately owned *Guyana Graphic* acknowledged in its January 7, 1973 edition: "ASCRIA in general, and Eusi Kwayana in particular are making a potentially serious approach to national unity in a country where there is so much superficiality and still an uneasy truce between the two races" (quoted in Hinds 1998: 49). In November 1974, ASCRIA, IPRA, WPVP, and Ratoon launched the WPA as a pressure group.[5]

Building on the work of these constituent members of the pre-party WPA, Rodney brought a quality into the Guyanese struggle that led Eusi Kwayana to call him, after his death, "the prophet of self-emancipation" (Kwayana 1998: 2). Kwayana did not mean that Rodney was a savior or a preacher, nor that he did not commit errors; Kwayana was acknowledging the extraordinary passion, conviction, and persistence (not quite "apostolic zeal," as his friend Gordon Rohlehr called it) with which Rodney drew out the lessons of history to hammer home the necessity of the working people's unity across race and of their leadership of the struggle. Their history, he taught, showed that they had achieved both in the past; they could do it again.

He repeated these messages in public meeting after public meeting, and, crucially, he trained two groups in this political direction: in his bottom-house, he held classes in political economy with workers and other interested persons, many of them women and men who already were or became members of the WPA; and in the bauxite mining town of Wismar/Mackenzie, he held classes with the bauxite workers where the training requested—which was on political economy and revolution—was "more concentrated and intensive"[6] (Kwayana 1998: 4, 8). According to Kwayana,

> [Rodney's] political students … did not leave his courses spouting slogans and quotations from the great masters, but with some competence in the art of examining the social relations and trying to discover the social motion … interested in discovering the story of the oppressed classes … and learning of their efforts and limited successes in the destiny of self-emancipation, for which, Rodney taught, there was no substitute. (Kwayana 1998: 4)

The third message that Rodney brought to the struggle was that the Guyanese could end the paralysis of spirit that had been carefully cultivated by the ruling party, the People's National Congress. Rodney's confrontational relationship to the leader of the party, Forbes Burnham, for which he has been criticized, was an enormous risk, but the criticism starts from the wrong premise if it claims it was an unthinking risk. It was a calculated risk to try to revive the will to defy. In the 1950–1953 period, Cheddi Jagan and others (but Jagan in particular) had aroused that will in Rodney's generation before the collapse of the multira-cial anti-colonial movement into what could be characterized as race camps by the 1960s. As I will try to show, the spirit of defiance that Walter Rodney was largely instrumental in restoring, while almost crushed by the manner of his death on June 13, 1980, came alive again in the food rebellion of 1982–1983.[7]

WOMEN IN THE RESISTANCE

1974–1980

Women were a distinct minority among the pre-party WPA activists who met every second Sunday. We were also a small minority in the executive committee, and we were Georgetown-based and middle class and either African-Guyanese or mixed.

The numbers of women slowly increased as WPA street activism increased, notably from 1978, with a campaign against a referendum designed to usher in a new constitution with sweeping powers for an executive president. With the civil rebellion of 1979, what had been a relatively small pre-party formation was bombarded with applications for membership, and those of us in the WPA tried to make a practical response, keeping a steady core inside the growing mass of members. Some membership was kept secret. As membership in the WPA as a whole multiplied with the launch of the party in July 1979 and the start of the civil rebellion, the numbers of women also grew significantly. The women whose entry into the party was fueled by the growing resistance were of different races and classes, from both urban and rural communities, and increasingly grassroots. One woman, Karen de Souza, (then employed at the Office of the Prime Minister), became a member in July 1979 after being arrested at the same time as Walter Rodney and Rupert Roopnaraine. She was charged with theft of National Service property following an arson attack that destroyed the Office of the General Secretary of the PNC and Ministry of National Development. She entered the WPA, as it were, from the street, carried on the shoulders of the crowd that had gathered outside the courts on July 14.[8]

There was little separation in the early WPA party between leaders and foot soldiers in relation to certain tasks, and a core of men was among those who distributed flyers and handbills, announced public meetings, picketed, and marched. By party decision, everyone was supposed to distribute *Dayclean*, the party newssheet, preferably house-to-house; and since we had no party vehicle and no working class members could drive, Walter Rodney and Rupert Roopnaraine often announced the meetings at which they would speak. Still, it is fair to say that grassroots women were (as they always are) the backbone of the party, and that in conditions of resistance they had a wider range of tasks than they would normally have had: for example, the hard and painstaking justice work of cooking and taking food to prisoners and monitoring cases in court.

At the level of the WPA leadership once the party was formed, women were still in the minority and still largely middle class and African-Guyanese or mixed. In practice, though not in name, we were in the second tier of the leadership. None of us had or could have had responsibility for caring for children—a responsibility that could never have been properly carried out given the number of hours we worked and the unstated requirement that we should always be ready to meet, ready to move, ready to respond to each emergency. Some of the wives of male party leaders were activists in the WPA—Pat Rodney, Tchaiko Kwayana, and Samia Bhagwan in particular—but the simple truth is that the more active the man was, the more responsibility the woman had for childcare and sometimes for ensuring that the household had some limited income.

In the 1979 civil rebellion, women were central to organizing actions from within the center, and a few were directly involved in what Rupert Roopnaraine has called the effort to create an insurrectionary movement (Hinds 2008: 36). Very many grassroots women were on the frontlines in the streets: as the civil rebellion grew, repression against the WPA escalated. (A *WPA Recognition Handbook* was produced by the security forces, with 22 of our names accompanied by photos, license plates of cars we might drive, and even in some cases physical identification marks). Women, like men, suffered dismissals from work, police searches, threats, official arrests, unofficial arrests (being picked up and carried miles away from home in some strange place and left to find one's way back was a regular occurrence), imprisonments, and beating. Eusi Kwayana spoke of one grassroots woman, Kathy Wills, then in her early fifties, who "became one of [the WPA's] living banners, [and] set an example in street action such as picketing, demonstrations and placing herself as a human barrier to wrongdoing" (*Dayclean Global* 2008). The visibility of grassroots WPA women was always less in rural Indian communities. However, on the Corentyne and in the West Coast of Demerara a few young women, mainly the wives of sugar workers who were WPA members, ensured the success of public meetings and bottom-house meetings and demonstrations, and arranged accommodation and food. But while treated with respect, they were assumed by many leading WPA men and women not to be "political activists" in their own right but the wives of the "real" activists (Karen de Souza, personal communication, September 2008).

On June 8, 1980, a mostly grassroots offshoot of the WPA, Women Against Terror (WAT), was launched by 16 women. Founding members included Kathy Wills, Thelma Reece, Tchaiko Kwayana, Gwennie Kissoon, Joan Ann Gravesande, Doris Loo, Ruby Ganeshdin, and Olga Bone. Members were mothers and grandmothers who came together in outrage after a day of what they described as "police terror against children" during searches under the National Security Act, which gave the security forces carte blanche to enter and search homes without warrants, acts the women described as "a part of a systematic plan of police terror" (Women Against Terror undated a: 1). In one home, a gun was placed to the head of a ten-year-old boy, in another, a gun put to the head of a four-month-old baby in an attempt to force the mother to reveal her husband's whereabouts; in yet another, a mother and four children were terrorized by a policeman holding a long knife "menacingly" at his side.

WAT's statements and reports reflected a wide definition of "terror," at the heart of which was "economic terror" (Women Against Terror undated a). In keeping with its definition, its activities ranged from protesting to publicizing to offering support to mothers and children. Other events it organized in its first year included a children's press conference on September 13, which "brought out that many children had had personal experiences of police terror"; and a Nutrition Survey, the results of which spurred WAT to call for an immediate relief program with a number of explicit demands, and to embark on what it called a rehabilitation program for those most in need (ibid.: 3–5). Surviving records of WAT's activities after the first year are few, but they show that in 1982, WAT was one of the groups invited by the Guyana Council of Churches to a unity meeting, and in 1983 the group held a discussion on the care of the child for International Children's Day and served hot meals to children at four centers in the city. Proposals for action made during the discussion included a soup kitchen, a mother support organization to deal with the "enormous emotional and physical stress placed on the mothers of our children," and a pot-a-month feeding program. The last record that has been found so far is a 1984 statement for International Women's Day.

Surviving records of WAT's activities are scanty. One record, the organization's report of "The First Year," recounts that as the founding members began to distribute an open letter to the police commissioner, in the city, nearby villages, and other areas where there had been "known incidents of terror," more women joined WAT. They soon found, however, that most women were too afraid of victimization to take public action, a fear that was no doubt heightened by the fact that Walter Rodney had been killed five days after they launched (Women Against Terror undated a: 2). On September 17, the report records, an Ecumenical Service at St. Andrew's Kirk in Georgetown organized by WAT for people of different religious backgrounds to "dedicate to the organization's goals of creating a healthy, safe and just society for the children of Guyana" was physically attacked by women leaders of the ruling PNC. Later that year, the group issued a statement condemning what it called the training of children "to become mindless terrorists," referring to reports that on November 25, 1980 "three youngsters not more than 14 who appeared untrained were standing guard opposite the Georgetown Prison with magazines and sub-machine guns at the ready" and that on December 2, "a truck carrying between 35 to 40 armed youths was seen in the vicinity of the Cove and John Police Station," reportedly on the way to attacking an opposition political meeting. The statement added that the recruitment of youngsters into the PNC terror squads was not recent but had its antecedents in a 1978 Early School Leavers Opportunity Programme, which included training 14-year-olds in sniper fire. Youngsters who had left the course claimed that they used life-size photographs of government's political opponents as targets (Women Against Terror undated b).[9]

WAT was an autonomous organization created by Guyanese women across class and race to act in defense of their children. While its membership was multi-class, its open letter to the police commissioner viewed the world from the perspective of those with least power: "Do you think," it asked the police commissioner pointedly, "that ideas of parenthood are not for those outside your class?"[10] The organization remained active at least until March 8, 1984 when it issued an International Women's Day statement.

The 1982/1983 Food Rebellion

In 1982, the government banned the most basic staples of the diet of both working class Indo- and Afro-Guyanese, including wheat flour and split peas. The stated reason was the need for Guyana to become self-sufficient in food, and thus to grow and buy local. The underlying reason was the growing foreign exchange crisis. This was not the first ban on food imports, and the adjustment that people had made to each preceding ban may have led the regime to under-estimate the resistance that would be mounted to a ban on a staple like wheat flour. As an editorial in *Open Word* explained on April 11, 1983, the government then enforced this disastrous policy by making the buying and selling of wheat flour illegal, and by seizing bread, poisoning it, trampling it in the streets, and prosecuting people for possessing it (*Open Word* 1983a).

Protests against the policy during 1982 came from every sector and from all types of organizations. For example, along with Vanguard for Liberation and Democracy (VLD, an opposition party), the Clerical and Commercial Workers Union (an independent union), and WAT, the WPA conducted a campaign that collected close to fifty thousand signatures demanding an end to the ban on basic staples. Among the immediate events spurring the signature campaign were the deaths of three women in food lines—Samwaria Milton, Parbattie Narine, and Irene Somerset (*Dayclean* 1982).

The most critical response was the immediate and sustained refusal of grass-roots Guyanese housewives to obey the ban:

> uncounted thousands of housewives defied the regime's ban on wheat flour by becoming, overnight, buyers and sellers of wheat flour … In the explosion of petty trading that erupted in a country with little prior history of that kind of trade, women traders had to confront hostility from local and regional police and customs officials, because their trade was illegal. Women from urban communities who had never visited the interior braved its rivers. (Andaiye 1993: 8)

One urban woman trader described crossing the Pomeroon River in a paddle-boat at three in the morning:

> The place black. The sky black. The bush black. The water black. The people up there can't swim. You, you who come from town, you can't swim. The place black. If you raise you hand in the air you can't see it. All you can see is the little lights from the candleflies blinking. (Andaiye 1993: 9)

In the factories and fields and on the streets, the protests did not gather momentum until 1983. Then, as always happens, a small spark in the right conditions ignited a huge fire. On May 4, 1983, when a worker at the state-owned bauxite company collapsed from hunger on the job, 42 shop stewards decided to go on a one-day-a-week strike beginning on May 6 (*Dayclean* 1983a). This decision catapulted what was until then a slow, rising tide of protest, to a new level. About a thousand bauxite workers, housewives, woman sellers, and teachers in Linden took to the streets demanding more goods and drugs in the bauxite community, carrying placards with various slogans: "Stop this eye-pass"; "less guns more food"; "hungry workers can't produce" (*Dayclean* 1983b). On May 19, 24 bauxite workers were arrested and held. With the momentum building, nearly two thousand housewives and children stormed the Wismar/Mackenzie police station demanding their release, faced down the riot squad, and forced the jailers to free them (*Dayclean* 1983a). Soon the action was taken up in sugar-belt communities along the West Coast Demerara, where a multiracial demonstration of two thousand sugar workers and housewives was carried out in solidarity with the jailed bauxite workers (*Open Word* 1983b). Shortly after, West Coast sugar workers shut down the two factories at Uitvlugt and Leonora for the second time in seven days, bringing repair work at both sites to a standstill (*Dayclean* 1983c).

Bauxite workers, sugar workers, housewives and children were each no longer alone in their rebellion. As the state seized more than 40 private vehicles during May—including hire cars, private cars and company vehicles, planes, speedboats and tractors (*Catholic Standard* 1983a)—taxi drivers protested (*Open Word* 1983c). The Guyana Human Rights Association issued an appeal to the Caribbean to join Guyanese in protest against the government's "inhuman food policy" (*Catholic Standard* 1983b). The National Association of Agricultural, Clerical and Industrial Employees (NAACIE), one of the two sugar unions, made a unanimous call on government to reintroduce the importation of wheat flour, split peas, and other foods at its annual delegates' meeting (*Catholic Standard* 1983c). The special delegates conference of the Trades Union Congress on May 21–22 passed a similar unanimous resolution, endorsed the strike action taken by the Guyana Mine Workers Union (GMWU) and condemned police harassment of workers (*Catholic Standard* 1983d). The Four Unions grouping,[11] also came out in support of the GMWU's decision to hold a one-day-a-week strike to protest "the dismal food situation within the mining community" (ibid.).

By early June, a Sugar and Bauxite Workers Unity Committee (SBWUC) had been formed. Strikes at the Leonora and Uitvlugt factories, and huge multiracial marches of sugar workers and housewives continued on West Coast Demerara, in spite of state violence and arrests.

Meanwhile, the strike spread to new branches. On the West Coast, taxi drivers answered a call by the SBWUC and staged a taxi stoppage, while gas stations refused to sell gas to taxi "scabs" (*Dayclean* 1983d). In Georgetown, a peaceful picket of 75 women and children organized by the WPA Women's Section was broken up and five women arrested, held overnight, and charged with disorderly conduct and unlawful procession.

Back on West Coast Demerara, the SBWUC supported a strike called by the Guyana Agricultural and General Workers Union (GAWU),[12] and in the ensuing march, riot police beat women and children and drove old people from the street (*Open Word* 1983b).

In Wismar/Mackenzie, after the government reduced the workweek to three days as a punitive response to the one-day-a-week strike, the bauxite union called a six-week strike demanding an increased food supply to the area and the return of the five-day workweek. An estimated 95 percent of the workers joined in (*Catholic Standard* 1983e, 1983f).

On the West Coast Demerara, the SBWUC held meetings in several communities to report back. From June 13 to 29, the WPA held Walter Rodney Freedom Festivals in Georgetown; in Wismar/Mackenzie; in Rosehall, Corentyne; in Buxton-Annandale, East Coast Demerara; and in New Amsterdam and Skeldon, Corentyne.

Action continued well into July. In a first Day of Rest called by the WPA on July 14, all Georgetown markets were affected, and the main business street in New Amsterdam almost closed down. With taxi drivers withdrawing their services within New Amsterdam and between New Amsterdam and the Corentyne in the county of Berbice, the action had spread to another part of the country. In saluting participants in the first Day of Rest, the WPA stated:

> Because of the actions of organized workers, housewives, youth and children, shoppers, vendors and especially taxi drivers, the protest against hunger is on the streets. Two strong parts of it were the resting of taxis and farm supply vehicles and the staying away of shoppers and market vendors in many places. (*Open Word* 1983d)

Beginning on July 15, the retaliation against the taxi drivers began with police pulling in an estimated fifteen to seventeen hundred drivers with their vehicles, fining them, and forcing them to remain idle for days. With the majority of taxi drivers Indian Guyanese, the action took on a racial slant.

Protests continued, some now in support of the taxi drivers. On July 21, a multiracial hunger march was staged on the East Coast Demerara public road; while in West Coast Demerara, Uitvlugt and Leonora sugar workers conducted a go-slow and sit-down strike, partly in solidarity with the taxi drivers (*Dayclean* 1983e). On July 23, the Guyana Mine Workers' Union issued a strong statement against the abuse of the taxi drivers. That week, 12 women were arrested in Georgetown for picketing in solidarity with the taxi drivers, charged, and remanded to prison before being bailed (*Dayclean* 1983f).

By the end of July, however, the rebellion was clearly in decline. One reason for this not usually considered, was that the geography of the actions worked against the development of a critical mass of resistance. At its height, between May and June, there were days on which more than one action took place but they were not taking place in contiguous areas. Most were in Wismar/Mackenzie and the West Coast Demerara, with a smaller number in Georgetown and on the East Coast Demerara, and later in Berbice. There was little chance that the news of action in one place would travel quickly and without prior organization to the other. This was before the era of internet, cell phones and text messaging, and at a time when the media was mostly in the hands of the state.

By August, although housewives continued their refusal to obey the ban, the street stage of the rebellion had broken decisively. On August 6, *Dayclean* reported that the SBWUC "called a temporary halt to food protests on the job so that the workers could catch themselves after the nine weeks of one-day protests" (*Dayclean* 1983g). Without the SBWUC to buttress them, taxi drivers, market vendors, and other similar groups were vulnerable. Some 1,721 workers in the bauxite sector were retrenched in August, including the president of the Guyana Bauxite Supervisors' Union, the treasurer of the Guyana Mineworkers' Union, and the shop steward.[13] WPA party phones were disconnected, and cars used by party leaders were seized.

There was another crucial factor. From the onset, the main opposition party, the People's Progressive Party (PPP) and the main sugar union GAWU (from which it drew much of its support) had been openly hostile to the rebellion—perhaps on the grounds that deprivation leads to revolution—and to the example of workers that the SBWUC represented organizing independently. Moreover, having always organized sugar workers where they lived (and therefore, deliberately or otherwise, on the basis of race), GAWU was all the more hostile to the SBWUC's attempt to create GAWU branches where sugar workers worked (i.e., crossing racial lines).[14] The interests of the PPP and GAWU, on the one hand, and the ruling PNC, on the other, finally converged in a smear campaign against the WPA, with "handbills from a pro-PPP group and fact sheets from a pro-PNC group ... linking the WPA with the CIA," while a GAWU statement accused the WPA of union busting and "in a fact sheet, not under its name, the PNC also accused the WPA of meddling in the affairs of the GMWU ... in order to overthrow the government." Significantly, the fact sheet "praised GAWU for discovering this alleged plot on the part of the WPA and refusing to cooperate with it" (*Dayclean* 1983h).[15]

An increase in violent crime around the same time deflected and slowed down the overall protest. For one thing, people were afraid to come out of their homes, and the WPA was increasingly preoccupied with organizing "community defence groups" (*Dayclean* 1983i; Nigel Westmaas, personal communication, September 1983). The "crime wave" also inflamed racial tensions. As the WPA said, "It is true that different races were hit (by crimes on the East and West Coasts of Demerara), but the main fact was that the vast majority of the victims, over 95 percent, were Indo-Guyanese and the vast majority of the bandits, over 95 per cent, were Afro-Guyanese" (*Dayclean* 1983j).

The nine-week activism of the SBWUC was a striking feature of the rebellion. For this period, the visible level of workers' leadership, across race, and of worker self-organization, was higher than in 1979, stamping this as an advance on the 1979 rebellion. The groundwork had been laid in 1979 for solidarity of the sugar and bauxite workers of West Coast Demerara and Wismar/Mackenzie, but it nonetheless remained significant because these two areas were arguably two of the bloodiest scenes of violence in the civil disturbances and racial violence of 1964 (Eusi Kwayana, personal communication, September 29, 2008).

In the leadership shown by grassroots women, however, the 1982–1983 rebellion was far more than a development of the 1979 rebellion. It represented a significant departure from the earlier years. For the first time, grassroots women—housewives—were visibly taking action as a sector. Why did this happen then? Not just because the issues in 1983 were "economic," but because they were issues that grassroots housewives saw as threatening the survival of their children.

This is exactly what inspired the militancy of WAT, who, in an open letter to the commissioner of police shortly after their launch in June 1980, said, "We do not have guns ... WE HAVE LOVE FOR OUR FAMILIES. We will not allow our children to be terrorized without coming to their rescue. You must be prepared to kill us all" (Women Against Terror 1980).

The sustained strikes and street protests would have been unimaginable without the ongoing refusal of housewives to accept the bans, their acceptance—even embrace—of "criminality" by giving their children wheat bread to eat, and transforming themselves overnight into traders braving unknown rivers, forms of transport, and officials. "What we are seeing in the small traders' struggle," said an editorial in *Open Word* in 1982, "is the most effective civil disobedience campaign ever carried out for such a long period in Guyana."

For the duration of the street demonstrations, housewives were present in large, sometimes massive numbers. In Wismar/Mackenzie, they responded immediately to the call for action by the bauxite workers. In the West Coast Demerara communities in particular, Indo-Guyanese and Afro-Guyanese housewives unhesitatingly joined solidarity action for Afro-Guyanese bauxite workers. They initiated protests. There were all-woman pickets and pickets of women and children. The women were in some ways more militant than the men. One of the extraordinary moments of the food rebellion was the storming of the police station in Wismar/McKenzie by thousands of women and children.

LESSONS FOR ORGANIZING WITH GRASSROOTS GUYANESE WOMEN

Left-wing parties and feminists have in different ways underestimated the power of housewives. Many feminists have argued that calls for the measurement and valuing of unwaged housework and payment for it will entrench women in their role (job) as housewives. The Left, in contrast, explicitly sees housewives as isolated and therefore lacking in what they understand to be consciousness, even though housework is seldom an isolated or isolating activity. At the level of the household it usually involves people, and it often takes place outside—for example in the Third World by the riverside or the fireside or in the market. In some conditions, as in Guyana in 1983, the crisis itself puts housewives in a position to become even more consciously part of a sector as they come together daily, across race, with other housewives, in food lines and in shops where they hunt and gather food. There is no frontier between home and street.

The theoretical argument had already been made by Mariarosa Dalla Costa and Selma James in *The Power of Women* in 1972: "What has been neither clear nor assumed by organizations of the working class movement is that precisely through the wage has the exploitation of the non-wage labourer been organized. This exploitation has been even more effective because the lack of a wage hid it" (Dalla Costa and James 1972: 28). It was an argument that influenced Walter Rodney, who had been part of a study group in London with Selma James (as well as C. L. R. James), to propose the inclusion of "housewives whose role in production is obscured by lack of a wage" in the WPA party program's definition of the working class. Indeed, once this is grasped, the question of class can no longer be narrowly understood.

The sources for this paper show that we in the WPA—specifically Eusi Kwayana, who was the principal writer for both *Dayclean* and *Open Word*—recorded the presence and the militancy of women in general and grassroots women in particular in the 1982–1983 rebellion. Notwithstanding the language of our party program, we did not fully grasp that what we were seeing was a sector of the working people in motion. We were not seeing what was in front of them, not looking to find a way. The language we used juxtaposed women and housewives with workers even as we were recognizing the value of their work, as for example in an *Open Word* editorial on April 11, 1983:

The food policy is bad for everybody, but worse for women ... when it comes to the things that can really ease ... [their] burden, what do we hear? Go back to the coalpot. Learn to bake bread with rice flour. In addition to new housework jobs, women must run around hunting for food and *risk conviction to produce the energy with which the nation works*. (*Open Word* 1983a; my emphasis)

The WPA facilitated the organization of the SBWUC that ensured the unity of sugar and bauxite workers across race. We helped produce weekly SBWUC handbills that were widely distributed and essential to informing and mobilizing both bauxite and sugar workers. The housewives were given no such support. We learned no lesson from the fact that, as the WPA Central Committee report put it,

> women cadres … found that their progress in bringing women into active functioning within the party, and in mobilizing and organizing non-party women was hampered by the fact that the food crisis in the country was increasing the burden of housework to a point where few women cadres could meet the requirements of nucleus [cell] participation and of active work in the Women's Section. (WPA 1983: 20)

Instead of moving towards and reinforcing the self-activity of the housewives, the WPA Women's Section organized at best parallel activities, like the July 4 conference of 102 women in Georgetown, which was one step forward in terms of its inclusion of Indigenous women, and more than two steps backwards in terms of its resolution to form a "national organization of women"—in other words, a mass organization attached, as mass organizations usually are, to the party. These activities were in effect a party (WPA) decision. Instead of looking to see where the women were at, we brought some of those we knew (who were not those in the forefront of the rebellion) into action with us, with the result that when they were jailed overnight they gave in, saying, "We don't want politics, we want money."

What could have been the alternative? The recognition of hierarchies based on the waged and unwaged sectors of the working class has immediate implications for organizing—that sectors should organize autonomously so that they can come together in a new way.[16] There is evidence that Rodney knew this. In the 1975 interviews later published as *Walter Rodney Speaks*, he spoke about autonomous organizing—though only in relation to racial hierarchies in class, and this, mostly in relation to black and white workers in the United States. Moreover, he never raised these issues of autonomous organizing, whether in relation to race or to gender, in the WPA. Understanding and consciously recognizing the housewives in the food rebellion as the unwaged sector of the working class (as distinct from individuals), might have led us to organize a housewives committee, meeting autonomously and then meeting with sugar

and bauxite workers in one unity committee, so that the sectors acknowledged and strengthened each other. Each would have been changed in ways
we can't know.

It took 15 years for two of us, who in 1983 were WPA women, to draw the
lessons and to begin to attempt—slowly and gradually (given a far less favorable
environment)—a way of organizing based on the recognition of grassroots
housewives as a sector of the working class and their unwaged labour as the
foundation of the whole economy. This is what informs our organizing with
Red Thread and Guyanese Women Across Race, beginning in about 1998, and
our relations with grassroots women in campaigns globally against all that
threatens life, from dams to war, and for all that is life-giving: affordable access
to food, water, health, education, and housing, for a start.

FOR WHOM DOES THIS MATTER?

In an interview with Rupert Lewis in 2001, David Scott identified my generation's task as being "to write the cultural-political history of that age of
Caribbean euphoria and self-sacrifice—the 1970s—in such a way as to inspire
another generation to utopian aspirations" (Scott 2001: 87). The language of
"euphoria and self-sacrifice" and "utopian aspirations" is not only partial; it also
runs the risk of trivializing the political history of the 1970s and 1980s. All
these qualities were there but these could not *all* characterize the events of these
two decades.

The question is: for whom are you telling the history? When I tell or write
the history of which I was part, the "audience" I have in mind is the women
in Red Thread and the Red Thread network, Grassroots Women Across Race
(GWAR) with whom I organize, and the children of these women. Like the
women whose resistance in "the Rodney years" I want to make visible, Red
Thread and GWAR members are Guyanese grassroots women across race—
now, not only Indo- and Afro-Guyanese and mixed, but also Indigenous. They
and their children are of more than one generation, ranging in age from their
teens to their twenties, thirties, and forties. The women are working their way
to believing that through their own organizing they can make change happen.
The small victories they have won encourage them, as does their relationship
with women struggling and sometimes winning in Haiti, Venezuela, Chhattis-
garh in India; Uganda, indigenous communities in Latin America; Ireland, the
United States, the United Kingdom, and Spain. The women of Red Thread and
GWAR don't have the option of escaping: they are not part of the "labor" whose
movement around the Caribbean is "free" (and all those of us who are entitled
to "the free movement of labor" more often than not unthinkingly accept this
discrimination!). US predators don't come to recruit them for their universities

and hospitals. They are women whose options are to go under, or to struggle where they are for survival and for change.

ACKNOWLEDGEMENTS

This essay is an edited version of an article previously published in a special Issue on Caribbean Revolutions, Nationalist Movements, Rebellions and Revolts, for *MaComère* (the journal of the Association of Caribbean Women Writers and Scholars) 12(2) (2010).

NOTES

1. Elsa Goveia was the first female professor at the University of the West Indies and the author of seminal works on West Indian history including *A Study of the Historiography of the British West Indies* (1956), and *Slave Society in the British Leeward Islands* (1965).
2. Houses in Guyana were typically built on stilts and the space underneath (the bottom-house) used for a variety of purposes: cooking, washing, lying in hammocks, entertaining visitors, holding meetings.
3. A note on three of the constituent members of the alliance: IPRA, unlike ASCRIA, had a small membership; its precursor, the Success Movement, had concentrated its work in certain villages: Better Hope, Success, Grove, and Triumph. ASCRIA, in contrast, had 32 "compounds" or groups at its height as an organization and was active in most of the major black communities. Ratoon, established in 1969, was a radical group comprising academics and students, whose birth led to a more multiracial dynamic presence among students and faculty (Professors Clive Thomas, Josh Ramsammy, and Omawale, and students Bonita Harris and Zinul Bacchus were prominent in this group). A multiracial grouping of students and faculty represented a new dimension in university politics. This multiracial unity was not long afterwards strained when Stokeley Carmichael, visiting Guyana in 1970 at Ratoon's invitation, said that Black power was only for people of African descent. Ratoon had its own monthly publication, like ASCRIA, with an estimated circulation of three thousand, according to Omawale in *Georgetown Journal* (Salkey 1972). Apart from its work in the university, Ratoon challenged foreign penetration of the economy while providing support for labor struggles, in which ASCRIA was also quite influential. Like ASCRIA and IPRA, however, Ratoon stressed its limits and clarified that it was not a political party and did not seek political office.
4. The sources cited tended to round figures off.
5. The principles outlined in the statement that appeared in the November 1974 issue of *Dayclean* to launch the WPA as a pressure group—i.e., before Rodney joined them—reflect how close their political views were to Rodney's. They included: (1) to teach and fight to bring about the unity of the working people (the definition of working people includes housewives); (2) to stand for the genuine multiracial power of the working people, expressed in organizational forms which guarantee the nature of this power, benefitting from the work being done in this respect by its member organizations; and to address itself to the contradiction between the Indian and African sections of the population and to the historical exclusion of

Amerindians from the political process; (3) to join in the day to day struggles of the people; (4) to develop, out of the struggle of the people, a political line of the working people based on the theory of their emancipation (Working People's Alliance 1983).

6. OWP also organized classes with C. Y. Thomas in labor economics, "with others of us holding a class or two as reliefs or on special themes" (Kwayana 1988: 8).

7. In September 1981, the WPA had held its first mass action after Rodney's death, a march for a living wage for which the authorities denied permission. Then, when the party went ahead with the activity, it was violently broken up (see Hinds 1988: 91).

8. The offices were a concrete manifestation of the doctrine of party paramountcy announced in 1974, which subordinated the state to the ruling party.

9. This recruitment of what were essentially child soldiers was, it should be said, a racial conscription of Afro-Guyanese children.

10. Another indicator of the group's political understanding was that in its International Women's Day 1984 statement, after outlining the ways that "the women of Guyana live hunted, fearful and depressing lives," it added, "In all of these areas of concern … Amerindian women in our country suffer even greater hardships."

11. NAACIE, the Guyana Agricultural and General Workers' Union (GAWU), the other sugar union, the University of Guyana Staff Association, and the Clerical and Commercial Workers' Union (CCWU).

12. After Independence the Guiana Agricultural Workers Union became the Guyana Agricultural and General Workers Union.

13. The full text of the complaint is contained in a submission to the International Labour Organization on April 9, 1985, filed as Report No. 241, Case No. 1330, and titled "Complaint Presented by the National Association of Agricultural, Commercial and Industrial Employees (NAACIE) and five other trade unions against the Government of Guyana."

14. In contrast, while not hostile to the food rebellion, the Guyana Mine Workers' Union was itself against independent workers' organizing, as was the ruling party, the PNC.

15. The failure of 1983 was preceded by the failure of 1979. The industrial front of the 1979 rebellion was precipitated by a strike called by the Guyana Mine Workers' Union for merit increments, which won solidarity action from the University of Guyana Staff Association, the Clerical and Commercial Workers' Union and the General Agricultural Workers' Union, but which collapsed.

16. In the 1970s, Selma James began to set out a new political perspective based on the autonomous struggle of each sector of the working class as the only basis for unity. Her starting point was the "hitherto invisible stratum of [Marx's] hierarchy of labour powers"—unwaged women in the home and on the land who were not seen as "workers" and whose struggle was therefore seen as less than the class struggle (James 1975: 6).

REFERENCES

Andaiye. 1993. "'You Got to Get Good Heart': Interviews with Guyanese Women Traders." Enterprise in the West Indies. Special issue of *Trinidad and Tobago Review* 15: 8–9.

——. 1995. "Democracy and Development." WAND Occasional Paper 1/95. Cave Hill: Women and Development Unit, University of the West Indies.

——. 2000. "The Red Thread Story." In *Spitting in the Wind: Lessons in Empowerment from the Caribbean*, Ed. Suzanne Francis Brown. Kingston: Ian Randle.

Catholic Standard.

——. 1983a. "Bauxite, Sugar Strikes Go On." June 5.

——. 1983b. "GHRA Appeals to the Caribbean." June 5.

——. 1983c. "NAACIE Demands Wheat Flour." June 5.

——. 1983d. "TUC Demands Wheat Flour." May 29.

——. 1983e. "Bauxite Strikes Worsen." June 12.

——. 1983f. "Bauxite Workers Regain Five Day Week; Government Backs Down." July 24.

Dalla Costa, Mariarosa and Selma James. 1972. "Women and the Subversion of the Community." In *The Power of Women and the Subversion of the Community*, Ed. Maria Dalla Costa. Intro. by Selma James. Bristol: Falling Wall, 19–54.

*Dayclean.*1974. Editorial. [1(2)] November: 2.

——. 1974. "Working People's Alliance Formed." [1(2)] November.

——. 1982. "Everyone Can Sign for Bread and Justice." [7(34)] August 7.

——. 1983a. "Food Strike Fires Guyana." [8(19)] May 20.

——. 1983b. "Bauxite Workers Lead Bread and Butter Fight." [3(17)] May 7.

——. 1983c. "West Coast Workers Strike for Food." [3(20)] May 28.

——. 1983d. "The Government Are Rioting." [3(21)]June 4.

——. 1983e. "People Unite in Hunger Marches." [3(24)] July 23.

——. 1983f. "WPA and People Fight On." [3(24)] July 23.

——. 1983g. "All Must Watch Out." [3(25)] August 6.

——. 1983h. "The Working People Understand This Attack." [3(24)] July 23.

——. 1983i. "Citizens Should Be Free to Organize Community Defence Groups." [3(28)] September 2.

——. 1983j. "Shame! Guyana Is Bleeding." [3(28)] September 2.

Dayclean Global. 2008. "It is in the Eyes: A Chat with Kathy Wills, Ultimate WPA Activist." June.

Goveia, Elsa. 1956. *A Study of the Historiography of the British West Indies*. Mexico: American Institute of Geography and History.

——. 1965. *Slave Society in the British Leeward Islands*. New Haven, CT: Yale University Press.

Hinds, David. 1998. "Authoritarianism and Resistance in Guyana (1964–1992)." Ph.D. diss., Arizona State University.

——. 2008. "Walter Rodney and Political Resistance in Guyana: The 1979–1980 Civil Rebellion." *Wadabagei* 11(1): 36–63.

International Labour Organization. 1985. "Complaint Presented by the National Association of Agricultural, Commercial and Industrial Employees (NAACIE) and Five Other Trade Unions against the Government of Guyana." Report no. 241, Case No. 1330. Report presented April 9.

James, Selma. 1975. *Sex, Race and Class*. London: Falling Wall.

Kilkenny, Roberta.1984. *The Radicalization of the Women's Movement in British Guiana 1946–1953*. Georgetown: Women's Studies Unit, University of Guyana.

Kwayana, Eusi. 1988. *Walter Rodney*. Georgetown: Working People's Alliance.

Open Word. 1982. Editorial. [40] November 8.

——. 1983a. Editorial. [62] April 11.

——. 1983b. "Sugar Workers on the Move." [70] June 6.

——. 1983c. "Hire Car Seizing: Now the Police Have Really Gone Too Far." [68] May 23.

——. 1983d. "WPA Says: They Have Made a Second Day of Rest Necessary." [76] July 18.

Rodney, Walter. 1969. *The Groundings with My Brothers*. London: Bogle L'Ouverture.

——. 1981. *A History of the Guyanese Working People, 1881–1905*. Baltimore, MD: Johns Hopkins University Press.

——. 1990. *Walter Rodney Speaks: The Making of an African Intellectual*. Trenton, NJ: Africa World Press.

Salkey, Andrew. 1972. *Georgetown Journal: A Caribbean Writer's Journey from London via Port of Spain to Georgetown, Guyana, 1970*. London: New Beacon Books.

Scott, David. 2001. "The Dialectic of Defeat: An Interview with Rupert Lewis." *Small Axe* 10 (September): 85–177.

West, Michael. 2008. "Seeing Darkly: Walter Rodney, Black Power and the US Diplomatic Mission in Jamaica and the Caribbean." *Small Axe* 25 (February): 93–104.

Westmaas, Nigel. 2004. "Resisting Orthodoxy: Notes on the Origins and Ideology of the Working People's Alliance." *Small Axe* 15 (March): 63–81.

Women Against Terror. 1980. "Open Letter to Police Commissioner." June.

——. Undated a. "Women against Terror: The First Year." Cyclostyle.

——. Undated b. "Statement." Cyclostyle.

Working People's Alliance. 1983. "Central Committee Report." August 7.

Four Letters in Defense of Workers, Unwaged and Waged,
and their Families
[2011, 2012, 2018]

1. ENDING POVERTY DEMANDS COLLECTIVE ORGANIZING; INDIVIDUAL SACRIFICE IS NOT ENOUGH

Dear Editor,

I write in response to the *Stabroek News* editorial of Thursday, October 18, last, entitled "Poverty," which salutes two mothers, both of whom had been subjects of earlier articles in *Stabroek News*—Ms. Vanessa Simon on September 30, and Ms. Dorothy Blackman on October 14.

Ms. Simon, whom the editorial calls "mother extraordinaire," is described as a "39-year-old single parent with five sons (who) holds down three menial jobs," and Ms. Blackman as "also a mother of five, (who) is a newspaper vendor, who scrimped, scraped and saved to send her third child to university and law school."

Both women deserve all the praise we can heap on them. That is not in question. But I want to challenge two aspects of the editorial.

The first is an old story: whether we end poverty by collective organizing against exploitation or by individual hard work within the exploitative situation; whether what we need is poor people in their numbers rising up against "the privileged few who most often have treated them unjustly" or individual sacrifice which—according to the editorial—can start "a revolution against poverty."

Which brings me to my second point. The editorial not only acknowledges the two mothers as extraordinary. It carries an underlying assumption that they are rare, in the sense that poor mothers who work themselves to the bone (and sometimes into the hospital, the mental asylum or the grave) are hard to find.

That is simply not true, and the stories of other women's lives often show that the revolution against poverty cannot and will not be made only by individual hard work. Many, many poor mothers work hard. A month or so ago, one of Red Thread's founding members, Cora Belle, died suddenly at the age of 62 after a lifetime of hard work. Nicola Marcus, her daughter, who is also a founding member of Red Thread, after attending the funeral of the mother of the pastor who had so recently officiated at the funeral of her own mother, said that listening to the tributes "was like looking into a mirror." What she meant was that the pastor's mother was a mirror image of her own mother, who had often worked three jobs to ensure that her nine children and many other foster children survived and grew, as they all did. Vanessa Simon herself was quoted in the *Sunday Stabroek* article of September 30 as saying that "she does nothing differently from the many women around her, who work hard to help maintain their families."

The problem is that many mothers do all that work without achieving what *Stabroek News* thinks is "a revolution against poverty." For today, I want to offer just one uncontentious example of why—one that Red Thread has written about before, very often: the fact that the economic model we are working with is fueling unprecedented migrations.

For us in Guyana, what this means is that a mother working under conditions of unbelievable exploitation as a security guard, a domestic worker, a shop assistant, or a cook, cleaner or waitress in a cook shop, often has no one at home, not even an older child, to care for the other children.

The other relatives, who would once have taken up the slack, including sometimes the other parent, are either somewhere else in the country or out of the country trying to earn money.

Worse, we have families without a single resident parent or guardian. We have mothers who are "catching dey hand" in one part of the country or another country altogether while their children catch their tail living on their own or moving from house to house, because both immediate families and extended families have scattered.

Only a fool would say there are no bad mothers among us; clearly there are. But there are far more who are "mothers extraordinaire." Some succeed in raising their children on the "straight and narrow" and deserve honor. But when we ignore or demonize the others who also deserve our respect even though their hard work does not lift their families out of poverty, then the mothers themselves, their children, and the whole society—all of us pay.

Signed,
Sincerely,
Andaiye
Red Thread

2. COMBATTING THE EXPLOITATION OF DOMESTIC WORKERS AND THE SUFFERING OF THEIR CHILDREN

Dear Editor,

There's a crisis in Guyana that almost everyone is ignoring—the crisis of mothers and other carers forced to work endless hours, often on no fixed schedules, and of the children they must leave to fend for themselves while they destroy their health laboring for a starvation wage.

Thousands of these women are domestic workers. Six of the 9 women in the Red Thread center know their exploitation firsthand: we have performed paid domestic work in the homes of respectable middle-class women and men who overworked, underpaid and sometimes verbally abused us, who could afford to pay us a decent wage but believed that while their labor is of value, ours is not.

Here's a summary of one true story.

One Domestic Worker's Story

M is employed by a couple on the East Coast Demerara to wash, iron, clean, mend and alter clothes for the whole household, and care for two young children: bathe them, fix their meals, wash their clothes, comb the older one's hair, help with her homework, read to the younger one and rock him to sleep and supervise both children. She is supposed to work Mondays to Saturdays, 9:00 a.m. to 5:00 p.m. but most days she is there till 6:00 p.m. when she returns home to care for her own child. She has an older child who doesn't live with her but who she supports. She has no agreed lunch break; she gets one if she asks. If the employers have to go out in the evening they ask her the same day to stay till they return, which might be as late as midnight. They don't offer her a taxi or a drop home so most times she sleeps over. For the past 6 months she has been told some Saturdays that she has to work on Sundays. Her young daughter is left alone when she can't find someone to keep her at short notice. Her monthly wage is G$36,000 (US$180) and basic expenses (food, rent, electricity, water, transport, school costs, phone) $52,445 (US$262) monthly. If she gets a day off it's without pay. When the employers have house guests her workload increases with no extra pay. She doesn't get extra pay for working holidays either. No NIS (national insurance) is paid for her. M says, "These people hard bad."

Domestic work is under-valued and under-paid because it is the same work that mothers perform unvalued and unpaid in their own homes. In other words, it is not real work and those who do it are not real workers. Domestic workers in Guyana are invisible in statistics and invisible to government, parties contesting elections, and even unions. They work in isolation, vulnerable to employers who "hard bad" because they have no protection either in law or usually in representative organizations that are recognized.

ILO Convention 189 Says this Exploitation Must Stop

ILO Convention 189, passed on June 16, 2011, demands that domestic workers have the same rights as all workers. Although the Convention if implemented will not end their exploitation it will reduce it. Among other provisions the Convention says that domestic workers must:

- Receive a written contract of their employment terms and conditions (Art. 7).
- Be entitled to minimum wage coverage where coverage exists (Art. 11).

- Receive equal treatment with other workers in relation to: normal hours of work, overtime pay, daily and weekly periods of rest, and yearly paid leave (Art. 10).
- Have conditions no less favorable than other workers, re social security protection, including maternity benefits (Art. 14).
- Enjoy the promotion and protection of their human rights and fundamental rights at work including freedom of association and the right to collective bargaining (Art. 3).
- Be protected against all forms of abuse, harassment and violence (Art. 5).
- Have the right to a safe and healthy work environment (Art. 13).

On October 7, World Day for Decent Work, domestic workers around the world launched a campaign to get Convention 189 ratified. In the Caribbean, Trinidad and Tobago's National Union of Domestic Employees (NUDE) and the Jamaica Household Workers Association of Jamaica (JHWA) took the lead. At the Jamaica launch the Labour and Social Security Minister committed himself to getting the Convention ratified. In Trinidad and Tobago the Labour Minister, former head of the Oilfield Workers Trade Union, had earlier promised ratification but has not followed through.

Red Thread has joined the campaign. NUDE, JHWA, Red Thread and other groups are also forming a Caribbean Domestic Workers Network which will meet in mid-November to fine-tune its agenda. Red Thread's big priority is organizing with domestic workers in all of Caricom, including Haiti, and connecting with others in the wider Caribbean, South and Central America— among them Peru's domestic workers' union SINTTRAHO. That will make us stronger as we will make them stronger.

Another key priority is winning the rights of Caricom's migrant domestic workers, whose largest contingents come from Guyana, Jamaica and Haiti. Since December 2009 they have had the right to work throughout Caricom once they are certified, but for many reasons, Guyanese domestic workers are still going to other Caricom countries as visitors and taking up jobs. They go in order to get the money to sustain their children although they have to leave them behind and often face inhuman treatment. In April this year, the Trinidad *Express* reported the Foreign Minister as saying that he had heard of Guyanese and "small islanders" being treated as "virtual slaves" in Trinidad and Tobago.

Most domestic workers in the world are migrants, from country to country or from countryside to city. They send massive amounts of money to families back home. Yet almost everywhere they are left alone to face terrible conditions.

All over the world domestic workers are organizing and beginning to win. The passage of ILO Convention 189 was itself the result of domestic worker organizing, including by NUDE and JHWA. In New York where most domestic workers are immigrants, many from the Caribbean, they have won a Domestic

Worker Bill of Rights which came into effect on November 29, 2010, and California is likely to have its own Bill of Rights soon. In Peru, they won protective legislation in 2003 but it is not being implemented so they are now using the new ILO Convention (which they helped to win) to pressure their government to force employers to sign contracts.

In Guyana we will take the example of the late Clotil Walcott, grassroots mother and grandmother, an extraordinary organizer who knew what workers must do to win: draw out the connections between domestic workers in Trinidad and Tobago and grassroots women (and men) globally. She saw that women did the unwaged and low waged work of caring for the whole human race—doing backbreaking work in their homes, in other people's homes, in factories and fields—to survive, and to feed, clothe and educate their children. Ms. Walcott, who spent decades working in a chicken factory, founded NUDE and joined the International Wages for Housework Campaign (later Global Women's Strike), which she coordinated in Trinidad and Tobago.

In Guyana, all of Caricom and across the Caribbean, that is what domestic workers must do to win—organize where they are and against the racial and other divides.

Signed,

Sincerely,

Andaiye, Joycelyn Bacchus, Joy Marcus, Halima Khan, Susan Collymore

3. WE ARE ALL LINDENERS (FOR BAUXITE WORKERS AND THEIR FAMILIES)

Dear Editor,

It is now five days since the deadly events in Linden, in which three men were shot dead by the police during a day of community protest. The last time protestors were shot at and killed by police was 64 years ago, when sugar workers were cut down by colonial officers acting on behalf of the sugar planters who ruled Guyana in those days. In *The West on Trial*, Cheddi Jagan offered us the following analysis of what happened and what it showed about relations between the rulers and the ruled:

> Without consulting even their company-dominated Manpower Citizens Association, they (the sugar planters) changed the system of work from cut-and-drop to cut-and-load … this action led to a 4½ month strike in 8 sugar estates on the East Coast of Demerara with its main slogan: "Sit and starve rather than work and starve." The response of the ruling class was characteristic—the resort to force.
>
> On June 16th, 1948, the police opened fire at the rear of the sugar factory at Pln. Enmore, killing 5 and injuring 12 persons. Thirty-year-old Lalla Bagi

was shot in the back; nineteen-year-old Pooran had a bullet through his leg and a gaping 3-inch wound above his pelvis; Rambarran died from two bullet wounds in his leg; Dookhie died in hospital the same day; Harry died the next day from a spinal injury.

This whole sordid and tragic episode could have been avoided. But the plantocracy was contemptuous of the workers, whose lives were regarded as expendable. (Jagan 1968)

Just last month, on June 16, 2012, many Guyanese, led by the PPP, rightly commemorated the Enmore martyrs, and their supreme sacrifice for the liberation of all Guyanese from colonial rule and arbitrary force.

But 64 years after Enmore, the PPP is in power in independent Guyana, and without Cheddi Jagan—who we believe would have fought against the degeneration that resulted in the police unleashing deadly violence on Lindeners on the evening of July 18, 2012. As we all now know, on the first of five days of action organized by the people of Linden to protest steep increases in electricity rates imposed without consultation with residents and to bring attention to the economic realities their community faces, the police used teargas and shot into a crowd of hundreds of women, children and men amassed on, and in the vicinity of, the Wismar-Mackenzie bridge.

Three men were killed: 46-year-old Allan Lewis; 18-year-old Ron Somerset; and 18-year-old Shemroy Bouyea. Another 20 women and men were sent to hospital nursing blunt trauma wounds and shooting injuries to the back, face, legs and chest: 34-year-old Alice Shaw Barker; 47-year-old Michael Roberts; 23-year-old Hector Solomon; 33-year-old Ulric Michael ; 56-year-old Reuben Bowen; 38-year-old Dexter Scotland; 5-year-old Janice Burgan; 35-year-old Yolanda Hinds; 45-year-old Brian Charles; 26-year-old Collis Duke; 35-year-old Cleveland Barker; 25-year-old Dwight Yaw; 39-year-old Marlon Hartman; 24-year-old Troy Nestor; 35-year-old Jermaine Allicock; 39-year-old Malim Spencer; 29-year-old Shandra Lyte; 34-year-old Andy Bobb Semple; 24-year-old Collin Adams; 21-year-old Trelon Piggot. Two people are in critical condition. One woman was shot as she tried to rush young children to safety.

And in 2012 as in 1948, there is an attempt to whitewash the atrocity. Writing about the murder of the five Enmore workers in 1948 in his book, *A History of Trade Unionism in Guyana, 1900 to 1961*, Ashton Chase noted: "the police claimed justification for the firing on grounds that a riotous mob at about 10:30 a.m. on 'massacre day' rushed into the factory compound and right into the factory building itself, and were overpowering the police who felt compelled to open fire so as to save the valuable property of the factory from destruction or damage and to protect the lives of those engaged in work therein." In *The West on Trial*, Cheddi Jagan described official explanations of the Enmore murders that were circulated before the setting up of the Bolland Commission of Inquiry as follows: "... the government had whitewashed the shooting of workers at Pln. Enmore. The police, it said, had been attacked and had opened fire in self defence."

Today, in response to the murders of Allan Lewis, Ron Somerset and Shemroy Bouyea, and even as the government has agreed to a Commission of Inquiry into the Linden shootings, a news story in the July 19 issue of the state-owned *Guyana Chronicle* had this to say: "Kudos to our police which did their duty at great risk to the lives of ranks. You stood your grounds in the face of much provocation and danger and you did your duty to protect the peaceful citizens of Guyana and Guyanese once more say thanks."

The commemoration of the martyrdom of Enmore workers in 1948 is a refusal to accept that the workers, not the police or the state of which the police are a part, were to blame for their own deaths. So too, today, we must categorically reject the efforts to whitewash the use of deadly force against women, men and children at Linden. Those responsible must be held accountable.

We must also reject the government's line that the opposition parties are to blame for the protests and the casualties of July 18. We must reject it whatever we think of the opposition parties because it is insulting to the people of Linden, a product of a political view disrespectful to "ordinary" people and an attempt to isolate Linden by making this into a party issue that can divide Guyanese. Linden has a proud history of self-organizing. In the 1970s the Organization of Working People (OWP), independently of party or trade unions that answered to the government of the day, organized bauxite workers and led many of the strikes that shut down the industry. Less well known is that Linden women have a history of organizing as mothers/carers, that housewives and children took to the streets in their thousands in 1983 at the height of the food rebellions, facing down riot police and forcing the release of 24 bauxite workers arrested for participating in a one-day-a-week strike. Both the OWP and the housewives allied with others across race and party and outside of Linden, most notably in the formation of the Sugar and Bauxite Workers Unity Committee.

Rising up against the electricity increases comes out of this proud history that holds many lessons for us today. In particular relation to women, what the history of their actions in 1983 shows us is that no mothers in Linden (or anywhere else) have to be led by political parties to protest. What leads them to protest is what they know from their daily lives—that the work of making ends meet is theirs, and that anything that increases that work is something that they must rise up against in defence of themselves, their children and their families.

The media, in their reporting and coverage of efforts to demonstrate solidarity with Linden, also have to do better. For the most part reports have focused attention on what either the government or political opposition are saying and doing. The protests in Georgetown on Thursday and Friday were organized by Red Thread to say what we have said before, that the struggle in Guyana is not about government and opposition parties. It is about we the people, starting with mothers and other carers, those who are always left to mourn their dead, comfort the ones left behind, and nurse the injured back to health.

Challenged about why we're organizing protests against the violence in Linden we point to the sign outside Red Thread's center that reads "Solidarity with Linden mothers." We are in solidarity with all Linden; the banner says "mothers" because our starting point is always mothers and other carers, the foundation of the whole society and economy. It is what we said in the statement we issued after the 2008 Lusignan massacre, in which we called on Guyanese to begin with "those who continue to pay the highest price of all" and added, "It is time we learn to listen to the anguish of a mother's cries, to recognize that her grief knows no race, no politics, no camp, only unspeakable loss and love."

Violence of the powerful against those with less social power is always criminal and to be condemned—and there is too often no condemnation except when it directly concerns us or "our race." The tendency of too many of us to respond to injustice only in relation to race, not to race as it interacts with class, and gender, and other social relations, always works in the interest of those with more social power. It keeps us divided from each other, and makes us all losers in the end.

The violence unleashed on the protestors by the state on July 18, 2012 has carried Linden and the country beyond the question of electricity tariffs. Violence is not violence is not violence. Whether in 1948 or in 2012 the violence of the state must be seen for what it is. The violence of the colonial state in 1948 carried that struggle well beyond the issue of cut-and-load to the central issue of how we will organize to live. It fueled the nationalist movement that began in the late 1940s, led by working people across race. The violence of the state in 2012 demands the same courage—that we stand up and answer the question: How will we organize to live?

This moment is about Linden but it is about more than Linden. As the placards held in the GT protests by women of different races proclaimed—in hope and determination—"We are all Lindeners."

Yours faithfully,

Andaiye, Joycelyn Bacchus, Karen de Souza, Joy Marcus, Alissa Trotz

4. RISE UP—TIME TO SPEAK (FOR SUGAR WORKERS AND THEIR FAMILIES)

Dear Editor,

Sometimes in political life, movements that promise relief to the majority of the population fail to perform and are left to flounder and crash. In the case of Guyana, there was much hope in the air when the Alliance for Change and the Partnership for National Unity reached an agreement under the Cummingsburg Accord to enter the 2015 elections.[1] Establishment of the coalition promised changes in several major areas of national life: ending governmental abuse at local and national levels; doing away with the seething corruption which was eating away at the fabric of the national culture; addressing the frequency of extra-judicial killings and bringing the perpetrators to justice (in excess of four hundred citizens, mainly Afro-Guyanese youth, gunned down during the reign of the previous government); transforming the country into a constitutional democracy, through much needed reform; creating a sustainable people-centered economy; and in the words of then presidential candidate, David Granger, ending "mediocrity."

These were and remain lofty ideals which Guyanese at home and abroad embraced and supported. As foundation members of the Working People's Alliance, we have watched from the side lines and with growing unease as this government committed error after error. Some of these errors, we felt, resulted from a newly sworn in coalition administration having to respond to situations which many of its ministers did not yet have the experience to address. Others may have been the result of the normal difficulties of coalition politics. But recently, we were shocked beyond belief when severance notices were handed out to sugar workers at the start of the Christmas season, without a plan regarding the future of the workers, their families, their communities, and the wider economy of Guyana.

This disastrous decision cannot be explained away with reference to inexperience. It is callous, foolish, ill-advised and economically unfeasible. The economy of Guyana has revolved around sugar since 1815, when the decision was taken to create a one crop economy. In that vein, the diversity that enslaved Africans had introduced, through the cultivation of provision grounds, came under attack. Some normalcy was restored to the people's economy through valiant struggles in the 1840s after the abolition of slavery when the village movement was formed. Over the long and protracted history of the second half of the nineteenth century, these villages supported the everyday existence of the mainly East Indian indentured sugar working communities. The wages from sugar workers resident in Indian and African villages was important to the survival of all the villages. The structure of economic and social relations in rural coastal Guyana is related to the integration of these two communities. For two hundred years, the wages paid to Indian and African workers on the sugar estates have helped in no small manner to sustain and bring vibrancy to every other industry and enterprise in Guyana, including the ice seller, the flutie producer, the hairdresser, the farmer, the haberdasher, the mechanic, the fisherman. This decision to shut down sugar is being taken as if it does not strike at the heart of the household and community economies of both those directly engaged in sugar production and those for whom there are ripple effects. This decision will affect every political constituency in the country. It will even affect the viability of the National Insurance Scheme (NIS).

The decision to hand out severance letters disrupts the micro economy of the working people, and is already affecting major sections of the country. We believe that Cabinet is duty bound to explain in plain language when the decision to issue severance letters was taken; when the decision to implement the decision to hand out severance letters by Guyana Sugar Corporation became government policy; what were the consultations and deliberations and with whom, what alternatives were discussed; why Cabinet did not consider a more reasonable phased approach; why, for instance, proposals from citizens' groups such as the National Farmers Organization for managed diversification were not given any attention and due consideration. Cabinet should also tell the public how much of the yearly subsidy was used to pay super salaries of Guyana Sugar Corporation officials.

The problems of the sugar industry are not new. As early as 1990 President Hoyte had raised concerns about its future, and had intimated the need for national consensus on the way forward for sugar. But this mostly fell on deaf ears, except for the WPA which made its position clear at the time. The WPA position then was that divestment of the industry should not mean and must not involve disposal of the sugar lands—they must remain public property. In 1990, Booker Tate was invited by President Hoyte to manage the industry on a management contract, an arrangement that came to an end in 2009. From that point a new Guyana Sugar Corporation management board was reinstated. The current government owes the people of Guyana an explanation for why it main-tained the structure of a top-heavy management board, even now as thousands of sugar workers, who have known nothing but sugar, are being sent home with no viable plan for their future.

Under normal circumstances, governments are expected to be even-handed. Given the lack of information on whether severance letters are also being handed out to the top heavy management board, we ask the question, how could the people who are part of the problem be relied on to find solutions? In light of the tragic news of two reported suicides by sugar workers since the layoffs, and to lessen despondency, uncertainly, and anxiety among sugar working families, it is well past the time for the government to fully explain its plans for the industry going forward.

What plans, if any, are in place to meaningfully involve people in the commu-nities in figuring out the future of sugar, the sugar lands, and the sugar assets? The time is never too late to change course. Government is serious business.

Government is serious business, period. In a country that now notoriously boasts the second highest suicide rate in the world, government must be more than serious business. In a country where domestic violence, and violence against women is now a sub-culture, government must be more than serious business. In a country where the families of the more than four hundred young men who were murdered extra-judicially still wait for justice, government must be more than serious business. In a country where the top 0.5 percent of the population owns and controls most of the wealth and decision making, government must be more than serious business.

As a country we can do better. The certainty that we could do better was the reason for the formation of the Working People's Alliance in 1974, and to see a government which includes the WPA falter on the most basic of ideals, gives us cause to pause and question. We think it necessary to remind our colleagues from the WPA in the government, that for decades our slogan was "*Bread and Justice*." Further, when the Economic Recovery Program (ERP) was put in place in 1989, the WPA called for investment in the people. It was not for nothing that the people renamed the ERP the Empty Rice Pot. Today, the government is following through on the approach of its predecessor, and is investing in the top 0.5 percent of the population to the detriment of the people. They invest in politicians, contractors, consultants, and those who seek to leech off the sweat of the working people. We remind those in power today of the APNU-AFC Manifesto for the 2015 elections, where they committed to "establish and entrench an inclusionary democracy through the appointment of a Government of National Unity which would create opportunities for the participation of citizens and their organizations in the management and decision-making processes of the state, with particular emphasis on the areas of decision-making that affect their well-being." We ask the government, were these empty promises?

We say now, and we say boldly, if this government does not recognize the wrong turns it has made, if it does not change course, if it does not embrace and lift up those most downtrodden among the population, it is doomed to failure like its predecessors.

Signed,

Andaiye, Moses Bhagwan, Eusi Kwayana

ACKNOWLEDGEMENTS

Letter 1 was originally published as "Recognising the Mothers Extraordinaire among us," *Kaieteur News*, October 19, 2012. Letter 2 was originally published in *Stabroek News*, October 16, 2011. Joycelyn Bacchus (d. 2017) was, and Joy Marcus, Halima Khan, and Susan Collymore are, members of Red Thread. Letter 3 was originally published under the title "The Violence of the State Demands that we Stand Up and Answer the Question: How Will we Organize to Live?" in *Stabroek News*, July 23, 2012. Karen de Souza is a former member of the Working People's Alliance and a founding member of Red Thread. Joycelyn Bacchus (d. 2017) was and Joy Marcus and Alissa Trotz are members of Red

Thread. Letter 4 was originally published in the Diaspora column of *Stabroek News*, January 8, 2018. Moses Bhagwan is a former member of the Working People's Alliance (see Essay 6).

NOTE

1. The coalition, which included the Working People's Alliance along with several other smaller parties, would defeat the incumbent minority PPP government at the 2015 polls.

PART THREE

THE POLITICAL IN THE PERSONAL

MY BREAST AND YOURS,
AND THE INEQUALITIES OF POWER

ESSAY 15
The War on Cancer as Seen by an Embattled Survivor
[2017/2018]

On International Women's Day 1989 I was diagnosed with cancer. Later I learned that it was Stage IVB diffuse large B cell lymphoma, an aggressive form of non-Hodgkin's lymphoma (NHL). Treated with chemotherapy, by the early 1990s I was in remission. But towards the end of 2011, I was told by one of the doctors who'd treated me that the protocol they used had been found to produce late effects, chief among which were three illnesses I was now suspected of having: a secondary cancer (mine was of the breast), congestive heart failure, and severe fixed obstructive lung disease. I also had a worsening of peripheral neuropathy. To quote the main character in a play called *Wit* by Margaret Edson which Susan Gubar cites in her memoir on surviving ovarian cancer: my treatment had imperiled my health (Gubar 2012: 3).[1]

During the nearly three decades since I had treatment for NHL I've been close to many people who've died of cancer—the youngest, 18-year-old Brad, the most recent, Garth, a man of 49, just two years older than I was when first diagnosed with cancer—so I *know* that being an embattled survivor means that I am one of the "lucky ones." S, a younger family friend successfully treated for Hodgkin's lymphoma around the same time I was treated for NHL, responded to my complaints about my treatment's late effects by saying quietly, "but the problem is that without the chemo we would probably both have died." I want to put the problem another way: for me, the problem is that the choice the medical system offered me and still offers too many others was between what Gubar calls, in relation to the unremitting horrors of her treatment for ovarian cancer "technologies and protocols that salvage ... cancer patients' lives by stunning, hurting or harming us," and death (Gubar 2012: 255). That is, when the high cost of conventional cancer care gives us a choice at all.

Gubar is not blaming individual medical professionals. She coined the word "loconcology" to describe "the double binds into which current protocols put medical practitioners and their patients," adding, "Physicians fully realize that standard treatments trigger destructive effects, but there is no alternative available to them" (Gubar 2012: 24). The skill, professionalism and kindness of an individual doctor,[2] nurse or lab technician can only reduce the pain of patients' experience of the war on cancer; they cannot alter the reality that once it uses the weapons it still uses, it is necessarily a war in our bodies.

While I was in treatment I'd tried to keep a diary but couldn't. In the years following this, I spoke about cancer in newspaper columns, speeches, a conference presentation or two, interviews, and tributes to friends who've died of cancer. I joined with others to organize a Cancer Society and a Cancer Survivors Action Group in Guyana, and with three women from other parts of the region, discussed forming a region-wide network of women cancer survivors.[3] I didn't write the story of my treatment because I saw no value in reliving what had been a brutal experience. But once it was confirmed that the breast cancer and heart and lung disease were effects of the treatment I had 22 years before,[4] there was no way I could continue evading the questions that had been at the back of my mind for many years—"Can what I feel be effects of chemotherapy after all this time?"—and faced with advocates of alternative treatments for cancer—"Should I have refused the chemotherapy?" Now I *had* to research the treatment, to understand where it came from, and to ask how anything so life-threatening, discovered on a literal battlefield, became a cure for life-threatening cancer; and I had to record what I'd found, how the treatment had affected me, and what I'd learned from the whole experience about the power relations that worked for and against my survival.

* * *

Many factors shape, even determine, survival from cancer—where your cancer began and how advanced it was when diagnosed; whether effective treatment has been discovered for that cancer; access to testing and treatment, meaning the availability of those services and the means to pay for them. Luck. I want to discuss two others, one which works against survival and one which works powerfully in its favor.

First, the one which I truly believe inhibits survival. For the great majority of cancer patients, a central part of the work of surviving is holding your own against the power of a medical system and culture which at best underestimate, at worst take advantage of your relative powerlessness. This imbalance affects most people who are sick, I think, but especially those of us whose illnesses leave us physically and emotionally empty. In relation to cancer (and other illnesses like HIV), a part of what disempowers the patient in the first place is how the disease is perceived.

Up to today, there are communities and countries where what Susan Sontag wrote about cancer in 1988 remains true: that it doesn't just provoke fear of a dreaded disease; it provokes dread of something unfathomable: it is treated as "an evil, invincible predator, not just a disease" (Sontag 1988: 7). In those countries and communities, the view that "culturally [in relation to cancer], everything has changed," is patently wrong.

People who live in places where cancer has come to be treated as just a serious illness may be as puzzled at the thought of cancer being seen as a predator, as an African-American girl I heard of in the 1970s was puzzled by the story of Rosa Parks. "Why would they expect her to sit in the back of the bus?" she asked. It wasn't that racism was dead in the US by the 1970s; it was that the struggle led by Black people had changed it, and that its earlier faces were unrecognizable to a new generation. But people for whom "culturally, everything has changed" in relation to cancer are a small minority. The face of cancer remains unchanged for millions. The cancer environment in which they struggle to survive is not dissimilar to the one I encountered nearly three decades ago. As late as 1989 when I was diagnosed people still didn't say cancer; they said "The big C." With very few exceptions, friends and family who were told of my illness initially responded with such fear that it fell to me to console them, and often, I was the only one who would name the disease. When I was first in hospital in Barbados, my aunt came into my room on tiptoe although she could see I was awake, and whispered when she spoke, as decent people did in the presence of death. Inside my immediate family it didn't help that our one direct personal experience of cancer at that time was my mother's sister, in her thirties, dying not long after she was diagnosed with leukemia—another cancer which, like lymphoma, is not located in any one organ and leaves you to imagine it crawling around inside your body and making it shrink mysteriously.

And so it was that in 1989 when I went for my first meeting with the hematologist/oncologist in Barbados who was to treat me, I took six women colleagues with me. (I had been doing a part-time consultancy with the Women and Development Unit (WAND) of the School of Continuing Studies, University of the West Indies since 1987). They were there to ask the questions I was too exhausted and afraid to think of and to remind me later what the answers were. But more importantly, they were there because I needed some power on my side of the doctor's desk. This is not a comment on the doctor whom I didn't know then but grew to like, but on that built-in imbalance of power between doctors and patients, particularly patients whose lives are literally in the doctors' hands.

And yet, compared to the other patients with whom I was treated, I had a lot of potential power on my side. My parents were both medical people— my father first a dispenser/nurse then a doctor, my mother a nurse. I had not only spent about seven years of my life living in the compound of the public hospital where my father worked and interacted with his colleagues/friends, but by the time I got cancer had been sick fairly often and had spent time with doctors and other medical professionals, including in hospitals. I knew the culture. Moreover, I had organized with women and men working to win economic, social and political rights for over 25 years, and had a developed sense of entitlement—that is, a belief that people (including me) are *entitled* to services including health care. And yet with all this, the size of the physical and emotional onslaught that cancer and its treatment inflicted on me was so enormous that I often felt powerless in the face of medical professionals and institutions.

I had several experiences of this, including one that began when I saw a strange rash on my cheek which I later learned was herpes zoster. Before me, another patient who was being treated for NHL at the same time as I was also developed the herpes zoster rash. When I advised her to call the doctors she said she would tell them at her next appointment, that she didn't want to "bother them." That was her general attitude to doctors—that they were busy people whom we shouldn't "bother." It is not stretching things too far to say that this is one of the reasons that she died; she never "bothered" her doctors with what she felt. I was less intimidated by our doctors than she was, but I *was* intimidated. When my rash came out, unlike her, I called in. But when the junior doctor who answered the phone said that my clinic day was imminent and it would be checked then, I retreated. It was no thanks to me that I was seen as urgently as I needed to be; the junior doctor called back and reported that the senior doctor, on hearing what I was complaining of, had said that I should come to the hospital right away, prepared to stay in.

I felt even more intimidated in the loneliness of the isolation ward. Sometime after I was put on a continuous drip my arm began to hurt. I don't know that the pain was unbearable but I know that on that day, in that environment, in that state of weakness, I could not bear it. I asked the nurses to put the needle into another vein; they said a doctor had to decide. I asked for a doctor to be called; they said none was available. I was insistent enough that one was called at her home but I could tell from the nurse's responses that she was saying she couldn't come; I subsided. The rational side of me accepted that she had a life; the frightened patient in me had no room for rationality. I don't know how long I was alone in this state; you exaggerate it, measure it by the size of your fear. Eventually, thinking only to avoid more pain, when the nurses came to inject more of whatever they were treating me with into the drip I said no, and learned by accident that at least in that hospital ward, refusing treatment was an infallible way to summon doctors: two arrived almost immediately and asked me solicitously whether I was refusing treatment and if so, why. The needle was adjusted. I understood the need for me to be in isolation. I didn't and don't accept that there is no alternative to ignoring a patient's terrors.

While the imbalance of power is not only between doctor and patient but between the patient and the institution of medicine, the doctor/patient relationship is key. Atul Gawande identifies three types: the interpretive (shared decision-making between doctor and patient); the paternalistic (the doctor has the knowledge and experience to decide what's best for you); and the informative (the doctor supplies up-to-date knowledge and skills, you make the decisions) (Gawande 2014: 200–201). I've experienced all three, but I believe that all of them can be deformed by the unequal relations of power between the doctor and the patient.

Doctors' power derives from our acceptance that they possess the knowledge that will determine our fate, and this is all the more true when their approach to medicine is purely as science, not also as art; I learned from my father that medicine was largely art. The more typical approach leads to a tendency not to deal with the patient's whole body and mind, and a frequent rejection of non-Western therapies. I know there are exceptions but what I'm describing is what I've experienced as the general rule.

The over-specialization which characterizes modern medicine became a particular problem for me as the several late effects of my treatment for NHL developed and I needed more help connecting if and how they influenced each other. But the problem was there even while I was being treated only for NHL, expressed in gaps ranging from an absence of counselling on nutrition to an absence of emotional counselling. There was no integrative care. Whether doctors practice the interpretive, paternalistic or informative doctor/patient relationship their angle of vision is too often their specialty and they limit themselves to the information that falls within that specialty. The (specialist) textbook rather than the (whole) patient is the main guide. This order clearly needs to be reversed.

The single-minded reliance on scientific evidence can blind a doctor to the evidence patients provide from their lived experience of both illness and its treatment. I have seldom found any Western-trained doctors, no matter how well they interacted with me, truly open to all I was reporting on my experience when the report did not fit neatly—or at all—into what the science says.

Medicine as science is about general truths; medicine as art, I think, about hearing the patient's specific truth. When I was being treated for NHL there was a woman in treatment with me, Marva—who was the same age, and had the same cancer, at the same stage. We were very alike in those essential ways. But we were also very unalike, above all in life experiences and belief systems. Those differences were fundamental to how we thought and felt and what we understood about our (shared) disease and how we interacted with our (shared) doctors—how we heard them, how we spoke to them, how they heard us. And we were very very different on the life-and-death question of in whose hands we believed our chances of survival lay.

Medicine as art requires awareness that differences matter.

I've found doctors' lack of openness to patient's experience when the experience went against the science particularly true in relation to the use of non-Western therapies, even as complements to Western medicine.

*   *   *

I didn't come to the question of the pros and cons of different approaches with any clear views or beliefs, much less dogma. At the time I started treatment for NHL I knew little or nothing about the use of alternative or complementary therapies in major illnesses. I hadn't yet read Audre Lorde's *Cancer Journal* or any other narrative by a cancer patient who'd used any of these therapies. I assumed Western medicine as a given. In my home, bush medicine (plants or herbs), though not disparaged, was left for my grandmother to prescribe for problems like period pain; not for a life-threatening disease. But since I did have at least that limited experience of using something other than conventional medicine to reduce pain and discomfort, from about midway in the treatment I decided that I couldn't bear much more chemotherapy unless I found ways to mitigate its negative side effects. Friends searched for and found a Western trained doctor in Barbados who'd also studied Chinese herbal medicine. I chose a doctor trained in Western medicine so that he could take the drugs I was using into account. Having listened carefully to my report and posing several questions he selected and prescribed some herbs. After taking them for a short while I felt better, less battered, and was not swayed from this by my knowledge that most doctors I knew would dismiss my response as a placebo effect. I continued to see this doctor.

In addition to the Chinese herbs I pursued other ways to give my body some ease. For example, I wanted to try meditation but at first found it impossible; my mind was too agitated to begin. Then the friend of a friend made a tape which worked—her words carrying me without steering me to a sense of being bathed in color—not as she expected, blue, which is known as the color of (other people's) healing, but the shades of deep pink and peach with flashes of burnt orange which are the colors of the sky when the sun in Guyana is rising or setting over the Atlantic, and which have always made me feel at peace. With my mind stilled, I could meditate, at least a bit.

Later, after the mastectomy, the oncologist to whom I was referred for management of my case, on reading the file on the treatment of my NHL said that he was glad that I'd had a mastectomy (rather than a lumpectomy) and that my cancer was found early because he would not have wanted to recommend further chemotherapy given the nature and quantity of the drugs that I'd already had. If he had so recommended I would have fought him but I was grateful not to have to fight, or to argue the efficacy of a mastectomy followed by homeopathy, as I'd decided on.[5] From about 2000, I had started using homeopathic remedies more consistently, increasingly attracted to it and to other complementary therapies whose approaches, though varied, were all non-invasive.

To recap, my first cancer, NHL, was diagnosed at Stage IVB; advanced and aggressive, it was treated aggressively with chemotherapy alone until I allied the chemotherapy with Chinese herbal medicine and other non-Western therapies like meditation. My second experience was of breast cancer, diagnosed at Stage II; caught early, it was treated with surgery which I allied with homeopathic remedies. My biggest self-criticism is that on neither occasion did I ensure that I did the complementary therapies in a truly informed and systematic way. However, on both occasions I was guided by qualified and experienced practitioners.

Most Western-trained doctors I know dismiss and disparage alternative and complementary therapies as not scientifically proven and/or unsound, sometimes illogical, sometimes dangerous—even when they have a long and proud history of use, including by doctors trained in both Western and non-Western therapies in a country like India. Other people I know, including cancer patients, swear by alternative and complementary cancer medicines, some dismissing conventional cancer drugs as ineffective and destructive products of a cancer industry whose priority is making profits, at whatever cost to patients.

The survival of patients with illnesses that are physically and/or emotionally disabling requires an abundance of unwaged caring labor. While details of what each of us needs will differ (for example, I needed certain kinds of practical help only because I was being treated away from where I usually lived), every such patient needs emotional and practical support. Once this is seen as integral to survival, the collaborations that need to be established in the particular environment where the patient is being treated will become clear—such as with families, friends, and/or groups of various kinds including cancer survivors' groups. This is something that our medical systems need to take on board. For one thing, people in poor communities, even where cancer is still seen as a predator to be feared, often have access to networks of support, but to the extent that they get in the way of the "work" of the medical system (especially hospital wards) they are not welcomed, much less encouraged.

Particularly during the two crisis periods—1989/90 and 2011/2012—the loss of power I felt, and the imbalance of power between me and the medical professionals and institutions, was in part redressed by personal and political friends and "family" who came with me to and from Barbados and to and from visits to doctors, hospitals and labs. They made me welcome to stay with them in their homes or lent me their homes to stay in; drove me around or arranged for others to drive me around. Made my bed. Washed my hair. Took photographs so I could see later how far I'd come. Left me alone or kept me company as I needed. Supplied me with special foods and complementary remedies and nutritional supplements and advice and books. Cooked for me (one friend grumbling all the while about "women's work," which made me laugh) or corralled or paid others to cook for me. Raised money or gave me their money,[6] (or in one case in 1989/1990, employed me to do writing jobs with long deadlines which I could complete by working on my good days). It was redressed (in large part) by women, some of them strangers, who organized medical help for me in countries where I was a stranger. Who mobilized what they called an international healing circle of women in my support one day in 1989/1990. By women and men who came together in nightly gatherings to eat, talk, argue, and drink wine (sometimes while I slept) at the home that had been made available to me and my friends/carers in 2011/2012. Who sent emails or, earlier, cards ("We never met but I met so-and-so at a conference and she told me about you so I'm writing to say ..."). Who phoned, visited, prayed (one woman telling me laughingly in 1989 what a fraud I was because while I didn't pray myself, I was willing to use other people's prayers). Who made me laugh even when they didn't mean to, like the one who, searching for how to help me build confidence that I could beat the NHL, urged me to take a herb which another woman she knew with cancer had taken. Me: "And how is she now?" She: "Oh, she's dead." That carried me for days.

During 1989/1990 the best bulwark against isolation and fear was often the nurturing of the community that Audre Lorde called "sister survivors." I've mentioned Marva—the woman who like me, had NHL and with whom I became friends. Marva became an almost daily telephone companion. Together with Jenny, a teenage girl whose chronic illness since childhood had made her far older than her years, we formed a small community. Like women and girls who, living in the same house, find their periods synchronizing, Marva, Jenny and I would find ourselves admitted to hospital at the same time. There, more than once we saw the same group of night shift nurses who greeted the second and third one of us to arrive with a "Soon as we saw the first one (or two) we knew you were coming!" and put us in beds from which we could see and speak to each other. Mercifully, they didn't have the attitude to patients that was displayed in what I once heard another nurse say to her colleague one morning, "So many patients came in last night I didn't get to do my work," meaning, record-keeping. They didn't see our interaction as making work for them. They saw that we helped bear each other up. Once, Jenny and I stayed half-lying in our beds all night talking to Marva as she fought her pain and frustration as one doctor after another attempted to find a vein that hadn't collapsed to restart her IV, and when—sometime in the morning hours—one succeeded in getting a needle into a vein in her foot, as we all finally turned to go to sleep Marva said quietly, "thank you for watching with me through the night."

Marva and I were both 47 or 48 years old then, but no matter how old you are, when you're in pain and alone at night there are monsters in the dark.

Part of what we fortified ourselves with was laughter. After Marva and I both had the high-dose methotrexate and leukovorin rescue to bomb us both into remission, we knew that the hair that had begun to grow back after the first six cycles of treatment and that we had been carefully tending, would fall out. Unable to bear waiting for the inevitable. I got rid of mine in one go by running my finger backwards from my front hairline to the back. All of it came out without my even pulling at it. Forty-seven/eight years old or not, I wanted to cry, till Marva laughed, boasting that she was keeping her hair on by covering it with a shower cap. Then she took the cap off and every single hair came off with it. Only my laughter stopped her tears.

The heart of the tribute I wrote for Audre when she died—a tribute that was written quickly, almost without conscious thought, as though what I was vomiting up this time was the poison of grief—was the recounting of an exchange we once had about lost teeth which started with me frozen with depression and ended with me shaking with laughter. Survival work. As with Marva and me, it was because we were both residents in what Susan Sontag called "the kingdom of the sick" (Sontag 1988), that we were able to laugh at each other and laugh at ourselves with each other over losses, some, or all of which we each suffered, that were a daily threat to our spirits: losses of hair, weight, teeth, skin tone; of attractiveness, sexual confidence, independence, privacy and dignity. I have since had pieces of that relationship with other women with cancer, and with a few men and one youth with cancer, relation-ships where the terrors of advanced cancer and its treatment formed a bridge across our other-life differences which we crossed with survival work. The downside is the unbearable pain you feel if they die, as almost all have. When I went to see Marva near the end of her life she looked angry that she was dying while I was not, and I grieved.

It's not only raising a child that takes a village. My survival has been due also to my brother's extraordinary, daily support for the whole year I was treated for NHL—support that ranged from the practical (cooking and cleaning and washing clothes to accompanying me when I went for treatment to wiping up vomit) to the emotional (knowing when and how to provide silent sympathy, and never, ever behaving as though my illness gave him grief that it was my job to assuage). It has been due, too, to the daily physical and emotional housework I've done for myself. And it has been due to the not always day-to-day but always life-giving caring work of a wider community of mainly (though not only) women across all these years.

POSTSCRIPT

More than a year after I finished writing the last several paragraphs I saw a report in the *Guardian* on an experiment in a town in the UK called Frome.

A General Practitioner named Helen Kingston had launched the Compassionate Frome Project in 2013 as an answer to the problem of "patients who seemed defeated by the medicalisation of their lives." The project established a directory of agencies and community groups, identified gaps, and filled them with new groups for people with particular conditions. It employed "health connectors" to help people plan their care, and trained voluntary "community connectors" to help their patients find the support they needed. The reporter, George Monbiot, commented that the approach used by the project "could, if the results stand up, be one of the most dramatic medical breakthroughs of recent decades," transforming treatment regimes, saving lives, and saving health costs. He called the approach not a drug, a device, a surgical procedure, but "a newfangled intervention called community" (Monbiot 2018). He reported that the results of the trial had been published informally, in the magazine *Resurgence and Ecologist* and a scientific paper had been submitted to a medical journal and was awaiting peer review. The provisional data, he said, appeared to show that when isolated people who have health problems are supported by community groups and volunteers, the number of emergency admissions to hospital falls spectacularly, and went on to discuss the scientific basis for this result. He ended by pointing out that the results of the Frome trial should not surprise given "A famous paper published in *PLOS Medicine* in 2010 which reviewed 148 studies, involving three hundred thousand people, and discovered that those with strong social relationships had a 50 percent lower chance of death across the average study period (7.5 years) than those with weak connections," adding that dozens of subsequent papers reinforced these conclusions.

It takes a village.

ACKNOWLEDGEMENTS

This essay is excerpted from a three-part essay on surviving cancer, published posthumously in a special edition of *The Scholar and Feminist Online* on Caribbean Feminisms (16:1, Winter 2020), edited by Tami Navarro and Tonya Haynes.

NOTES

1. The original is in the present tense—"My treatment imperils my health."
2. As part of that kindness, some of the doctors who treated me across the 30 years since I was diagnosed with NHL did so without charge.
3. The Cancer Society and Cancer Survivors Action Group are defunct, although some members have gone on to other cancer-related organizing; while the idea of the region-wide network was abandoned after the death of two of the women concerned.

4. While the diseases were confirmed in early 2012 it's not clear when they started, especially the congestive heart failure and the lung disease. In relation to the latter, one doctor told me that I have both chronic obstructive pulmonary disease and lung fibrosis.
5. For the background to this see Ramakrishnan and Coulter (2001: 196).
6. This was years before the concept of crowdfunding was born.

REFERENCES

Gawande, Atul. 2014. *Being Mortal: Illness, Medicine and What Matters in the End.* London: Profile Books in association with Wellcome Collection.
Gubar, Susan. 2012. *Memoirs of a Debulked Woman: Enduring Ovarian Cancer.* New York: WW Norton.
Lorde, Audre. 1980. *The Cancer Journals.* San Francisco, CA: Spinsters/Aunt Lute.
——. 1988. *A Burst of Light.* Ithaca, NY: Firebrand Books.
Monbiot, George. 2018. "The Town that's Found a Potent Cure for Illness—Community." *The Guardian*, February 21.
Ramakrishnan, A. U. and Catherine R. Coulter. 2001. *A Homeopathic Approach to Cancer.* Berkeley Spring, WV: Ninth House Publishing.
Sontag, Susan. 1988. *Illness as Metaphor.* New York: Farrar, Straus and Giroux.

ESSAY 16
Sister Survivor: For Audre Lorde
[1992]

I met Audre Lorde toward the end of 1988 at the Caribbean Association for Feminist Research and Action (CAFRA) meeting. I was chairing (they call it facilitating) a session. CAFRA members were being—as usual—disorderly; and why not? I was in my best head teacher mode. Audre came in late. I recognized her face from the back of books but I had to make a point; she was late. I asked her to identify herself. She said, looking a little surprised (she was not humble), "Audre Lorde." I led the acknowledgement by thumping the table. She acknowledged the recognition with a slight raising of the eyebrow, a ducking of the head.

A short time after I was asked if I could be interviewed with Audre. I agreed. It took some time to get the interview together. When I was free, I heard she was tired. When she wasn't, I was busy. I wasn't trying to be difficult. I hadn't read the cancer books. I didn't know about her struggle with cancer. Eventually we did the interview at a table (I think; my memory is bad) in a room full of people and smoke. I think, too, I was smoking myself. As I said, I didn't know she had cancer. And I didn't know I had cancer.

Somewhere in the next six months I learned she had cancer. Somewhere in the next six months—on International Women's Day, 1989—I learned that I, too, had cancer. I remember only fragments of what happened over the next few days. I remember being at my father's house and people coming in, the women breaking the silence of awkwardness by asking me what I needed washed or ironed or bought for the hospital; the men, not socialized into housework, having nothing to break the silence. I remember my friend, Jocelyn Dow, taking me to see a play that was on in celebration of IWD: *For Colored Girls who Have Considered Suicide/When the Rainbow is Enuf*. I remember going to the home of another friend, Alice Thomas, where I cried and Alice said, "Done, done, never mind, the diagnosis probably wrong." Mother words. I remember yet another friend, Nesha Haniff, saying angrily that we all know Guyana's medical services had fallen apart so why were we so stupid as to believe they could read any slides? I remember my father sitting with Jocelyn making arrangements for me to go to Canada for the diagnosis to be checked even as he denied the possibility it might be right. I remember him calling my mother, who was in England, and who did what she did best—pretended she was coping well; how was her daughter? I remember my brother, Abbyssinian, calling to say that he would leave his job in New York (as he did) and come wherever I would be, to be my nurse (as he was). I know I spoke during those few days, too, to other women who became major supports; the thing I call not yet a women's movement called in.

I do not remember when I wrote Audre, but I did, and I remember that she answered immediately and sent me a copy of *A Burst of Light* with the inscription, "Sister Survivor—May these words be a bridge over that place where there are no words—or where they are so difficult as to sound like a scream!"

And so began my friendship with Audre Lorde, around the sharing of the fear of living with, perhaps dying from, cancer. She wrote often, mostly on cards. She'd said, "I need your words too." I couldn't write too many. So I called, often. And she called too.

West Indians are a people who, for good or evil, express the serious as joke. So across all my weekly and monthly phone calls with Audre in four years, here's what I remember most sharply.

I was well into my treatment and had developed a reputation as a person who was dealing well with cancer and chemotherapy. And I was brave. I knew from reading that the drugs I was using would cause me to lose my hair. I arranged to shave it all off when it began to fall. I was determined that I would be in control. Every time I went for chemo I vomited my guts out, then, vomiting over, called for soup with pigtail which my Aunt Elsene or mother made. I watched people watching me with pity—hair gone, cheeks deformed by steroids—and managed to laugh. My friend Karen de Souza, a photographer, would come from Guyana to visit me and climb up high to take pictures of the sun shining on my head and my cheeks, so she said, I could see later where I had been and acknowledge the journey. I genuinely found that funny. At least she assumed there would be a later.

I was brave until the day I was told I had to lose several teeth which, given the teeth I had been losing since childhood, meant that I had to get a plate.

A plate, teeth in a cup, at night; worse than cancer, a metaphor for old age. I went back to the home where I was staying with my friend Elsie Yong, entered my bedroom, closed the door, climbed into my bed, went into the fetal position and lay.

Somewhere within this—the same day, next day?—Audre called. "Hi girl-friend," she said. "Hi," I muttered, the first time I had ever felt or sounded not glad to hear her voice. She chatted and then eventually asked what was wrong. I said, "I have to take out teeth and get a plate and soak it in the night like old people." One breath, whining.

I heard a noise like a person who hadn't managed to get her hand over the phone before she giggled. Then Audre said, "I lost my two front teeth. Which teeth are you losing?"

"The remaining ones on the right side," I answered.

"Oh, that's bad," she said. "But not as bad as front teeth." I sucked the teeth I had left. "Listen," she said. "You know I'm supposed to be so brave? Well, when I lost my two front teeth I felt worse than when I lost my breast. I mean, you don't have to show your breast or use it every minute, but your teeth!"

I giggled, then said, "But this is it. This is the end. This is teeth in a cup, in the night. The end of …"

"No," she interrupted. "Here's what I do. In the night, I go into the bathroom and close the door, firmly. I take out my two front teeth. I brush the teeth in my mouth, then the teeth in my hand. Then I put the teeth in my hand in my mouth. I go to bed. Now, if you have expectations (and girlfriend, you and I might seem to have different expectations but they're really the same expectations), you wait till the expectations are met or if none are forthcoming you raise some …"

I giggled.

"Stop interrupting," she went on. "After your expectations are met (she/he approaching, you approaching), you wait for the right moment (she/he asleep) and you take out your teeth (if you think you must) and place them strategically under your pillow."

I giggled.

"Girlfriend, you put them so you can get at them quickly if any further expectations come up. And if they don't, in the morning you get up, take them quickly from under the pillow, go to the bathroom, close the door firmly, brush the teeth in your mouth then the teeth in your hand, put the teeth in your hand in your mouth and you're ready to meet any further expectations …"

"OK, OK, OK," I giggled. "OK."

It occurred to me then, it occurs to me now, that the story had been made up out of whole cloth. But what does that matter?

A few times Audre called me because she needed to find company in the place she was in. When the alternative therapy that had helped her stay alive for so long wasn't shrinking her liver tumor anymore or even keeping it the same size; and the question was whether to finally take chemotherapy, even though she was tired of carrying her life every day in her hands.

"Girlfriend," she inquired, "Tell me about methotrexate." I answered; she hummed. She asked, "You think I should take that, you who've felt it?" I tried a balancing act. I wanted her to take anything that might keep her alive. I wanted to support her in her determination not to switch gears from a form of therapy that was about strengthening the immune system to one that could destroy it. I wanted her to take poison if poison would keep her alive. We spoke when, after she had taken the chemo, her locks had fallen out and she asked, "Do you understand thin with bloat?"—because she had lost weight while parts of her body had grown fat. She called when, for love of those for whose love of her, she was considering more chemo although her heart and her body and her mind said no. And all she asked of me, at those moments, was that, as a person in a place similar to hers (although never the same), I would listen to her weigh options I had weighed, and tell her the truth of what I had discovered so she could use that in her weighing of the options.

A person in a similar place. For we were never, Audre and I, "sister survivors," surviving in the same place. No one else I came to know who had cancer had travelled such a road, from breast cancer to liver cancer to ovarian cancer. From mastectomy to hysterectomy. From a person who started like the rest of us with little knowledge of cancer and its treatment to a person fully informed about the disease and the options for treatment; from a person just living to a person having to make decisions every day about what to do or not to do just to live, who found the courage to choose a road with no one ahead to guide her— no person who had chosen that road and walked it for so long through such pitfalls and reached the places she wanted to be.

Audre told me, as she told countless others, that I should write—a diary entry each day, poems. I didn't. When Gloria (Joseph) said she had died I thought (I didn't know what else to think) I would write her a poem. I couldn't. I wrote, "I want you in this world." Nothing else. What I meant was that although I believe she will always be in this world in her children, her partner, her blood and non-blood sisters, all her life's work, I wanted her in this world—at the other end of a phone or postcard, talking about the loss of teeth and hair, about bloating bellies and cheeks and Bush and the Gulf War; about where she was going/had been to see an eclipse of the sun; about why something I had written was OK but not good enough because I had chickened out on homophobia; about why she would forgive me that (for a while) in the face of CNN images of Rodney King, Ethiopia, Brazilian street children, the thing they call "black on black violence" with its origins in white on black violence, in New York, DC, the townships of South Africa. About living with and dying from cancer. About her loving me and I, her.

For I loved her, this woman who came so late to my life but whose death leaves a void in the center of my life.

Audre, there's rosemary. That's for remembrance.

ACKNOWLEDGEMENTS

This essay was originally published by the Caribbean Association for Feminist Research and Action (CAFRA). It was reprinted as "Andaiye, For Remembrance, For Audre Lorde," in Gloria I. Joseph (Ed.), *The Wind is Spirit: The Life, Love and Legacy of Audre Lorde.* (Villarosa Media, 2016); and as "Audre, There's Rosemary, That's for Remembrance, in Margaret Busby (Ed.), *New Daughters of Africa: An International Anthology of Writing by Women of African Descent* (London: Myriad Editions, 2019).

ESSAY 17
Asylum: Diary of the Last Seven Days in a Women's Psychiatric Ward
[circa 1973]

TUESDAY

Today marks three weeks that I've been here. The day I came I felt safer; for weeks before then I had frozen each time I reached the door of my apartment building, terrified by the brightness of the sun and the noise of the traffic.

Over the next few days I learned the geography of the ward: the open space of the lobby which led on all sides to other spaces that close you in: in front, rooms for group meetings, arts and craft therapy and eating; to the left, a long narrow corridor with a blank wall on one side and a glassed-in nurses' station, a washroom and a 24-bed dorm on the other; to the right, two doors, one leading to stairs, the other to a short passageway off of which was the solitary. These spaces together made up the women's ward.

The solitary. I learned about that, too: a dark, airless cave into which guards manhandled any woman who wasn't compliant. Twice since I came here I've heard a woman scratching at the walls, the door, the floor of that room, crying softly, like a whipped dog.

The day I came I didn't know any of this. All I saw as I was being escorted to the nurses' station to book in were the women—about 18 or 20 of them, aged between about 15 and 50, a few white, most Puerto Rican or black. All, as it turned out, poor. Most were turned in on themselves; a few looked alive, even combative. Later I found out that two were immigrants who had come to New York to make a better life.

WEDNESDAY

A woman shuffles to the end of the corridor and back, forward and back, moving as if by instinct, avoiding as if by instinct things and people that make no effort to avoid her.

"Hi, Jackie," a voice says.

"Hi," she answers, not pausing or lifting her head. When she reaches the far end of the corridor she stops and crouches between the couch and the wall. Hiding in plain sight.

Later she sits in her chair, head thrust outwards like a turtle's, eyes staring at the stains and dirt on the clothes she never changes, skin and nails full of grime, mouth rimmed with old spittle. Strands of dark, greasy hair part around her face to reveal sudden, arbitrary streaks of bleached white. Near her Elizabeth sits as she does every day from 8.00 a.m., dressed and made up for the office, never talking or moving except to answer the summons of a bell or light a cigarette or throw a quick, bright smile at a male aide passing by.

The morning share-out of medications and cigarettes-on-request and the counselling and arts and crafts and group discussion sessions are done for today. By now I understand that they're all part of the system—the bell which summons us to begin and end our days and for meals and meetings; a sort of roll call for medications; privileges granted or withheld through a careful arrangement of reward and punishment; guards who they call attendants whose job is to enforce order when medication can't.

There he goes—the guard in charge—a fat, joyless man who boasts that he preaches in church on Sundays.

It's our free time now, time when we're allowed to regulate our own activities within their tight boundaries. In the lobby Pam, Wanda and I draw chairs around a table to play cards with Kay. I deal, my hands shaking. Wanda whistles the tune she always whistles. Pam complains that her psychiatrist told her that morning that he's leaving, that she hates him but doesn't want him to leave because she's accustomed to him. "The sonofabitch!" she screams. "He don't care what I feel!"

"Quiet," Ellen mutters. "Ain't nobody interested in your games." Kay calls, "Diamonds." Then, "John, you know, my boyfriend?"

We play cards until the bell sounds for lunch; afterwards all of us are sent to the dorm to rest for an hour, then the four of us play cards again until dinner. The business of the ward goes on around us. New women enter, some already quiet and subdued, others loudly resistant. A few have been here before and when they enter some of the nurses greet them like old friends. "Hey Debbie, how ya doin'?" they shout, as if in welcome. "How ya doin'?" At night we're allowed music, and a middle-aged woman sits near the stereo spreading rouge carefully over her face, listening to Isaac Hayes lament that one woman's making his home while another one's making him do wrong. A baby-faced young girl stands over the card players, staring at us with old, watchful eyes, chattering in a high-pitched voice in a language no one else understands. We play cards until the bell sounds for bed.

THURSDAY

Another morning. Psychiatrists and nurses and aides and guards bustle about, rushing to meetings, checking charts, preparing the day's routine. Elizabeth sits silent in the lobby; Jackie hides in the corner of the corridor; Wanda whistles the tune she always whistles; Pam, Ellen, and Debbie bicker; other women sit and stare, their days shaped only by the bell that summons them to food and medication.

For the group meetings they put us together as usual, the women who they've given limited freedom of movement. Pam complains about her psychiatrist leaving. Wanda asks if she can go up to the top floor whenever she chooses, without escort now, to buy sodas and we vote yes.

Debbie and Ellen, too, get what they request. Pam asks if she can get back her street privileges so she can go for short walks and come back, and when we vote no she throws a chair across the room. We fall into a guarded, measured silence then the psychiatrist murmurs soothingly.

"God damn you," Wanda shouts. "It's as if we was idiots or children." The bell sounds for lunch. The day stretches long; when we've finished eating it's only one o'clock. Four of us draw chairs around the table and play cards. Near the door a new patient draws shapes on a board like a child, smiling eagerly, like a child, asking if her pictures are pretty. Someone groans softly, "Ohmygodohmygodohmygod." Debbie goes to another room to look for an aide to teach her how to put on her make-up. "I'm gonna make that man beg me to come home!" she yells. We call out to Kay to come play cards in Debbie's place and she smiles, sucking the end of one long braid and saying, "I don't know why John left me." Wanda calls "spades." Ellen shouts out "Cigarette time!" and we rush to form a line outside the nurses' station, to wait to be handed one cigarette each from the boxes kept there behind a locked door. We play cards and talk, not answering each other. Learning nothing about each other. Conspiring with each other to remain invisible.

And yet, holding on to each other for dear life.

SATURDAY

Kay died yesterday.

In the morning, early, she came to me and said, "John, you know, my boyfriend?"

"Later, Kay, later," I replied. Then I ran behind her as she walked away sucking the end of her braid, and repeated, "Later."

"Wanda," she said "you know ..."

"Later, Kay, later."

Later.

Later Kay stood in the corridor, stopping each patient, each nurse, each psychiatrist, each aide and guard to ask, and they all answered as they rushed by that they would talk to her later.

Later she went to the elevator and when the guard there told her she didn't have street privileges she waited till his back was turned, crossed the room to the door, found he'd left it unlocked and unattended behind some visitors who had just left, and went out.

Later we looked for her to play cards. She wasn't there. I ran to the sixth floor, the ninth floor, the eleventh floor, using for the first time the privileges I'd recently won. I couldn't find her. I ran to the exit door of the building and stopped, frightened by the brightness of the sun. Suddenly I saw some nurses coming back from lunch and I ran towards them screaming "Kay's gone!"

"It's alright," they said soothingly. "It's alright." And I went back, grateful to hand over responsibility.

Last night we sat talking about everything except Kay. Across the room Jackie sat slouched in a chair, her mouth slack and dribbling. Wanda said suddenly, "You know when I first came here I was frightened by Jackie, frightened I'd get like her ..."

"Hey," objected Pam; "she's better off than me. She's numb."

"No she ain't," said Wanda. "Remember the day that Elizabeth fainted and Jackie loosened her clothes and then went to tell the nurses Elizabeth fainted?"

"Yeah," we replied wonderingly. "Yeah."

"Then she went back to sit on her chair and stare, not talking. Like she'd decided long ago she couldn't bear how things were in her life no more so she'd come here and be crazy."

We looked at each other from inside our separate fears. "Who're you?" we enquired tentatively, as you might of a shadow in a room where you'd thought you were alone. And we discovered that we'd been born continents and generations apart. "Who're you?" we asked again. "Why'd you come here?"

"Police brought me in for fighting."

"Brought myself in cos I couldn't hold it together."

"Too much load to carry."

And Debbie volunteered that she had five kids and her old man was always losing jobs because black men aren't allowed to mouth off and she'd bitch at him because she couldn't feed the kids and he'd beat her and she'd go crazy and come back here, here where she'd been sent the first time, at 13.

"Aw, screw it," Pam said quickly. "Let's play cards." We played, holding our cards up high like children holding their hands over their faces to hide. The aides brought food and drink and put on the stereo. "Get up! Get up!" they invited. "Dance!" So we danced, danced and sang like immigrants holding on to ceremonies that have no meaning in this other time and place.

Last night, no one rang the bell to send us to bed at ten.

SUNDAY

At nine o'clock they call us all to a meeting. As we enter we see more psychiatrists than usual sitting, silent and nervous. Wanda says, "Kay's dead," her voice
flat and certain.

"Noooo!" Pam screams, throwing herself to the floor, hard, banging her head
over and over and over again.

Someone whimpers. Someone else cries. They tell us she jumped from a roof
right around the corner. The guards have been waiting and run to hold us so
the nurses could administer injections. Then they led the other women away,
leaving only those of us who had played cards with Kay—and in my mind was
an image of her falling, her hands reaching up and out, clutching the wind, her
body twisting until it splintered against the concrete, pieces of flesh and bone
saying "I don't know why John left me."

"We have to leave sometime," Wanda says, and we stare at each other. A
nurse comes to call us for extra medication the psychiatrists have prescribed,
and we go with her into the almost empty room and stay there talking, each of
us wondering each time we fall silent how soon she would leave.

M: A Daughter's Tale
[circa 1982]

The police band marched in their dark, heavy uniforms, brass trumpets glistening in the sun. The children stood for hours in the heat, the boys pulling at the ties choking their necks, the girls, hair straightened and oily, protecting their starched white collars with their handkerchiefs, and when the governor came they all lifted their heads and sang "Rule Britannia." Then the boys went to college—to London, Montreal and Washington—and the girls to marriage. And M, to mothering the children she taught in school, mothering her mother as she grew old and mean into second childhood.

* * *

By the time she retired from teaching in 1975, M and her mother C had lived on top each other for more than ten years. To C's mind, the rules of blindness confined her to three rooms—her sleeping space, the washroom just off of it, and the living room to which she groped her way slowly each morning, coming to rest in the Berbice chair lined up alongside the front windows where she remained till afternoon. Although M occupied more of the terrain of the flat than her mother, they shared too much of its intimate ground, sleeping in a single bedroom divided only by two wardrobes set back to back with each other. To go to the washroom M had to pass through her mother's section; to go to the living room C had to pass through M's section; each almost never stopped as she made her way.

M would get up at six, careful not to wake C. Make her way to the washroom, careful not to startle her. Make her breakfast and call her, careful not to rush her. Take the tray to her chair, careful not to jostle her. Careful. Careful.

* * *

The two tiny bedroom sections were crowded. M's, marginally bigger than C's, had a double bed, her wardrobe, and bookshelves with the whole of her small collection of books. C's was stuffed with furniture inherited from a larger place. In addition to her double bed there was a two-door wardrobe where after her death they found all the bedroom slippers she'd received as Christmas gifts for about 20 years; next to it, a large armchair where she sat to have her morning and afternoon meals; and at its foot, an old-fashioned washstand with a basin and water pitcher decorated with tiny lilac flowers surrounded by joined-up leaves. The spaces between these four pieces of furniture were so small that she could guide herself around the room by holding on, in turn, to one piece with each hand—first the bed and wardrobe, then the wardrobe and chair, then the chair and the washstand, last the washstand and bed. Picking her way. Slow. Uncertain. The placement of the furniture in both sections, like the placement of the furniture in the living room, had not been changed in the 35 years since C became blind.

*   *   *

For the eleven or so years before M retired her physical world had not been much larger than it became afterwards. The school where she taught was less than two blocks from the house in one direction, the church she visited occasionally two blocks away in the other. For all those years she seldom went anywhere except to those three places—home, church, school—except for an occasional foray into a shop. Food for the household was bought in the market by a woman who cleaned, cooked, washed and shopped for them and occasionally provided conversation but drew the line at being used as their buffer or punching bag. Inside the school classes were divided only by blackboards over which the children's voices converged, the chant of "London is the capital of? England / And Edinburgh is the capital of? Scotland" clashing with the chant of "six ones six / six twos twelve" building to "six elevens sixty-six / six twelves seventy-two"; while somewhere close by other voices declaimed or sang "I wandered lonely as a cloud / That floats on high o'er vales and hills / When all at once I saw a crowd, / A host of golden daffodils."

*   *   *

C had been confined to the flat much longer than M, who had started to stay home all the time only when she retired. Ever since C had become blind she'd left the flat only once a year, at Christmas, when she was taken to spend the day with her son. Thirty-five years, eleven of them with both women locked in. Oh, everyone knows that the majority of people in the country lived with less space than M and C had, but other people didn't live only indoors. It's the living only inside that made the geography in which they lived their lives too small for the two of them. It's living such unmediated inward-looking lives, while physically living only inside, that did them in.

*   *   *

"Mother," M would call from the dining room. "I goin' out this afternoon." C wouldn't move from her seat in the Berbice chair or answer.

"I goin' put your tray out before I go." Still no answer.

A few minutes later, "Mother," M would say. "Here's your tray; I already carry it to your chair."

"I ain' hungry."

"Is four o'clock. That is when you always eat."

"I tell you I ain' hungry."

"I goin' leave the tray on the table in the dining room for you to pick up," M would try. "For my tea to get cold?" C'd retort.

M would wait a while longer then she'd try again. "You goin' eat now?" she'd plead.

C wouldn't answer.

"I late," M would say. "I have to go."

Still no answer.

"Mother!" she'd shout.

"Why you shouting? I blind, I ain' deaf," C would mutter.

"Is past five o'clock. You still not hungry?"

She wouldn't answer.

"I'm leaving," M would say. "Drink your tea while it still hot."

"I ain' ready," she'd answer. "Turn on the radio let me hear Dr. Paul."

M would take off her shoes and put on her house slippers and when C heard the shuffle of the slippers against the floor, she would smile.

*   *   *

Even when M was a girl she had a sense of her life being stifled, though she couldn't put the feeling into words. Sure she was happy sometimes but she was the youngest and a girl and there were too many bosses over her. Besides, all of them were restricted although the rest didn't seem to mind. Their father was an important man in the village and their bad behavior was a reflection on him, or so he said. For years she thought that when it was her turn for secondary school she'd get to escape like her brother who'd been sent to Georgetown when his time came, but no one even considered it. At least, no one ever said anything at all about it to her.

But there was one moment, later, much later, when her life seemed to open up. From the carved-in-stone of "Rule Bri/tan/nia/Bri/tan/nia rules the waves" and "girls mustn't do this and mustn't do that" and "my children can't play this or can't say that," she learned first the idea of change, and then the possibility of change, in what had seemed an immoveable world. All over the colony (as the country was in 1953) it was as though people were cleaning themselves of trench mud that had dried hard on their bodies and spirits, shrinking them. Near their flat there was a house in which women and men, old and young, different races, though most black—town workers like domestics and waterfront laborers, teachers, nurses, doctors, lawyers, small-scale farmers, clerks, unemployed women and men, even some businessmen—gathered for hours every day to do all kinds of things they'd never done before with people they'd never done anything with before. Like everyone around her M had always found it so important to hold on to her hard-earned status as a schoolteacher that she would refuse menial jobs; now she would turn her hand to any job that needed to be done. She felt connected to things and people around her, and when she heard people on the campaign platforms speaking about things and people she had only ever read about or heard about on the BBC, their names differently pronounced, having nothing to do with her, she felt connected to them too. She was taken out of herself, transported. She didn't have a clue what would become of her private life; she didn't dwell on it. She wasn't thinking now about whether she would marry or not (though sometimes it crossed her mind still that she was already 33), whether she would have children or not. Nothing in the conditions of her immediate life had changed, but she had changed. Nothing in those conditions had changed but she had changed, and so everything had changed. Everything seemed possible. Everything was possible.

Inside the home which she shared then not only with her mother but with her three sisters, and inside the homes of their closest relatives, everybody was working in the election campaign, the first time most of them would be able to vote, and the first time they had women and men to vote for who said that life could and would change. At home, M and her sisters shared the work of looking after their mother and she made the work of looking after her something that didn't feel like a burden. Taking her a meal, helping her find the clothes she wanted to wear (she could do that pretty well herself, by feel), they could talk, and did, about things outside themselves, outside the everyday, outside the old limits.

*   *   *

The years passed. Outside in the street small girls and boys were taunting a woman who walked for miles each day, a cloth covering her eyes.

"Mad lady, mad lady, why yuh tie up yuh eye?"

"Because Guyana not fit tuh be seen," she answered.

"Like you ain' mad lady," laughed another woman passing by.

The election had been won; leaders had quarreled for power then reached a compromise; troops had invaded; a constitution had been suspended; leaders had been imprisoned; leaders had split first this way then that way till town workers and country workers went their separate ways, and rich and poor lined up on the same side provided they were the same race, and she went one way then the other, trusted by neither, and to cut a long story short (but how to cut it short when it has never ended?) people who had been together ratted on each other and killed each other and raped girls and women and said that all they did was in self-protection or at worst in revenge for what was done to them— and her sisters, married, left, and she was left, her life closed tighter and more airless than it had ever been before, whittled down to less than it was before, till all that was left was the life of the unmarried, youngest, grown girl child, all alone mothering her mother as she grew bitter into old age.

ESSAY 19

Against the Beating of Children: Submission to a Parliamentary Sub-committee on the Corporal Punishment of Children
[2013]

The Clerk of the Committee

Special Select Committee on Guyana's Commitment to the United Nations Human Rights Council with Regard to the Abolition of Corporal Punishment in the Schools, the Abolition of the Death Penalty and the Decriminalization of Consensual Adult Same Sex Relations and Discrimination against Lesbians, Gays, Bi-Sexual and Transgender Persons (Resolution No. 23 of 2012 Committees Division)

Dear Sir/Madam,

Re: Submission on the attitude of Guyanese, especially parents and children, to corporal punishment and its possible abolition

My name is Andaiye and I am a member of Red Thread which is making other submissions, but I also want to make a brief one in my own name.

More than 40 years ago, when I was 27 or 28 years old, I was an acting head teacher, part of an experiment introduced by then minister of education Shirley Field-Ridley, to see whether young head teachers could break with the old authoritarian practices of our schools, including corporal punishment. The day I informed staff members that there would be no beating in our school, a teacher near retirement age told me that I had taken away his "authority."

I believed then, as I do now, that in the relationship between teacher and student the teacher has to have authority. I understand that it's not a relationship between equivalents. Equals but not equivalents. These are two people of different ages, different levels of experience, different responsibilities, and different roles to play in ensuring that the school carry out its teaching/learning function. But I was amazed then, and I remain amazed now, that any adult would be willing to signal to a child that the basis of his/her "authority" is a cane or a ruler or a belt or a whip. Just like the man on a horse, subduing enslaved women and men with his whip while they seethe inside with a rage that will either burst out in rebellion or be turned inwards.

I don't tell this (true) story because I'm unaware that conditions in the society and therefore in our schools have changed drastically. I tell it only because what I hear proponents of corporal punishment in our schools saying today is exactly what my colleague was saying to me all those many years ago: that removing the teacher's right to inflict corporal punishment removes his/her authority. What they really mean is that it alters the power relation between teacher and student in favor of the student; it makes it impossible to get the student to submit. But submission should not be what we want to teach.

I grew up at a time when few would argue against the proposition that corporal punishment was not only acceptable but necessary. Various letter writers of my generation have argued that it is because we "got licks" that we've turned out well. These included men whom I knew (not thought, knew) to be wife-beaters. They had never been taught how to reason. Reason is what we need to teach.

No one I know is advocating that teachers who have been taught reliance on corporal punishment be suddenly cast adrift without any knowledge of alternative ways of exercising authority. What we want an end to is a policy that says that hitting any adult is a bad, even a criminal act, while hitting a child is for his/her own good.

All human history is a battle between two broad tendencies: one, pushing for expanding rights and freedoms, the other, resisting change and holding on to a status quo which works for those who have power. I'm not a great believer that parliament as an institution can lead change, but I would never deny that in Guyana, successive parliaments—some with a PNC majority, others with a PPP majority—have done a good job of increasing the legal rights of women in particular, especially their right to live free of violence. Those changes in the law were opposed too, sometimes from within the parties themselves. No one took a poll to ask the people whether they agreed that it was wrong to beat women, not because they were less democratic than you are, but because—talk for sun, talk for rain—they had the courage not to hide behind a pretense of democratic consultation. You can do no less for Guyana's children.

Yours sincerely,
Andaiye.

ESSAY 20
Three Letters against Sexual Violence against Children
[2010]

1. JUSTICE FOR CHILD VICTIMS OF SEXUAL VIOLENCE NOW!

Dear Editor,

Kaieteur News (May 9, "Rights of the Child Commission sworn in") reported President Jagdeo as describing the recent and ongoing protest by the Coalition to Stamp out Violence as "cheap" because the protestors "knew that the government had to take care of a busy parliamentary agenda which included crucial security legislation, such as wire-tapping …"

The report has not been denied. If it is correct the criticism is unworthy of a head of state. If we are so short of people to draft legislation that the government has to choose between "crucial security legislation" and providing children with crucial security against acts of sexual violence which destroy their lives, then finding the personnel and expertise we need is a national emergency.

Do we hear the children when they cry?

- The four-month-old girl with "thrush" in her mouth which turned out to be layers of a neighbor's semen.
- The three-year-old boy whose policeman father tore his anus open.
- The six-year-old girl whose womb was destroyed by a 35-year-old neighbor.
- The 13-year-old girl raped by a 72-year-old man.
- The five boys, aged 6–8, raped by a businessman.
- The two boys aged 9 and 11 whose father has been raping them since they were 7 and 9.

These few examples come from newspaper reports and from cases which have been brought to our attention.

Why have we come out on the streets *now* to call for justice for children who have been victims of sexual violence?

1. We decided at a meeting in March 2009 sponsored by Red Thread and Help and Shelter to mark International Women's Day to step up the campaign to stamp out sexual violence against children. We want to bring the attention of all—government, opposition, what is called "civil society" and the general public—to the horrors of this violence because we believe that if more

people and groups and institutions could "see" this violence they would be spurred to immediate action.

2. We were pushed to come out onto the streets when a man was recently charged with buggery of a 15-year-old boy because we have no legislation at present to charge him with what he would have been charged with if his victim had been a 15-year-old girl—rape. In fact, it is only the homophobia of our present laws that permitted him to be charged at all.

3. We decided to follow through with our plans to come out onto the streets after we heard that the legislation may shortly be placed before parliament because we wanted to say to the government and to the opposition that we are watching and that any further delay for any reason whatsoever would be intolerable. We want the legislation and we want it now.

We also want to say to all those organizations in the private sector and the trade unions that say they are concerned with "national" issues—bringing an end to sexual violence against children is a national issue, surely one on which we can all agree and around which we can all unite in active struggle. We want to say to the ethnic organizations—this brutality is being inflicted on children of all races; are children not part of the race you defend? We want to say to the religious organizations which rise up against what they define as evil—rise up against sexual violence against children in Guyana, which is one of the worst evils imaginable.

Do we hear the children when they cry?

Signed,

Andaiye

Red Thread

2.   RED THREAD IS NEVER SILENT ON ANY ISSUE, PARTICULARLY SEXUAL VIOLENCE

Dear Editor,

We write in response to recent letters attacking Red Thread, among others, for our public silence on the allegations made against C. N. Sharma.[1]

The most recent we've seen is one published in the *Guyana Times* of Thursday, April 22, titled "Is the response to Sharma's case because of the girl's poverty or the accused prominence?" No doubt it has also been published, or soon will be, in the *Chronicle*.

Red Thread deals with all too many cases of child sexual violence. In all of these cases, we think that we and all who care about children need to take the following steps:

1. work (if possible with the relevant authorities) to ensure the safety of the child alleging the violence;
2. again with the relevant authorities, if possible, take care that the child's statement will be admissible in court; and
3. avoid any action, including any publicity that might compromise the case.

We have found this last to be especially critical for two reasons:

One, the readiness of some of our most prominent and "respectable" lawyers to use any ammunition provided to destroy children to save their clients and justify their fees; and two, the readiness of people with power to use that power completely without scruples to protect their friends.

This is why we believe that while our institutions are very weak and frequently don't respond as the law requires them to, our task is to "kick start" them rather than attempt to go around them in ways that act against the interests of the victims of sexual violence.

In relation to the allegations made against C. N. Sharma, Red Thread was asked to see the child and we did what we always do: we heard what she had to say, advised her about her options, and reassured her that she was doing nothing wrong by coming forward. We then stayed in contact with the Child Care and Protection Agency about the safety of all of the children named in the affidavit she made.

C. N. Sharma's supporters outside the court, the prison and the police station and in minibuses everywhere have been drawing parallels between the treatment of the earlier allegations against Kwame McCoy and today's allegations against him.[2] Some of them are proclaiming his innocence, but many are in effect saying that it doesn't matter whether or not he is innocent. Their line is, "You (the Government and ruling PPP) din lock up McCoy, loose Sharma." In other words, "you protect you own, we protecting we own."

This is what we get when people in the highest places play politics with the lives and safety of children.

The reported statement by the PPP that all, high and low, must stand equal before the law, is a level of hypocrisy that would be hard to beat.

While we must ensure that adults who are innocent of charges of child sexual abuse are exonerated, we have an absolute obligation to see to it that every single one of them who is guilty as charged is locked away in jail; all, regardless of which party they belong to, or none. Till now, the law has been stacked against the children who allege that they were sexually abused.

That is why we picketed every week for almost a year for the Sexual Offences Legislation to be passed. We believe that properly implemented, it will serve as protection against the barbaric acts that too many adults (overwhelmingly men) are perpetrating against our children.

But we will still have to deal with how our increasingly party-politicized culture works against the interests of the children. While we piously mouth that "children are our future," we are destroying their present as we play political games on their bodies.

Signed,

Andaiye, Karen de Souza

Red Thread

3.   FOR NEESA GOPAUL[3]

Dear Editor,

Nothing can make up for the last tortured year of Neesa Gopaul's life and the failure of adults to give her the help she asked for; the least we can do now is to face her without defensiveness, scapegoating and/or political game-playing.

Minister Manickchand [Minister of Human Services and Social Security] has initiated an investigation into the breaching of protocols by officers of the Child Care and Protection Agency who allegedly failed to report to supervisors that they had lost contact with Neesa. Minister Rohee [Minister of Home Affairs] has blamed the Leonora Police Station and the community policing groups of D division in West Demerara. Dr. Luncheon, Head of the Presidential Secretariat, proclaimed that "a range of entities" were at fault. On his own behalf or on behalf of the cabinet, he also found that the Sexual Offences Act and other aspects of the criminal law "all failed to operate in the interests of this young child," apparently unaware that the structures and procedures to implement the Sexual Offences Act have not yet been put in place.

The old Minister Manickchand (she's changed) would have been open to the view that while the tragedy of Neesa Gopaul is unique in the horror of it, there is a broader failure to protect our children in spite of all the good legislation we have passed.

To address domestic and sexual violence against the vulnerable, the government has prioritized legislation and produced laws which have often been well in advance of the laws in other parts of the region. But as has been remarked repeatedly, laws are only a beginning. Our co-worker Alissa Trotz made the point in her "Diaspora" column on October 25, that what we have to face is that as laws proliferate, so does the violence.[4] We don't pretend to understand all the reasons why, but for now, we want to raise examples of two kinds of issues that must be faced, practical and political.

First, the practical:

1. Laws need to be supported by the mechanics of implementation, which is where the first failing lies. It is quite possible that the investigation will find that officials of the Child Care and Protection Agency breached protocols.

Red Thread as just one organization has its own experience of officers of the Ministry of Human Services and those of the police and courts ignoring protocols. Or it might find that the fault lies with supervisors. Whatever conclusion it reaches, we know that there are incompetent, uncaring check-back-tomorrow bureaucrats in the various protective services. We also know that the services do some good work, although whether one's business is dealt with well can seem largely a function of luck. But anyone accessing the social welfare system would also recognize that it is seriously under-skilled, under-resourced and over-tasked. The laws we are so rightly proud of in fact add to the officers' burden of work, without a proportionate rise in resources to do the work.

Officers have too many cases, and are responsible for too much territory. They are inadequately supported by other institutions, for example, by the Ministry of Education honoring its promise to have a welfare officer in every school. The physical environment in which they deal with those who come to them for help does not reflect a valuing of caring work—either the unwaged caring work of the parents and guardians who consult the services, or the waged caring work of the child protection officers, both groups mainly women. There are no built-in arrangements for the officers to receive the emotional support they need after the hours they spend dealing with other people's crises. Nothing in all this helps to produce what we need—social workers who are not narrow bureaucrats but people who are passionately on the side of the vulnerable, with the skills to support children staying with their families/mothers as long as this is the best option and to save children from their families/mothers where this is necessary. In the Ministry of Human Services and Social Security as in other Ministries, it is too easy to lay blame (only) at the door of individual officers at whatever level, while the Government responsible for providing the conditions in which they can work effectively is not held accountable and does not hold itself accountable.

2. Laws also have to be supported by an informed public. Minister Manickchand has made much of the protocols which were not observed in the case of Neesa Gopaul. It would help if the protocols were not treated like a secret but made public knowledge. All public agencies which have contact with the vulnerable or injured need to publish the protocols and procedures for dealing with reports and complaints, to begin with schools, health centers, hospitals, social services, and police. We must know what we have a right to expect from these agencies, and we must have some place where we can effectively appeal if the promised attention is not being given to a matter. In other words, we must demand that the system open up to organized monitoring from outside to ensure that weaknesses and malpractices are corrected before more tragedies occur.

These practical steps would help. The legal reform of which many have repeatedly spoken and written is essential. But none of this would be enough.

There must be political change—that is, change in how we treat caring work and carers. Laws designed to protect children, in particular, can reduce their vulnerability only when the work of caring for children, whether one's own children or the children of other parents, is counted; and when the society does not find it acceptable that so many poor people, in particular mothers, are earning money to feed their children under conditions that force them to neglect their children's other needs—earning money as security guards with 12 hour shifts, or as waitresses in small restaurants sometimes with shifts as long as 16 hours, or as migrant workers who leave behind children who have to look after themselves for weeks, months, and even years.

And finally here, political will demonstrated in more than good legislation is also required. Laws designed to protect the vulnerable against abuse also have to be supported by an unshakeable political will that those who are abused will be defended regardless of the power of their abusers. What we have instead is an attitude that says that "if the abuser is one of us, we duck the issue; if he is one of them we go after him."

As we said, nothing can make up for the last tortured year of Neesa Gopaul's life and the failure of adults to give her the help she asked us for—but we can try to identify and implement the reforms we need, which go far deeper than defensiveness, scapegoating or political game-playing are willing to see.

Yours sincerely,
Andaiye, Karen de Souza
Red Thread

ACKNOWLEDGEMENTS

Letter 1 was published in *Stabroek News*, March 16, 2010. Letter 2 was published in *Kaieteur News*, April 24, 2010. Letter 3 was published in *Stabroek News*, October 13, 2010.

NOTES

1. C. N. Sharma, a well-known political party leader and television station owner and host, was charged in April 2010 with carnal knowledge of a 13-year-old. A Preliminary Inquiry committed him to stand trial, but when the case came up for trial in the High Court, Sharma's reported ill health caused numerous delays. (The case did not come up for trial till 2016, by which time his victim was 19 years old and said that she did not wish to give evidence; the charges against him were dismissed.)
2. Kwame McCoy served as the press and publicity officer at the Office of the President under the PPP Administration; allegations (that remain unresolved) of sexual abuse of a child were also made against him.

3. This letter has been very slightly edited. Accounts after 16-year-old Neesa Gopaul's death indicated that she had been physically and possibly sexually abused following her father's death in 2009. School and Child Care Agency interventions resulted in her living with her grandparents for a while, but it would appear that at some point the responsible agencies dropped the ball. Neesa was murdered and her body stuffed in a suitcase which was dumped at an abandoned resort 45 minutes from the city. Her mother and the mother's lover were found guilty of her murder and sentenced to life imprisonment in 2015.
4. D. Alissa Trotz, "Law and Violence," *Stabroek News*, October 25, 2010.

Knife Edge: Living with Domestic and Economic Violence
[2013]

Asked to speak about violence against African-Guyanese women, I was perhaps expected to deal with domestic violence alone, but I thought I could best bring alive the totality of the violence against African-Guyanese women in the short time I have by describing the violence in the life of one African-Guyanese woman—first, after years of emotional violence from her partner, the single, barbaric act of physical violence which altered her life permanently; and second, the everyday economic violence inflicted on her as it is on other women like her. My objective in putting these together is to make what is for me a self-evident point—that the life of this woman cannot be transformed except if we confront the power relations that underlie both the domestic and the economic violence.

On August 5, 2000, Sonia Hinds was crippled by her male partner. A later video interview with Red Thread shows her leaning over a large wooden tub washing clothes. She is rubbing them with soap, using the stumps of her arms, both of which had been chopped off below the elbow. She recounts how on the day of the assault the man had come up behind her and dealt her a blow with what she thought was a leather belt. As he continued she put up her arms to bar the blows. It was only when he stopped and she tried to use her arms to get up from the floor where she had fallen that she realized that she had been chopped, not hit, and that her lower arms were hanging, attached only by pieces of skin. He had also chopped her across her face. That one day she lost her hands and the sight in an eye. The man who disabled her for life received a 15-year sentence. In the video she recounted that she had entered a relationship with him because she wanted a decent and stable life, the father of her children having been a married man. Sonia Hinds was in her early forties at the time of the assault.

Before then she had worked as a security guard and a seamstress, supporting herself and her children. Afterwards, she received severance pay since she was unable to continue the security guard work. Now she depends on an NIS disability benefit and public assistance, which together give her far less than she needs for basic expenses.

Sonia Hinds lives with the results of her partner's violence: permanent impoverishment (no employer would want her); loneliness (no man would want her); isolation (she goes out very little); dependence (while she does some of her housework herself—her daughters are now grown and live away—she can't cook or clean so she needs the help she gets from a niece). Her life having been upended by her partner's brutality, she lives every day with the memory of it, and with the silence that is the response of too much of our society to the war against women which results in one of every three or four women in Guyana being victims of domestic violence. It is a war not only against African-Guyanese women but against Indian-Guyanese and Indigenous women and women of other groups. It is waged not only against women of the working class but against women of all classes; but women of the working class have the least resources to escape it.

There is another kind of violence that affects African-Guyanese working class women. Like Sonia Hinds before she was chopped, many thousands of working class African-Guyanese women work in very low-waged areas of work with little or no legal protection. Usually, like her, they operate in at least two areas of work at the same time, often more. Most work in the massive informal sector which exploded into being in the 1980s.

This violence is assaulting African-Guyanese women, in particular. It is not that there is no economic violence against grassroots women of other races or against grassroots men. There is plenty. Among African-Guyanese the situation of working class men is also dire. But the economic violence against poor people has a particular impact on African-Guyanese women and therefore on African-Guyanese children.

On October 7, 2012, I had a letter in the press responding to an article celebrating a 39-year-old African-Guyanese single mother of five boys who also worked as a security guard, sweeper/cleaner, drainage worker, including on Sundays, maker and seller of pointer brooms, grower and seller of plants, and maker and bottler of products like pepper sauce with other women. That's one woman. She had no electricity, which made most household tasks take longer. Her workday added up to at least 20 hours (not counting many of her household tasks, including checking that the children had done the tasks they were assigned to do; that they'd attended the lessons she sent them to in part so they would be "meaningfully occupied" while she earned money—$10,000 of which went to pay for the lessons; and all the other tasks of raising five boys aged 9–13 to not become statistics of "failure." She also took Home Economics, Maths and English classes in the hope that they would lead to better-paid jobs.

For every mother who manages to ensure that her children don't become statistics of failure, at whatever cost to herself and them, there's a larger number of mothers who don't succeed. They are all around us. In the main, they fail not because they are "wutless." To say only that they are examples of the continuing legacy of slavery doesn't make sense, because if that is the whole story then why is the situation today worse, as we can all see that it is? No. They are also continuing victims of a way of organizing the economy which creates poverty and then criminalizes it; which imposes on poor families a choice between being superhuman or being beaten down by inhuman conditions;

which destroys families without a care—today, via a massive migratoriness of labor in a world where capital can travel freely but not labor,[1] and where labor therefore migrates under conditions that tears families apart, and is tearing apart the kind of extended family and community which was the bedrock of African-Guyanese survival. Look, for example, at what's happening with the CARICOM Free Movement of People where CARICOM says you can travel, but individual governments fail to introduce the mechanisms which would allow you to place your children in school in the country you're migrating to work in. So you have to leave them. For me, these are root causes.

In most discussions on African-Guyanese and the economy, the focus tends to be on the deliberate acts of economic sabotage against our ancestors as they worked to build the villages they bought after slavery; plus today, on the impact of corruption, nepotism, cronyism and discrimination on the African-Guyanese economy. But if we found a way to end today's corruption, nepotism, cronyism and discrimination, as we must, and maintained the dominant economic model and policies, the problems would not be solved. There would still be fundamental problems deriving from how capitalism and most clearly, unregulated, unbridled, unrestrained, predatory capitalism works; how it is set up to work even if racism is not the prime motivator; the role played by International Monetary Fund (IMF) policies which here we call Structural Adjustment and in Europe they call "austerity." We know those policies are not class-neutral, but seem to ignore the fact that they're also neither race-neutral (in Guyana cuts in the public sector, including in the 1980s, put many African-Guyanese women and men out of work), nor gender-neutral (when you cut public spending you increase the unwaged caring work that is done mainly by women).

Ending the corruption, nepotism, cronyism and discrimination would not by itself solve the problem of what is happening at the level of the household economies of poor people—which requires us to look for the solution where it belongs, and that cannot be just at the level of the individual household. A *Stabroek News* editorial of Thursday, October 18, last, which salutes two mothers, the one we just heard about and the other, a newspaper vendor, who, it said, "scrimped, scraped and saved to send her third child to university and law school," seemed to be proposing that we can end poverty by individual sacrifice, which—according to the editorial—can start "a revolution against poverty." On August 2, 2013, less than a year later, the media had another report on the same woman: she is the mother in Sophia whose husband chopped her and their children on Emancipation Night, including the one who is now a lawyer.

Even if you do not encounter these women in your daily life you see them on the TV when someone has interfered further with their ability to earn—not a living but a partial living: "I'se a single mother with five children and now they want to move my stall and wuh they expect me fuh do?" They are security guards, street vendors, domestic workers, low-cost seamstresses or street-side givers of pedicures and manicures, mini bus conductors, shop assistants, cooks, cleaners or waitresses in cook shops, sex workers. They work unbelievable hours. They often have no one at home, not even an older child, to care for the other children. The other relatives who would once have taken up the slack, including sometimes the other parent, are either somewhere else in the country or out of the country trying to earn money. Worse, we have families without a single resident parent or guardian. Men are part of the huge migrations we are seeing today but more women than men are migrating in the Caribbean. We have mothers who are "catching dey hand" in another country while their children "catching dey tail" living on their own or moving from house to house, because both immediate families and extended families have scattered. In the letter I went on:

> Only a fool would say there are no bad mothers among us; clearly there are. But there are far more who are "mothers extraordinaire" (the term *Stabroek News* used). Some succeed in raising their children on the "straight and narrow" and deserve honor. But when we ignore or demonize the others who also deserve our respect even though their hard work does not lift their families out of poverty, then the mothers themselves, their children, and the whole society—all of us pay.

What a member of the audience has called a "vision of liberation" has to be seen from the point of view of Sonia Hinds, the woman whose story says to me that we have to build a movement not only against the injustices of sex or the injustices of race, but against the economic system that we increasingly treat as a given, immovable, and which exploits and oppresses Sonia Hinds via the unequal power relations of sex, race, class, age, dis/ability and nation. Nothing less can liberate her.

ACKNOWLEDGEMENTS

An earlier version of this essay was presented at a forum on "The State of Black African Guyana: a time for renewal and empowerment," organized by the Ghana Day Committee in collaboration with the Cuffy 250 Committee held on Sunday, August 4, 2013. Since that original was lost, it's been recreated here partly from memory and partly from a newspaper report on the talk in *Stabroek News*, August 5, 2013.

NOTE

1. One of the Global Women's Strike demands is "Capital travels freely—why not labor?"

Women as Collateral Damage in Race Violence
[2002]

We're discussing race relations in Guyana in a context of increased violence, some of it reportedly aimed at forcing the government to a political solution. Some non-violent protest is said to have the same aim. Various players have said that the costs we are paying are necessary costs to achieve this solution: there's an echo here of George Bush's collateral damage. At the risk of being called (again) hopelessly naïve and "typical of a woman" I want to ask again—on whose bodies will this solution be constructed?

In all the calculations made by different sides, the bodies counted are those of the police or civilians killed by usually unknown and uncaught assailants and the bodies of those killed by the police on the grounds that they are wanted. But a woman's perhaps naïve body count would include bodies hurt in another kind of assault. Let me back up a bit to make the point.

Women and children are always, everywhere, the main victims of war—for example, we are 80 percent of refugees worldwide. But women are also the main victims in other ways. In Guyana, African-Guyanese mothers have been the main victims of incidents where police have shot into unarmed crowds of protestors, because they have been at the forefront of street protests, and it would strike those who are willing to hear them, how often they say that they are fighting because they want the means to feed and school their children. To say that they are shot because they are protesting is to agree that there is no right to even peaceful protest.

But there are other women in Guyana who are victims, this time of the sexual humiliation and abuse that is typical of all race/ethnic/religious conflict—and these victims are overwhelmingly, though not exclusively, Indo-Guyanese women. This is the body count I choose to talk about today.

I choose it firstly, because I am Afro-Guyanese, and secondly, because our inability to say factually what the acts of humiliation and abuse have been without either exaggerating numbers or dismissing their importance, and to collectively condemn them as unequivocally wrong, is the clearest example of how, in Guyana, race and ethnicity have come to supersede class, sex, and all other markers, including humanness. I choose it finally, to remind other Guyanese women that in times of peace, we have agreed, across race, that the sexual subjugation of women—no matter who the subjugator(s)—is the worst expression of the subjugation of women, and one against which we would fight.

I want to begin by referring briefly to three examples outside Guyana of the sexual abuse of women as a military objective in racial/ethnic/religious conflict, in the hope that reminding ourselves of how global the phenomenon is, can help us out of our normal attack/defense mode, when the issue is seen as "only" local. Two of my examples are deliberately from Africa and Asia:

- *One*: During the Rwanda war, hundreds of thousands of women were individually raped, gang-raped with objects such as sharp sticks or gun barrels, held in sexual slavery or sexually mutilated. During the trial of a former mayor for war crimes, Rwandan women testified that they had been subjected to repeated collective rape by militia in and around the commune office, including in view of the mayor.
- *Two*: During the partition war in India, as many as one hundred thousand women from different communities were abducted and raped, and recently, during the surges in communal violence in Gujarat, rape and sexual violence against women were prevalent, with women telling of being gored in the stomach, having a foetus ripped out, or having sticks inserted in their vaginas.
- *Three*: During the breakup of Yugoslavia, untold numbers of women were victims of sexual violence, and it was the horrors of Yugoslavia which gave us the description of these violations as rape not out of control, but rape under control.

And in Guyana:

- In the 1960s, while we know that the reporting was not comprehensive, the overwhelming evidence is of the sexual humiliation and abuse of Indo-Guyanese women and girls (there is the Wismar report, as well as recent information via Eusi Kwayana).

There is also evidence of some incidents of sexual humiliation and abuse of Afro-Guyanese women (see documentation by Eusi Kwayana 1999):

- In the 1990s, according to the Guyana Indian Foundation Trust (GIFT) report whose numbers I have no reason to reject, 34 percent of the 228 victims were women, and of these, 52 percent were physically and sexually abused. The sexual abuse was often stripping. The fear in the testimonies, as in similar testimonies from women elsewhere, is palpable, but a few of them give us hope that we can move out of this zero sum position.
- In the present upsurge of conflict, I know of at least one incident of a man putting his penis in a woman's mouth. There are uncontested reports of incidents of the stripping of women during attacks on mini-buses and

robberies; and there is the chopping off of Anita Singh's hair, accompanied by a verbal racist assault.

All the incidents, except one recently reported during a robbery, were against Indo-Guyanese women.

I want to intervene here to suggest that the media contribute heavily to the growing fragmentation of the society by what they choose to focus on. On March 8, 2002, 140 women were organized by Red Thread to march in Linden as part of a global strike of women held every year since 2000 in more than 60 countries. Most of the 140 Indo-Guyanese, Afro-Guyanese, Amerindian, and mixed race women in the march were not alive in the early 1960s. But as a new generation they were willing to subscribe to the following words in the handbill we distributed:

[Ours] … is a struggle of women of all races for women of all races. Because Wismar was a symbol of the terrible racial violence of the 1960s, we, the women, send out this call—Let us make Linden a symbol of how women can cross race divides and fight for a world which values all women's work and all women's lives!

Red Thread informed all the media about our action, but none of them found this attempt at reconciliation important enough to cover.

I'll close with a number of general points about the sexual abuse of women during violent ethnic, religious and racial conflict:

- Across the globe, all the kinds of conflict I've mentioned—ethnic, religious, racial—result in the same atrocities, whether on a small scale or a large scale. (Look at the recurrences in testimonies—stripping naked, sexual taunting, objects being inserted in the vagina, women being forced to take penises in their mouths.) In different degrees, all the conflicts are also about politics and about power.
- The point about sexually abusing or humiliating a woman of the "other side" is to humiliate the men of the "other side." As Devaki Jain said, it is "the idea that women are the 'nation' and dishonoring them is dishonoring the nation." She adds that in these cases men rape or brutalize women, meaning it as an insult to the honor of the men of the nation. Himani Bannerji says we are talking about the conversion of women into metaphors for a race or country, not as real persons.
- Women who are sexually humiliated and abused in race/ethnic/religious conflict are silenced in four ways:
  1. *through fear of reprisal;*
  2. *through shame and fear:* a Kosovo Albanian woman, Drita, raped by a Serb policeman and another man who waited till the policeman

finished before taking his turn reported that when she asked her husband what would happen to their marriage "if" she was raped, he answered "I would never keep you";

3. *through the response of men* of their own "side" who, in defense of "their" women, think of the assault in the same way the rapists did— as dishonoring them or their group, the women only the objects of the dishonoring; and

4. *through the response of women* of the same race/ethnicity/religion as the abusers who participate in the abuse or incite it, or just as bad, fail to condemn it.

In Guyana, the reasons for silence vis-a-vis the violence against Indo-Guyanese women include fear of playing into the racism of others, particularly about black men; and resentment that the ways in which Afro-Guyanese are oppressed/ assaulted/humiliated are not taken into account. I feel and have felt both of these.

As we all know, sexual humiliation and abuse are not only carried out during race/ethnic/religious conflict by men of the other race, but daily, within the family, often by men of the same race. The point is not to downplay the first kind of abuse but to show its connections to the other kind. The woman of "the other side" who is sexually humiliated and abused is being humiliated and abused both because of her race/ethnicity/religion, and because of her sex. We do not find, in any country, many examples of men stripped naked or having objects pushed into their bodies. Being female is almost a precondition to this kind of assault.[1]

The clearest expression of how race hate and woman hate can converge is from a self-styled revolutionary of the 1960s or 1970s who explained that he was raping black women to improve his skills to rape white women for the liberation of black people. He was raping me to practice how to rape you to liberate me. Sexual violence is targeted, but any of us may become an incidental victim of men who think in this way.

Finally, we do not have to agree on whether a cause is legitimate to agree that not all means are legitimate. I choose to single out the sexual violation of women as manifestly illegitimate and immoral except to people who are sick. It doesn't matter if it is still on a small scale. It doesn't matter whether it is planned or unplanned. Leaders are guilty not only when they plan these assaults or incite them, but when, knowing that they will occur because they always do, they do nothing to prevent them; and when they happen, excuse them or dismiss or call them regrettable but acceptable side effects of a necessary struggle. Collateral damage.

In Guyana, our refusal or inability to see the fears and oppressions of the "other side" is crippling us and will cripple us even if a "political solution" is created on top of it. And our preoccupation with the conflict between Afro-and Indo-Guyanese continues to deafen us to the demands of the Indigenous people. So far, the way we have been talking about power sharing has been dangerously limited to how the two main race groups, as represented by the two main political parties, will share power there—at the top.

Even though the efforts that women have made so far to come together across race and party in defence of women who have been abused have yielded little, we have to keep working. Most women are incapable of being as cavalier as most men about "collateral damage"—perhaps because we give birth to and raise and care for the persons who constitute this "collateral damage." This is the point that Mothers in Black has been making for two years now[2]—that they gave birth to and raised children only to see a society accept that their lives were worth nothing.

It is clear that for most Guyanese women, the strongest identity they feel is their race/ethnic identity. But maybe, if we see ourselves as women, capable of thinking freely, without party blinders, we can return to the position that we reached so readily when we were organizing for Beijing—that the sexual subjugation of women can never, ever, be acceptable to us, whoever the subjugator(s), whatever the cause.

ACKNOWLEDGEMENTS

This essay was originally titled "Notes on Women and Ethnic Conflict, Part 1" and presented on Thursday, August 15, 2002 at the National Library, Georgetown. The presentation has been lightly edited.

NOTES

1. This last point is not one I would make in that way now. The evidence still is that many more women than men are subject to sexual assault, but being female is not "a pre-condition."
2. A collective of mothers founded by Denise Dias, following the death of her 17-year-old daughter by a drunk driver, and which seeks justice for their children killed in "traffic accidents" caused by drivers who use vehicles like weapons, and by a justice system whose response to the epidemic of those "accidents" has been woefully inadequate.

REFERENCE

Kwayana, Eusi. 1999. *Next Witness: An Appeal to World Opinion*. Free Press. [Booklet first published in July 1962 by Labour Advocate.]

Sexual Violence is a Question of Whose Honor?
[2000]

In the *Stabroek News* of February 2, there were two stories on pages facing each other—the first, on page 18, headlined "Sophia man charged with rape of 11-year-old," the second, on page 19, titled "Fifty-year-old Rupununi woman gang-raped at party." What struck me in the two stories is probably not different from what struck other readers—they were stories of routine brutality.

Two rapes, one of a child, the other of a middle-aged woman. The child allegedly raped by one man, the woman gang-raped. The child allegedly asked by the rapist, whom she knew, if she liked him and after she said "No"—twice—lifted bodily into his home and raped. The middle-aged woman allegedly gang-raped by men taking turns: the report says that one took the woman into the bushes, overpowered her and raped her, then went and called the number two accused who raped her, then the numbers three and four accused were called and they went and raped her. (What did each say to the next, "Come and get some"?)

Laws (which we have) and mechanisms to make sure they're implemented (which are weak, but can be strengthened) are not going to be enough, here or anywhere else, to stop this everyday evil. Something has to change in the culture of how women are seen. But here and everywhere else, the first problem women seem to face is that rape is simply not high on the list of human wrongs which women and men can unite in opposing, across race. Rape is an evil against which large numbers of people will speak out, it seems, only when it is used by men of one race against women of another, and then only for those of the same ethnic background as the women raped.

Otherwise, it seems, rape does not really happen at all, except to a "normal" degree. In a "60 Minutes" programme on the night of February 1, two South African government ministers vehemently denied that "South Africa is the rape capital of the world." Reports that a woman in South Africa is raped every 26 minutes were dismissed as propaganda being used to discredit the country and by implication, its black, post-apartheid government. Among the rape victims interviewed were two who wept for what they had lost. One, a white South African woman, said that given a rise in what she clearly understood as revenge violence turned against women, there was no future for her children in South Africa. The other, a black South African woman, said (doubtless because in addition to the loss she and the other woman shared, she had the pain of having less choice of where to go), "Now I am futureless."

In some cases, rape is overtly a weapon of ethnic conflict. This is not unknown in Guyana, certainly in the ethnic warfare of the 1960s. It is not unknown anywhere. In the "Monday Review" of the *Independent* newspaper of May 10, 1999, there is a story headed "Rape as a weapon of war" which begins, "'They came into the village and put everyone in a warehouse. They took twenty women for two days and two nights during which they were raped continuously, and then returned to the warehouse half-dead.' So spoke one witness of the action of Serb soldiers that took place recently in Kosovo." The article points out what we know: that rape is "a common feature of war against a civilian population, and of political or ethnic persecution." It cites Pakistanis raping more than two hundred thousand Bengali women during the independence battle of 1971; Japanese raping thousands of women during the occupation of Nanking in 1937; and Americans, for whom "rape was a routine method of demonstrating their contempt for the people of Vietnam" during the Vietnam war. There are countless other examples.

What makes rape so useful as a weapon of war? An Arab expression says, "a man's honour lies between the legs of a woman." *Time* magazine of January 18, 1999 carried a story titled "The Price of Honor" which started with a 35-year-old man saying of the 16-year-old sister he had murdered, "She came to the house at 8.15, and by 8.20 she was dead." Her offence was that three days before, she had reported being raped to the police. "She committed a mistake," the brother says, "even if it was against her will." And so he restored his honour with her life.

Earlier this week, perhaps on Monday, January 31, the author of a new study reported on a "Today" TV show on the study's finding that rape was natural— not defensible, but resulting from how men are genetically programmed. I am sure that what the study has to say is more complex than that, but like the woman put to debate its author on the show, I wasn't hearing him too well. I was deafened by the sound of the main argument, which seemed to me to insult men, and by the implications that follow from it, which put women in their usual place. One of the implications is that women should avoid provoking men to rape, including by their provocative dress.

"For women, display is dishonour," says a Swahili proverb. There are similar proverbs in other cultures. You have to wonder whether anyone needed to run a whole study to find what has always been said about rape victims: "They asked for it." They asked for it, people say, perhaps even in Kosovo where in every picture we have seen, women wear long dresses and have their hair, sometimes their faces, covered.

Even when victim and rapist are of the same ethnic background, women can be treated as "collateral damage" in the ethnic war. Very recently, prominent women in England protested against boxer Mike Tyson being allowed into the country (for a boxing mismatch), because he had served time in the United

States for raping a young woman (who was African-American). Let into England nonetheless, Mike Tyson was reportedly greeted as a hero on a visit to Brixton, a largely black community. Some feted him as a role model. And we know why. He is seen as an example of a black man from a poor background who made it, and who was attacked and dragged down by white America for that reason alone. In this scenario, the woman who accused Tyson of rape is at worst, an accomplice of white racism; at best, incidental to the only real story of injustice and the abuse of power. It is easier to be against racial injustice than against injustice to women.

Thus, as I said earlier, it often seems as though rape is evil only if it is understood as attacking the honor of the men of the group to which the victim belongs. It is never a question of the victim's honor. Not in the race wars, nor in that wider war in which an 11-year-old girl in Sophia and a 50-year-old woman in the Rupununi are random victims.

ACKNOWLEDGEMENTS

This essay was originally published in Women's Eye-View, *Stabroek News*, as "A Question of Honour"; February 6, 2000.

Sexual Abuse and the Uses of Power
[2018]

Many groups of people are vulnerable to sexual abuse—people who by reason of age or dis/ability are less strong, LGBTI+ youth, women and men, especially in those territories where homophobia and transphobia remain rampant, and others who are marginalized in the society. A recent case in Guyana brought this to the forefront when a 15-year-old boy, taken into custody for the offence of loitering (which makes it likely that he was working class), was then raped by a city constable (*Kaieteur News*, February 6, 2018). Marginalized sectors also include people forced to live wholly outside the protection of the law, like sex workers and undocumented immigrants.

Among children, while girls of any age are the most frequent targets, young boys are also frequent prey. Two cases involving young Guyanese boys attracted particular attention because they involved multiple victims, not one of whom has received justice to date. In the earlier one, a businessman was charged for raping four schoolboys aged between six and eight years old. Only one of the charges went to trial. In the second, a 33-year-old imam was charged with raping nine male students who at the time the allegations were first made, were between four and ten years old. When the case finally came up for trial it was further postponed because the children's birth certificates and medical reports had "disappeared" (*Kaieteur News*, February 12, 2018). (*Update: In March 2019, the imam was found guilty and sentenced to 45 years imprisonment*).

Legal language describes the sexual abuse of children by persons whose function involves responsibility for children as a violation of trust. Hence, for example, a sexual abuse charge against a teacher earlier in Guyana in 2018 read that he engaged in sexual activity with a child under the age of 16 by abusing his position of trust (*Kaieteur News*, March 15, 2018). In another case where a religious leader was sentenced to 40 years for raping a child aged 15 years old between January 29 and 31, 2016, the State Prosecutor had reminded the judge that when considering the sentence he should bear in mind that the accused "had breached his position of trust by engaging in repeated acts with the minor" (*Stabroek News*, February 9, 2018).

Condemnation of sexual abuse is unequivocal when its victims are babies and toddlers. I remember the revulsion of people long accustomed to dealing with all kinds of depravity at a case where a four-month-old's mouth was found to be encrusted with the semen of a care-giver who habitually put his penis into her mouth, taking advantage of the fact that her reflex would be to suck.

While targets of sexual abuse include everyone rendered vulnerable by inequalities of power, when the abuse is directed against women and girls as a group it is at once an expression of misogyny and a tool of misogyny.

Female targets are not just girls of any age, but females across their life cycle. One newspaper listed cases from this year and called out a number of perpetrators as pedophiles, including the following: a man sentenced to 28 years imprisonment for the rape of a six-year-old girl twice in August 2013; a 55-year-old man sentenced to 30 years for the rape of an eight-year-old girl; a man sentenced to life for raping a girl twice, once when she was 10 and the second time when she was 12; a man sentenced to life for repeatedly raping a child (sex not given) over a period of two years; a 31-year-old man given 25 years for luring a 15-year-old girl into his house by pretending to be a doctor, then raping her; and a 66-year-old man found guilty of raping a ten-year-old girl twice in 2014, but not yet sentenced (*Stabroek News*, July 19, 2018). Older women are not safe from sexual violence either. A selection of cases reported in the press included: July 2009, a woman in her 80s raped at a senior citizens' home (*Kaieteur News*, July 8, 2009); February 2015, a 73-year-old woman raped and murdered (*Kaieteur News*, February 21, 2015); October 2015, a 78-year-old woman raped, sodomized and murdered (*Kaieteur News*, October 9, 2015); July 8, 2017, a 75-year-old woman raped and badly beaten, dying later the same day (*Stabroek News*, July 16, 2017); April 2018, an 85-year-old woman, visually impaired and hard of hearing, raped and left unconscious (*Stabroek News*, April 21, 2018).

While the rape of the youngest and oldest among us is particularly heinous, the range of sexual abuse we must confront goes from the sometimes invasive crudities of greetings from males to females (and not always on street corners either), to all acts of sexual violence in and out the home, where its perpetrators are parent, partner, stranger, preacher, teacher, business leader, policeman, politician—and it is always about power:

> Despite its name, sexual abuse is more about power than it is about sex. Although the touch may be sexual, the words seductive or intimidating, and the violation physical, when someone rapes, assaults, or harasses, the motivation stems from the perpetrator's need for dominance and control. In heterosexual and same-sex encounters, sex is the tool used to gain power over another person. It is sexual assault whenever words and actions of a sexual nature are imposed against another person's will. The perpetrator may use force, threats, and manipulation or sweet talk and flattery (or a combination). (Yonack 2017)

At every level of our society, much of this abuse is not recognized as abuse but as our "culture." The wit of sexual innuendo in many old calypsos is conflated with the threats of violence against women or LGBT+ persons in some of our newer music. One former Guyanese president said to a Red Thread coordinator in the hearing of other attendees at a meeting in his office, that it was very "North American" to make a fuss about boys "calling off" girls as they walk by, since the girls enjoy it and "it is part of our culture," ignoring the frequent slide to open hostility when a girl does not respond as desired. In the case of a young woman in Barbados, Ronelle King, who later used the hashtag "Life in Leggings" to recount the incident, a man tried to pull her into his car in broad daylight after she refused his offer of a lift. The police were dismissive of her report. The Life in Leggings hashtag pre-dated the global "Me-too" hashtag. This is not about patterning our responses on North America.

The sexual abuse of women and girls is about entitlement. Perpetrators do not only *need* domination and control; they assume they have a *right* to them. My sharpest personal experience of this came one night nearly 40 years ago when I was raped three times by a man I knew because we were part of the same political movement. He was, in terms of a narrow view of political comradeship, on the same side as I was. He was not a party leader so his power didn't derive from having a higher political position than I did. It seemed to derive simply from the sense of male entitlement which had been bred in him. In fact, that sense of male entitlement—coupled, at least in some cases, with a conscious desire to put the victim in her place—is to my mind what is central to the sexual abuse of women and girls. It is at the heart of what sections of the church are supporting when they oppose laws against rape in marriage.[1]

On top of the pervasive sense of entitlement among men of all classes, races, colors, and creeds, there are often other bases of power wielded by perpetrators. There are acts of sexual abuse where the perpetrator's sense of entitlement derives from the position he holds, and not just the sense of impunity it gives him, but the *assurance* of impunity it gives him. Religious and political leaders, especially, have long been accustomed to being given a free pass, although in some of our territories, religious leaders are increasingly being made to face the law.

The continued grant of impunity to political leaders who are sexually abusive (usually of younger women and women in lower positions) is of course not limited to our region. The widespread social impunity enjoyed by former US President Bill Clinton is a case in point. Within a few days of looking chastened after he was forced to admit the truth about his exploitative sexual conduct with a young (though not underage) intern, he entered the UN General Assembly to a standing ovation. Years later, when he entered the stage at a Hollywood award ceremony, he was again greeted with a standing ovation. It was enough for all of them in those two gatherings that he was (said to be) pro-black, pro-poor, pro-Third World, and pro- what in the United States is called the left, meaning liberal. He was "on their side," and so both the UN General Assembly and the

Hollywood elite were ready to turn their backs not only on the intern he'd abused and the other abused women that women on his staff dismissed as "bimbos," but on the black men and women in the United States his policies as president filled the jails with, and the Haitian women, men and children exploited by the sweatshop approach to development his Clinton Foundation pursues. While lower-level US politicians are being called out (and sometimes were before the Me-too movement started), neither past nor present top US leaders have so far been held accountable—and they will not be as long as each is able to draw on the continued support of those on their side of the political divide.

But at least in the United States the media report on sexual abuse by political leaders. In the Caribbean, that is not likely to happen, and women who might want to bring such abusers to justice have to contend directly with the problems arising from small size: the reality of being in the direct line of sight of political leaders and the readiness of these leaders to abuse their political power, including by threatening the women's jobs. This is particularly the case for working class women.

The stance of progressive men is not unique to the region, nor is it new. The black political and cultural movement of the 1970s was revolutionary, but not in its treatment of women. Black leaders too often argued that raising the issue of male violence against women divided the race; that it was "counter-revolutionary" and "white" in the context of the level of anti-black racism in the United States (and the world), and the weight of the assault that the US state was mounting against black people and the black movement. The struggle was a struggle of black people against white supremacy.

The best answer I know to that persistent accusation of divisiveness was made in 1981 by a black American woman called Wilmette Brown, speaking specifically about the struggle against sexual violence against women in the UK, the country where she then lived and organized. What she said went to the heart of the politics of women who are no less dedicated to the struggle against racism than progressive black men are, but are determined that this would not be in place of the struggle for another kind of justice for themselves and other women:

> We are campaigning as Black women so that the anti-rape movement is not used by the establishment to attack the Black community; so that neither racism by white women, sexism by Black men nor intimidation by the police, the law and the courts can keep Black women from getting justice; so that all rapists are punished but Black men are not persecuted; so that the money which the Establishment now uses to police and terrorise Black people be used instead to protect all women and to eliminate the poverty which makes Black women the most vulnerable. (Hall et al. 1984: foreword)

The criticism that men in the Caribbean progressive movement have made over the years of women they disparage as "those feminists," is of the same order as the criticism that black leaders in the 1970s made of women at that time: organizing in defense of the rights of Caribbean women is a diversion from the struggle against capitalism and imperialism. Worse, it is an attack on that struggle. In particular, accusing any male comrade of violence against women is doing the work of the enemy. In taking this position, they allow leaders who abuse women to set the standard for the kind of Caribbean civilization we are building.

ACKNOWLEDGEMENTS

This essay is previously unpublished.

NOTE

1. In Jamaica, for example, six churches advised a parliamentary committee reviewing the country's Sexual Offences Act not to pass laws against sex without consent in marriage. See "Tambourine Army Accuses Churches of Condoning Rape of Married Women," *Gleaner*, June 29, 2017.

REFERENCES

Hall, Ruth, Selma James and Judit Kertesz. 1984. *The Rapist Who Pays the Rent: Women's Case for Changing the Law on Rape*. Bristol: Falling Wall Press.

Yonack, Lyn. 2017. "Sexual Assault is about Power." *Psychology Today*. Posted November 14, 2017.

*Letter to the Police Complaints Authority on an Allegation of Rape
against a Police Commissioner*
[2012]

Dear Editor,

The following letter was delivered to the Offices of The Police Complaints Authority, The Office of Professional Responsibility and the Police Service Commission on March 30. To date (Thursday, April 5, 2012), we have not even received an acknowledgement of receipt from any of the three. This raises the question whether the Office of the Commissioner of Police is above the law.

March 30, 2012

Complaint against Mr. Henry Greene

Mr. Henry Greene, Commissioner of Police, in connection with the DPP's advice that he be charged for rape, swore to an affidavit which was proffered in the court of the Chief Justice.

The Commissioner of Police swore in his affidavit that he engaged in a sexual encounter with a woman who came to him for assistance in his capacity as Commissioner, and that he engaged in the sexual encounter with her knowing that she was the subject of an active police investigation.

This behavior of the Commissioner breaches the most permissive codes of accepted ethical behavior, and certainly, in a professional of Mr. Greene's position, at minimum, it amounts to (1) potentially perverting a police investigation; and (2) abusing his official position to secure sexual favors.

We anticipate your urgent examination and institution of disciplinary measures in relation to this complaint.

Sincerely,

Karen de Souza, Wintress White,[1] Andaiye

ACKNOWLEDGEMENTS

Published in *Stabroek News*, April 6, 2012. On April 13, a letter from the Chairman of the Police Complaints Authority was published in the same newspaper, complaining that Red Thread had criticized the Authority in the press without giving it sufficient time to respond to its letter, which had been received on March 30, 2012 while an answer had been sent by mail on April 4,

2012. Red Thread's view was that a complaint of rape against any Police Commissioner was of the utmost priority.

NOTE

1. Wintress White is a member of Red Thread.

PART FOUR

TOWARDS STRENGTHENING THE MOVEMENT

ESSAY 26
Gender, Race, and Class: A Perspective on the Contemporary
Caribbean Struggle
[2009]

INTRODUCTION

I want to thank the Department of Government, Sociology and Social Work of the Faculty of Social Sciences at UWI Cave Hill for inviting me to present the 2009 Patrick Emmanuel Memorial Lecture, and especially Dr. Wendy Grenade for making all the arrangements and for the good humor with which she dealt with my delayed and irritable responses to her emails—delayed and irritable because of Guyana's interminable blackouts. Secondly, I want, as always, to acknowledge the women I work with not only for what we are learning together every day, but for their specific assistance with this presentation and everything else that I write.

I knew Pat Emmanuel in the early 1960s when we were students at the Mona campus of UWI, and tonight, as I come to speak in his honor, both my 18- to 19-year-old self and my present self are here—the first, with a sense of disbelief that more than 47 years have passed, the second, with a sense of pleasure and fulfilment at being asked to speak at an event which recognizes Pat's life and life's work. I'm not using his work as a direct basis for my presentation, but want to acknowledge that along with the work of others of our generation, including Walter Rodney, it nourished my political thinking.

*   *   *

Recalling the labor uprising in Trinidad in 1937, Kathleen Drayton said in a speech delivered at a ceremony in her honor at the University of the West Indies' Institute for Gender and Development Studies two nights before she died, that her most enduring childhood memory was of the sound of the bare feet of working class women and men marching down the road, cutlasses and paling staves in hand, challenging privilege.[1] Hearing of this I thought again (it occurs to me often) that the radicalization of many of my generation of Guyanese began as Indian- and African-Guyanese working people mobilized together in the early 1950s to stand up to the colonial state in then British Guiana. To choose three seminal moments in just four decades of the history of that part of the Caribbean is my main focus (the territories that had an experience of British colonization): to be a child in British Honduras (now Belize), Jamaica, St. Kitts, St. Vincent, St. Lucia, Barbados, Trinidad, or British Guiana during the labor resistance of the 1930s; or in British Guiana at the high point of the anti-colonial mobilization in 1953; or in Trinidad during the Black Power rebellion in 1970, was to learn—early—that power that seems impregnable can be confronted, and sometimes beaten, by the collective power of so-called ordinary people.

The theme of this 2009 Patrick Emmanuel Memorial Lecture is "Gender, Race and Class in the Contemporary Caribbean" and I've stretched that somewhat so that my topic is "Gender, Race and Class: A Perspective on the Contemporary Caribbean Struggle." By contemporary Caribbean I mean the Caribbean post-Grenada 1983, using Grenada 1983 as a marker for a moment of serious rupture for the region, a moment when the defeat of the Grenada revolution, in the context of the rise of neoliberalism, destroyed our self-belief. The effects of this continue today.

UNDERSTANDING GENDER, RACE AND CLASS

There are limits to how far you can take an analysis of economic, social and political relations if gender, race and class are used as separate categories, though separating them can have some value. For example, a key measurement of the exploitation of women as a group was the UN's 1980 declaration at the Conference of the United Nations Decade for Women in Copenhagen that women do two-thirds of the world's work for 10 percent of the income (the ILO says 5 percent), and own 1 percent of the assets. Similarly, when in 2009, the United Nations Development Programme Human Development Report said that in waged work, Caribbean women earn far less than men—the figures ranging from 37 percent in Haiti to 58 percent in Jamaica—it was providing a smaller but nonetheless useful measurement of women's exploitation as women.

But gender, race and class are not separable in the lives of real people. An example: while in the coastal political economy of Guyana, African-Guyanese as a group are increasingly on the economic margins (Indigenous peoples are the most marginalized of all), this of course does not mean that all African-Guyanese are in the same position regardless of their class or gender, nor that a working class woman or man of another group is at the economic center. Listening to the enraged complaints of African-Guyanese women in a network called Guyanese Women across Race organized by Red Thread, the women's collective I help coordinate, an Indian-Guyanese member said in exasperation, "I ain' know why Black people always talkin' bout how Indian get everything. You mean big Indian like ... wit' he big hotel and ... wit' he big business! Look at me! You ain' see I Indian? What you see I get?" She was contesting what Shalini Puri, writing on Trinidad and Tobago, calls "the fiction of one seamless and monolithic racial community with common interests pitted against another seamless and monolithic racial community with common interests" (see Puri 2004: 183). Intellectually we all know it is a fiction, but it nonetheless orders our politics and often, how we relate to each other.

The violence that women suffer from husbands and partners, who are more often than not of the same race, is a brutal, daily reminder of how gender works *inside* race, while the burden of poverty and overwork shared by working class women is an indicator of how gender works *across* race, though with differences arising from factors including access to running water, electricity and other technology. Red Thread produced proof of this in relation to Guyana in a time-use survey carried out by four grassroots members of the group among Indigenous, Indian-Guyanese, African-Guyanese and Mixed race grassroots women in Guyana in 2001–2002.[2] There are of course many other useful examples but these are enough, I think, to make the point that as far as possible, we have to integrate gender, race and class in our analysis of the contemporary Caribbean situation.

Finally, by way of introduction, I know that a number of you may think that talk about "struggle" and "resistance" is old-fashioned, even a little embarrassing. That's no longer how most of us think about organizing today. You may even feel uncomfortable with the use of the word class, although the fact that you are able to be at the university means that many of you live in conditions of some class privilege.

I don't accept these discomforts. Above all, I reject any notion that discussion of capitalism belongs to the past. I just came from the United States where millions of people have been jolted out of their complacency about their future under capitalism by the recent economic collapse in parts of that country. I visited Detroit, sections of which people who saw New Orleans post-Katrina say look similar—broken and abandoned, the similarities with New Orleans sharpened by the fact that the great majority of women and men I saw were people of color. Here in this region, if we are complacent about our future our complacency is utterly misplaced. We are in crisis.

The presentation that follows is in four parts:

1. it describes the post-Grenada 1983 crisis from as many angles as it can, in the process looking at its gender, race and class implications;
2. it discusses how neo-liberal policies and the main strategies adopted to survive in the face of them, further exploit women's unwaged and low-waged work and undermine historic family coping mechanisms;
3. it examines formal organizing in the region (as against the informal organizing people do as part of their survival strategies) and suggests that the main organizations "of the people"—the left, trade unions, and the feminist movement—have been characterized by exclusion, and are not positioned to confront the multi-faceted crisis we are facing and its root causes; and it ends with

4. brief and preliminary proposals on what we might do to confront the crisis—what campaigns would allow us to unite all the sectors in the face of the divisions on which capital feeds, and to speak both to the needs and interests of each sector and to something we can truthfully call our common good.

While its main focus is on what is called the English-speaking Caribbean or the West Indies, the presentation also pays attention to Haiti, not only because Haiti is now a member of CARICOM (the Caribbean Community), but also because it is a laboratory for the worst excesses of neo-liberalism. Besides, as I will expand on briefly later, we owe Haiti.

THE CRISIS OF THE REGION

Sometime in the 1980s I attended a forum in Barbados where a panel discussed the (male) West Indies cricket team—then filled with world class talent and brio—as exemplifying what some have come to call "our West Indian civilization." Fast forward to an interview with one of our most internationally sought-after cricketers, where he was asked whether, of all the places he played for, he felt most commitment to playing for his country and he answered "Yes!" and quite unselfconsciously identified his country as one of the islands. Which of course it was and is. But the interviewer was speaking from the perspective of international test cricket where the Trinidadian's "country" was the West Indies. In the heyday of West Indies cricket, any of our cricketers would have instinctively known that, because there truly was a place called the West Indies in the pride we had in our collective regional mastery of the game. And if in good times cricket was product and producer of that pride, surely its failures are product and producer of what we have today, our loss of assurance.

Old foundations are crumbling, and new ones are not yet being imagined. In the economy, many thousands of working people are losing jobs and other sources of income. The tourism sector in parts of the region is in decline. Sugar prices in the European Union (EU) are being reduced by more than 60 percent over a three year period, beginning in 2006. Estates in Trinidad and Tobago, St. Kitts/Nevis, and Barbados had already closed as the EU dropped sugar prices even before it abandoned the Sugar Protocol. Of the traditional producers only Belize and Guyana remain in the business. Former bauxite workers are unemployed and underemployed and environments damaged in Guyana and Jamaica.

Climate change is a massive issue for the region. While it is a global phenomenon, changing weather patterns across the region, and micro-climate events in specific countries and areas of these countries, pose special problems for the Caribbean. Because climate crises, which are huge events with enormous implications for our small states, are small in comparison to those in other countries, especially in terms of the numbers of people affected, we cannot rely on international solidarity to help us meet their economic and social costs. At the level of international agencies the talk is about building resilience, but what precisely this means at the regional, national, community and household levels is unclear. What we can see is that old assumptions about weather patterns and how these shape major economic occupations are no longer valid. Farmers, in particular, have to cope with more unpredictable rainfall and drought. So do those whose task it is to protect workplaces and homes. In the great flood in Guyana in 2005, for example, women as caregivers and subsistence farmers carried a visibly increased burden as they struggled to safeguard their children and their livestock from disease. The catastrophe also taught other lessons, as Guyana lost some 60-odd percent of its GDP in a flood that covered a very small area of its coastline, measuring some 25 of its over two hundred miles (Jocelyn Dow, personal communication, undated).

In CARICOM territories like Belize, Suriname and Guyana which still have Indigenous populations who occupy savannah and forest, conservation and economic development often come into conflict. Environmental and social costs have to be factored in, in determining economic choices. The issue of Indigenous rights and their access to customary resources is often a contentious one, especially for coastal communities and businesses which in the main want unfettered access to areas that are Indigenous. In Guyana, for example, the conflict pits the demands of conservation and Indigenous collective rights to the lands which they have protected for generations on the one hand, against the needs of coastal people who want to use the lands for small gold mining— that is, for private accumulation on a micro scale—on the other. This has race, gender, class and age implications since the small gold miners are typically young African-Guyanese men, although increasingly young men of other races as well, who are unable to find alternative economic avenues on the coast. Most sublet the claims on which they work from large gold-miners and eke out a marginal existence, finding little gold, prey to malaria and other diseases and to crime. The fact that they go into the interior alone often places a strain on families and makes their female partners de facto single parents.

The CARICOM country most severely affected by climate change is without doubt Haiti, where the effects of denudation and impoverishment and of inequality in access to safe infrastructure, is exposed during frequent hurricanes. We pay the price for economic choices made by the developed countries. The obvious lesson that climate does not have boundaries can be drawn by the entire Caribbean.

The continued inequality of our relationships with Northern countries and institutions has been laid bare. In analyzing the expected impact of the Economic Partnership Agreement (EPA) signed by CARIFORUM (CARICOM plus the Dominican Republic), Jason Jackson and Judith Wedderburn (2009)[3] conclude that to the extent that Caribbean states are not competitive, they can be hurt by a change in the trade structure with the EU, and that the concerns of Caribbean states as regards the potential negative effects of the EPA are well-founded given, for example, Jamaica's experience with NAFTA. According to the authors, this saw steep declines in the manufacturing share of GDP and employment in the 1990s with the erosion of preferences in the apparel sector due to high capital and operating costs and competition from other foreign producers with preferential access to the US market, particularly Mexico. After rising steadily through the 1980s with the policies promoting "free zone" labor, much of which was in the textile sector and targeted women, women's share of manufacturing sector employment fell from a peak of 44 percent of total sectoral employment in 1994 and 1995 to 29 percent in 2001. Women's manufacturing employment fell by more than half from 46,500 in 1995 to 19,400 in 2001 while men's manufacturing sector employment also suffered heavily, falling from 59,600 to 47,500 (20 percent for men versus 58 percent for women).

In some countries in the region the loss of paid work in the formal sectors seems almost terminal. In the Windward Islands, while in 1992 there were 24,000 banana farmers creating livelihoods for at least 120,000 women, children and men, only 4,000 remain. Even before a recent plunge in prices "Dominica had seen a 50 percent reduction in the number of farmers exporting Fairtrade bananas to Britain while the number in St. Vincent and the Grenadines had declined by more than 30 percent" (*The Observer*, October 11, 2009). It is in a seeming spirit of desperation (and not ideological conviction) that territories such as Dominica and Antigua/Barbuda have joined the Bolivarian Alliance for the Americas (ALBA).

As the regional crisis deepens there is a rising incidence and viciousness of violence which expresses what is most negative in many of our relations—those of sex, age, race, and sexual identity most directly: domestic and sexual violence against women, children and gay and trans women and men, older women, sex workers; the beating of children; in Guyana in particular, suicide and race violence.

There are other forms of violence exacerbated by the crisis. In at least two countries (Guyana and Jamaica), there are credible reports of torture and extra-judicial killings executed by the law enforcement arm of the state and/or extra-judicial violence perpetrated by gangs and phantom squads with party, state and/or drug connections. In Jamaica, Jamaicans for Justice (2009) reports that the latest figures provided by the Bureau of Special Investigations (BSI) indicate that 157 people were killed by the police between January and August of 2009, suggesting serious abuse of power. This was 14 more than in the same time period in 2008. In all of these forms of violence, young males are overwhelmingly both the perpetrators and the victims. One of the worst dangers of the male marginalization thesis in the hands of unserious men is the insufficient attention paid to the very real marginalization of working class young men. There is a relationship between this violence and the drugs and arms trade, the increase in the use of illegal drugs and alcohol, and some of the content of popular culture, but there is another, deeper relationship between the present priorities of a world where money is funneled to the military instead of to the careers needed for the survival of families. According to the Stockholm International Peace Research Institute (SIPRI), global military spending in 2008 was $1.46 trillion, and a few years' expenditure would cover the whole backlog in official aid promised since 1970.

The economic and political stagnation of the region has contributed to a situation where in 2001, Guyana (83 percent), Jamaica (81.9 percent), Haiti (78.5 percent) and Trinidad and Tobago (76 percent) topped the list of non-OECD countries with the highest percentage of highly-skilled 15+ immigrants in OECD countries. Figures for Antigua and Barbuda, Belize and Dominica are also high. In many of our countries, including those with higher per capita incomes, our children, asked what they most want in the world say, "to migrate."

THE IMPACT OF NEOLIBERAL POLICIES AND POPULAR SURVIVAL STRATEGIES ON WOMEN AND FAMILIES

In response to the crisis Caribbean governments—including Jamaica, Barbados, St. Kitts/Nevis, Dominica, St. Lucia, St. Vincent and the Grenadines and likely Grenada and Antigua/Barbuda—are turning or returning to the IMF. Their conditions have not fundamentally changed since the 1970s, when Caribbean (and other) women showed how, for example, IMF Structural Adjustment Programmes (SAPs) increased the inequality between women and men, predicated as they were on a heightened exploitation of women's unwaged labor to take up the slack of cuts in social services.[4] The requirements of IMF SAPs are an example of the anti-caring, anti-humanizing priorities which create the conditions for violence. In increasing the load of women's unwaged caring work they not only affect women's health; but since women's time is not elastic, must lead to the neglect of their children.

SAPs have sharpened other divisions at the economic level. For example, the miniaturizing of the public sector and propelling of the private sector as the "engine of growth," have created the conditions for increased race conflict in Guyana where historically the public sector has been dominated by African-Guyanese, the private sector by Indian-Guyanese.

Among working people, in the face of the crisis in traditional economic sectors and the near-absence of new sectors, a main strategy for survival is a burgeoning informalization. The preponderance of women in the informal sector, especially in small/micro trading (higglering), domestic work and sex work, is visible. The second main survival strategy is increased migration across the region, much of it undocumented. This kind of migration is not new, but it has intensified. As in the informalization of work as a strategy for survival, women are very visible in the movement in and out of territories of the region, again as micro-traders, domestic workers and sex workers. Insofar as this migration is undocumented, it means work and lives that are precarious, unstable and uncertain, with negative effects on children, families and communities.

The terms of even "legal" migration are often unfavorable to families staying together. Where identified categories of people have been officially accorded free movement between CARICOM member territories, there are major hurdles still to be overcome including the rights of dependents and the avail-ability of housing, education, health and social benefits in receiving countries. A mother who migrates without her children has to find ways of mothering from across the seas, negotiating how to emotionally and practically sustain her newly trans-territorial family.

All this also imposes a terrible burden of survival work on children. Migration out of the region, leaving children behind, is also not new. But it, too, has intensified, in a context where the communities of female kin at home are less available to take care of the children, the networks of support are seriously weakened. While remittances, especially between Caribbean working class migrants and their families, are key in Caribbean household and national economies, as they are in economies throughout the Global South, they do not compensate for the devastation that migration can leave behind.

The rise in migration inside the region is leading to an upsurge in narrow nationalism. This has been a problem since the end of the Federation project. "In the aftermath of the collapse of the West Indies Federation," writes Gordon Rohlehr, "in each country that went its separate—national way, 'the Other' became the 'other Caribbean person'" (in Trotz 2009). But it has reached new levels. Today's crisis-fueled movement in and out of regional countries is breeding serious conflict between working people of the receiving and sending countries. This is especially true of the relations between the main receiving countries (The Bahamas, Barbados and Trinidad and Tobago) and the main sending countries (Haiti, Jamaica and Guyana). Race is also a factor as increas-ingly, intra-regional migration includes large numbers of Indian-Guyanese workers. Indian-Caribbean people are a sizable part of the region's population, but since they live largely in Trinidad, Guyana and Suriname, the influx of Guyanese of Indian descent into territories whose populations are overwhelm-ingly of African descent sometimes provokes fear of change, and hostility. And here is the level to which the very idea of "region" has descended. "Progressive" women and men accept the concept which should be anathema to us all, of the "illegal" migrant from a sister Caribbean country.

In these conditions, market forces have free rein as migrants undercut native-born workers, recruited precisely because they can be more exploited. Those who migrate "back-track"—that is without official documents—are of course in even more danger of exploitation since they often lack the skills that are most desired, and must work for extra-low wages, without any benefits. In some territories there is the problem of space. For example, Barbados is densely populated, with limited land, and thus the cry of inadequate room is legitimate. But a different sense of region, of how much we would collectively be strengthened by strengthening it, of who belongs in it, of how we are connected and interconnected, of how migration flows around the region have historically shifted depending on need (for example, post-Emancipation there was large-scale migration from Barbados to then British Guiana)—all this might produce a different response. For example, workers in Barbados could give solidarity and support to workers in Guyana in their struggles, and it would certainly lead to different language in the debate over "outside" migration.

In her 2008 Dame Nita Barrow lecture, Alissa Trotz (2009) recounted that on checking the online national newspaper archives to see how a mass deportation of Guyanese from Barbados in 2005 was being discussed publicly she was stunned:

Words like flood and swamp suggested that Barbados was vulnerable and open to invading hordes (the gendered dimension is clear here) who threatened the country's social equilibrium, notwithstanding statements by the Barbadian government that the numbers of Guyanese in the country could not support such a conclusion. In letters to the press, images emerged of squatting and overcrowding (the dirty, anti-social Guyanese), of illegal access to scarce social services and free medical care (the duplicitous and greedy Guyanese), of threats to law and order (the criminal Guyanese), of a political imbalance, with at least one opposition politician speculating that the voters' list could be artificially inflated (the cheating Guyanese), of immigrants accepting lower wages and undercutting Barbadian labour (the Guyanese scab). Indian-Guyanese were singled out and racialized as particularly incapable of integrating, and of threatening to import Guyana's "ethnic" problem into the island … Anxieties around borders also turned crucially on questions of sexuality. In some of the online blogs, women were singled out as preying on unsuspecting Barbadian men in order to get themselves legalized (the immoral and sexually loose Guyanese).

The worst case of racist, anti-immigrant hostility against a CARICOM people is meted out to Haitians in the neighboring Dominican Republic where they face unimaginable brutality. Amidst an anti-Haitian campaign in the Dominican Republic, four Haitians were decapitated, shot and burned, killed while burning trees to make charcoal in the Dominican border town of Jimani. Dominicans blame Haitians for cutting trees there to make charcoal, a practice that contributes to deforestation, erosion and flooding in Haiti (*Latin American Herald Tribune*, October 23, 2009). The UN Special Rapporteur on Racism and Related Intolerance and the UN Independent Expert on Minority Issues recently reported finding in the Dominican Republic "a profound and entrenched racism against ... Haitians, (and) Dominicans of Haitian descent" (*Stabroek News*, October 31, 2007). Over one million Haitians are said to have migrated "illicitly" to the Dominican Republic where they are employed in sugar fields, factories and on cattle ranches in conditions which human rights groups describe as not far from slavery, and face periodic expulsions. Haitians are also to be found—largely informally—in the tourist industry, ghettoized in particular jobs because of their precarious legal status. (A book by Steven Gregory, *The Devil Behind the Mirror*, gives examples of Haitians not being allowed to work in front of bars and restaurants where interaction with customers is required.) Yet the fact remains that they are indispensable to the tourist industry, and are also in demand in relation to particular skills like hair braiding (including by Dominican Republic women living overseas). Children born of undocumented Haitian parents are denied birth certificates in contravention of an Inter-American Court of Human Rights order (see Human Rights Watch 2002).

The precise size of undocumented intra-regional migration, while unknowable, is clearly massive. In reference to the wider Caribbean, one writer, Ferguson says that "Throughout the region, undocumented labor fuels a boom in construction, provides the bulk of domestic service, and accounts for much street vending and other small-scale commerce" (Ferguson 2003: 4). Those who provide domestic service, who are overwhelmingly women, use the demand for domestic workers to pursue different strategies to expand their economic opportunities or increase their survival chances. They migrate temporarily to engage in domestic work, saving money on accommodation, food and clothes so they can send home remittances to meet an immediate expense like paying school fees or repairing a house, or to make a larger investment such as building a house. They enter into one territory as domestic workers and use it as a jumping off point to another. According to Ferguson, "some territories, less economically developed, act as trans-shipment points for undocumented migration" (ibid.). In addition, domestic workers with work permits may use household domestic work as a stepping stone to similar work in the tourist sector, moving back into household domestic work in times of economic downturn when the number of tourist arrivals shrink, and then out again if tourism picks up.

In spite of all the negatives associated with the upsurge in migration, CARICOM people are ahead of CARICOM institutions in claiming the region as a single economic space. Another upside of some of the trading has been the collaboration the work fosters: when intra-regional trading from Guyana started, for example, a frequent sight at airports and in planes was Indian-Guyanese and African-Guyanese women and some men huddling together to work out which one should carry what for the other one to try to fool customs officials that neither was a trader, "illegally" taking in dozens of the same items to sell or with more money than the authorities would think reasonable for just a "normal" visitor. I've seen similar collaboration between women and men from different islands. I've seen, in other words, higglers and traders crossing divides of race, territory and sometimes age and gender to stake their claim to the region.

GRENADA 1983, NEOLIBERALISM, AND FORMAL ORGANIZING IN THE REGION

The psychological impact of the 1983 defeat in Grenada was amplified by the effect of neoliberalism. It destroyed the sense and reality of community and fostered individualism. When Margaret Thatcher said "There is no such thing as society" or the neoconservatives in the United States went on the assault after Hillary Clinton repeated the African proverb "It takes a village to raise a child," they were predicting the fragmentation that the neoliberal policies they were imposing were deliberately creating to undermine resistance to the same policies.

It's beyond the reach of this presentation to analyze the errors which con-tributed to the defeat in Grenada beyond what I have written elsewhere (see, for example, Essay 3, this volume). The point here is that its impact was region-wide. The immediate post-Grenada years saw the complete shut-down of many left parties, with the notable exception of those in Guyana.[5] Regionally, the left was drastically diminished in size and influence. As David Scott puts it in a brief analysis:

> By the mid to late 1980s ... the whole landscape of political opposition in the Caribbean was in a state of considerable upheaval. Sheltered by the new political context of international capital (these were the Reagan/Thatcher years, remember), the political right in the region reasserted itself with great ferocity, and the left began to spiral into crisis. The assassination of Walter Rodney; the collapse of the democratic socialist experiment of Michael Manley; and most damaging of all, the implosion of the Grenada Revolution and the US invasion—these seemed to mark the beginning of the end of the Caribbean left as a revolutionary project. (Scott 2004: 123)

Today, the main survivors of the actively anti-imperialist left are to be found in usually small but strong Pan-African groups including in Barbados and Trinidad and Tobago. Meanwhile, the radical trade union movement has also been weakened. In addition to the loss of public sector jobs resulting from SAPs or other austerity policies and an increase in the confidence of private sector employers vis-a-vis the workers and their unions, labor organizing has become less and less representative of the working people as they are now reconstituted, given the rapid informalization of work. In some territories, trade unions are increasingly vulnerable to accepting the neo-liberal diktat that capital, government and labour collaborate in keeping workers quiet.

Workers' rights continue to be undermined by the impact of migration on its present terms; this is true of both migration into, and migration between territories of the region. There has been, for example, a large inward migration of Chinese as shop owners, building contractors and workers across the region including in the Windward Islands, Suriname, Guyana and Trinidad and Tobago; and of Brazilian men as miners and shop keepers and women as shop assistants and sex workers into Guyana (and perhaps elsewhere). The exploitation of the Chinese workers in Trinidad and Tobago has been condemned by the National Workers Union of Trinidad and Tobago as permitted by a government policy to contract Chinese construction firms "based on savage exploitation of sweated migrant labour imported from halfway across the globe" for the purpose of giving Chinese construction firms a competitive edge, and of workers "made to pay a bond to secure their jobs ... worked mercilessly for unconscionably long hours and ... treated like twenty-first century indentured labourers" (National Workers Union, October 15, 2009). This is foreign investment and capital accumulation based on the importation of super-exploited labor in a context in which insufficient local employment is being generated.

In relation to the migration of workers across the region, there seem to be only a few national organizations which defend "illegal" migrant workers, including those trade unions which honor the principle of defending workers' rights regardless of their legal status.

The growth of the informal sector has meant that more and more of the working people have been consigned to working without security of employment and income, union protection, and the strength that can come from working collectively. Labor movement organizing is thereby weakened. There is little attempt to organize women and men in the informal sector although this region has prior experience of trade unions organizing with informal sector workers. I don't know much about the history of worker organizing in Barbados and other parts of the region, but thanks to the work of Rhoda Reddock, we have information about Trinidad and Tobago. Describing the process by which trade unions in that country began to exclude sectors of working class women and to base themselves on a limited definition of labor, she recounts that the

1937 labor uprisings "had resulted in a great mobilisation of women and men into trade unions which continued into 1939 and early 1940" (Reddock 1994: 254–257).

In the early 1940s, the Oilfield Workers' Trade Union (OWTU) membership included unwaged housewives. The Federated Workers Trade Union (FWTU) organized self-employed market women, with the union President personally collecting their union dues in the absence of a check-off system. However, in the 1940s and 1950s British trade union officials, the Fabian Colonial Bureau and the colonial labor department instituted what they called "responsible trade unionism" which "made the unions simply agents of mediation between capital and labour" and divided the working class along industry and sex lines, with only wage workers to be unionized and with a clear separation between the political struggle and the trade union movement. The Butler movement went against the trend by organizing all workers—wage-employed, self-employed, unemployed and housewives (ibid.).

The feminist movement which emerged as a strong force in the region in the 1980s, expressed organizationally in the Caribbean Association for Feminist Research and Action (CAFRA), arose in part out of the failure of the left to take the needs and interests called women's interests into account (such as domestic violence, unwaged work), or to accept, still less promote, women's real leadership in the parties. I joined CAFRA in the mid-1980s (and co-founded Red Thread in Guyana at around the same time) because I wanted to work with women outside of a political party formation. Some other women in the leading organ of the early CAFRA were also from the left. As explained by Reddock, one of its founders, "the conflict between the primacy of 'class' or 'sex' was one of the main reasons which led to the formation of … CAFRA." But even if CAFRA was founded to give sex "primacy," the view of feminism that it promised related sex to other power relations. "In choosing, despite opposition, to use the term 'feminist' in its title," wrote Reddock, "the early CAFRA membership sought to create its own definition of Caribbean feminism which was inclusive in relation to class, race or ethnicity and colour. It also sought to be pan-Caribbean in its outlook and composition" (Reddock 2007).

CAFRA's signal achievement was that it *was* pan-Caribbean in outlook and composition, including as it did members throughout the region, from all language areas. But in terms of membership, we were not inclusive. "CAFRA in those days was "made up mainly of predominantly Afro-Caribbean women, with Indo-Caribbean women in a small minority and little or no connection with Indigenous women, the poorest in the region. Working class women of all races/ethnic groups formed another minority. The age range was … narrow" (Essay 1, this volume). The exclusions I saw when I wrote that in 2002 related to race, class and age; of course there were lesbian and bisexual women in CAFRA, but they were not really out, and neither sexual identity nor dis/ability was in the forefront of our thinking. Nor did we carry out what was, to my mind a most important part of our mission: "To develop an approach to women's problems from the perspective of race, class and sex, specifically to show how the exploitative relationship between men and women, facilitates the continuation, maintenance and reproduction of exploitative capitalist relations, and how the capitalist system benefits from this approach."[6]

The continuation of David Scott's (2004: 123) comment on the period highlights what he sees as the paradoxes in the rise of feminist organizing in the region in the 1980s:

> [the] period of left decline was at the same time a period of remarkable growth and transformation in Caribbean feminism; it was a period in which women's organizations and networks that were independent of male-centred political formations emerged—the Caribbean Association for Feminist Research and Action, for example—and they set about recasting the agenda of women's activism. In short, "gender" emerged as a visible category of criticism, and in so doing destabilized the very idea of radical politics ... But there is a sense in which this is paradoxical. The context is one in which the hope of an alternative to capitalism is rapidly receding, and a politics of identity is displacing a politics of social transformation.[7] Moreover, it is a context in which transnational capital is focusing surplus-value extraction on women's labor (in free trade zones, in service industries, and so on); and therefore capital itself now has a vested interest in the question of women in economic development. In other words, just as what constitutes "politics" and the normative consensus on its "progressive" direction becomes ambiguous, "gender" emerges as a site for the proliferation of NGO development work. And as the Age of Projects arrives, the old political left, both men and women (understandably looking for sources of income in a hostile neoliberal environment), are urged to transform themselves into technical experts writing assessment reports for international funding agencies.

Where this comment ends is with what I and others have described as the NGOization of political space in the region. While we still use the word "movement" in relation to say, trade unions or women, increasingly we think of these "movements" as part of "civil society," especially in those countries where neo-liberalism is virtually unchallenged. While many claim to use the term without ideological bias, it is not neutral. It is the anti-movement—a kind of amorphous, neutralizing, lumping together of everything that is not government or business or sometimes religious groups, consigned to carrying out some not-too-militant action, and open to friendly, even dependent relations with the representatives of Western governments. Relatedly, as Scott suggests, civil society is often dominated by NGOs implementing "projects."

This in itself may not seem like a bad thing and indeed we have NGOs in the region which use donor funds to work in the interests of Caribbean women, youth, children and men. But the Caribbean has a history of the most sustained covert and overt interventions into our politics by the United States, Canada and Europe; a history which should make us alert to what a number of recent books have analyzed as the growing use of NGOs for covert intervention across the globe. These analyses do not emanate only from left-wing writers. For example, in *Foundations and Public Policy*, Joan Roelofs describes how the role of philanthropic foundations has been "unduly obscured," so that research on money and politics focuses on campaign contributions and generally ignores "the funding of ideas." Roelofs cites Robert Arnove in his anthology, *Philanthropy and Cultural Imperialism* (1980) as explaining how "foundations like Carnegie, Rockefeller, and Ford have a corrosive influence on a democratic society; they represent relatively unregulated and unaccountable concentrations of power and wealth which buy talent, promote causes, and, in effect, establish an agenda of what merits society's attention. They serve as 'cooling out' agencies, delaying and preventing more radical, structural change" (Roelofs 2003: 5).

Within CARICOM, the most extensive work on NGOization has been done on Haiti. For example, in the view of Peter Hallward, author of a book on Haiti called *Damming the Flood*, NGOs are being used

> to control populations that do not accept the global order of things, that resist the global division of labour, and the grotesque inequality that structures much of the world (particularly in a place like Haiti) since the end of the Cold War. What's remarkable about both the Intifada in Palestine (that began in the late 1980s) and the Lavalas movement in Haiti, is that they had to be managed with different kinds of tactics—certainly a mixture of military force, but other kinds of mechanisms as well, and the NGOs have been very important there.[8]

The 10 to 15 thousand NGOs in Haiti—the highest per capita figure in the world—now deliver about 80 percent of Haiti's public services. Among the significant consequences is that Haitian sovereignty is being sub-contracted out to other organizations and other governments. In 2004 almost without exception, NGOs—particularly political NGOs, human rights groups or NGOs interested in political process, in parliamentary systems, in electoral procedures, or media-related NGOs that receive funding from USAID and the National Endowment for Democracy—supported the overthrow of the Aristide government (see endnote 9). There were many of us in the Caribbean who were persuaded by their propaganda.

My argument is not that old and new forms of organizing in the region have won nothing in the post-Grenada neoliberal environment but that those victories are limited. Two examples—one from the feminist movement, the other from the Indigenous movement—may suffice. First, increasing the number of women in decision-making positions including in the political leadership, has made little substantial and lasting difference to policy because those women, even the ones who are consciously anti-sexist, have to operate within the same political party, governance and economic structures and environment that predated their arrival. Second, while Indigenous organizations in the region have won collective rights to land which they have protected for generations, these victories are under constant threat of destabilization and must be constantly defended.

Rights that can be won in the interstices of policies and institutions designed to maintain the existing disparities of power are always either partial or temporary, or both.

NOTES ON MOVING FORWARD

Under capitalism, exploitation, subordination and discrimination based on differences including gender, race, class and nation are fundamental to how we are divided against each other. Selma James puts it clearly in a paragraph which is always, now, at the heart of how I understand what Marx calls "a hierarchy of labour powers":

> A hierarchy of labour powers and scale of wages to correspond. Racism and sexism training us to develop and acquire certain capabilities at the expense of all others. Then these acquired capabilities are taken to be our nature and fix our functions for life, and fix also the quality of our mutual relations. So planting cane or tea is not a job for white people and changing nappies is not a job for men and beating children is not violence. Race, sex, age, nation, each an indispensable element of the international division of labour. (James 1986: 6)

I'm not suggesting that if we get rid of capitalism we will free ourselves from racism, sexism and other forms of exploitation, subordination and discrimination; but I am making two propositions. The first is that since they are fundamental to how capitalism functions, if we try to tackle them without confronting capitalism our victories will remain partial and temporary. The second is that since capital thrives on keeping us divided we will win lasting gains only if we unite.

But what we want is not unity on the old terms. We don't need a superficial unity based—even if unconsciously—on the interests of those among us who have the most power. The standard against which we must assess where we are today in the struggle/s to challenge the power/s against us is where we are in our determination to challenge the power relations among us.

Post-Grenada, most organizing in the region has been on the basis of identity politics—not only (as Scott mentions) groups organizing as women, but groups organizing as LGBTI+ people, people with disabilities, and people of one race/ethnicity or the other. Because the term "identity politics" is used to mean different things we need to be clear how we are using it here. Some use it negatively, contrasting it with what is seen as the wider politics of social transformation, while others use it as, for example, Orlando Patterson does, as a politics that "emerged [during the second half of the last century] as an eman- cipatory mode of political action and thinking based on the shared experience of injustice by particular groups—notably blacks, women, gays, Latinos and American Indians" (quoted at Merriam-Webster undated).

In my view, those who use the term to question all self-organizing by sector should recognize that much of this organizing has brought to the fore sectors which were either not organized or collectively not visible, and whose issues were not given the priority they deserve by traditional organizations or even understood as related to capital. Sector-based organizing becomes identity politics in the negative sense only when it means to divide the sector off from other sectors, and when it is without any goal beyond the rights that the sector can win for itself, and that it can win without challenging the domination of the market. We need to distinguish between those groups which are narrowly focused and those which are open to working with other sectors in their shared interests, while ensuring that their own sector's needs are kept on the table. The first type of group is engaged in separatist organizing; the second in auton- omous organizing, which opens the way to sectors with less power coming together with sectors with more power on a new basis (see James 1986: 8–10).

While we need organizing that is anti-capitalist and anti-imperialist, our orga- nizing must also be anti-racist, anti-sexist, anti-homophobic, anti-transphobic and against all forms of exploitation, subordination and discrimination. The left says that identity politics is narrow, but the left's definition of what is political and who is political has its own narrowness. Identity politics challenges those of us rooted in traditional left organizing to move beyond the narrow view of class or put another way, to recognize all the sectors that capital makes potential allies of.

Similarly, while we need organizing against the forms of exploitation, subordination and discrimination that the left has traditionally ignored or downplayed, our organizing must also be anti-capitalist and anti-imperialist.

I don't pretend to know how we will rebuild the movement to change the (Caribbean) world, and build it better than it ever was, but I am sure that divided action is not taking us in that direction.

Where might we begin to organize differently? We can begin organizing at any point; if we do it right it will lead us to every other point. My choice of starting point would be a cross- sectoral struggle against SAPs whether formally imposed by the IMF and World Bank or adopted by our governments as though independently designed. This would be a renewed, not a new struggle.

As far back as the 1970s and 1980s, women across the Global South, including in this region, led the way in uncovering the destructive impact of SAPs on our countries (see endnote 8). In January 1985 there were country-wide protests in Jamaica against a rise in fuel prices implemented in accordance with SAPs (see Danaher 2001) and in October of the same year, Jamaica's (conservative) government, "fearing a violent public reaction, told the IMF that it would not institute (further) price hikes for food and petroleum and other belt-tightening required under the program" (Director of Central Intelligence 1985). Elsewhere, anti-austerity struggles were (and still are) also waged by unions in some countries—often couched as struggles against layoffs and/or restrictions on the size of the public sector, wages and pensions. But today the active struggle against SAPs or austerity is dormant in our part of the region, while there has been a recent upsurge in protests in other Caribbean countries. I want to describe some of these in detail so you can see the broad range of organizations in nearby countries which understood their common interest in what was in effect anti-capitalist action.

In January 2009 a mass strike shut down Guadeloupe for 44 days "and launched the largest political movement in the island's history," winning agreement from the French government on 165 demands including an increase in the minimum wage and reduced prices for public utilities (Yarimar Bonilla, in *Stabroek News*, April 27, 2009). The strike was organized by a coalition of 48 organizations, including trade unions from a wide spectrum of industries, environmental groups, peasant organizations, political parties, pro-independence activists, consumer rights advocates, associations for disability rights, fair housing proponents, music and dance groups, and a wide range of other political, cultural, and civic leaders. This range of activists came together under the name Lyannaj Kont Pwofitasyon (LKP), which can be loosely translated as the Alliance Against Profiteering.

The Guadeloupe protests caught fire in Martinique where a general strike was launched by 12 unions on February 5 against a decrease in purchasing power "which has especially affected the 70,000 people on the island living below the poverty line" out of a total population of 401,000 (Francoise Thull and Pierre Mabut, in *BayView National Black Newspaper*, February 13, 2009). The strike ended March 14 with the signing of an agreement with terms similar to those won in Guadeloupe between the government and the February 5 Collective, a coalition of trade unions and other social movements named after the day the strike began. Thousands gathered outside the signing ceremony chanting "*Matinik leve*" ("Martinique stand up").

On October 15, in Puerto Rico, 200,000 people took part in a strike against recent economic and labor policies of the government, including the dismissal by the government—the largest employer—of thirty thousand government employees in the name of fiscal stabilization. The strike was called by a coalition of unions, religious leaders and community organizations called Todo Puerto Rico por Puerto Rico (All of Puerto Rico for Puerto Rico) and labor leaders of the Union Coordination for a Broad Front of Solidarity and Struggle. Local artists, university professors, students, school teachers, environmentalists, lawyers, senior citizens, gay rights activists and other labor unions participated, with college students "highly vocal." The strike was preceded by numerous acts of civil disobedience and there were solidarity protests in New York by Puerto Ricans resident there (Bonilla in the Diaspora column, *Stabroek News*, October 26, 2009).

For us, here, a key aspect of anti-austerity organizing we would need to take back up is the search for an alternative economic vision with people and nature at its center; and by putting people at the center I mean at the center of decision-making about economic development. C. L. R. James's decades-old analysis is not out-of-date:

> any new and genuine economic development of the Caribbean has to begin first of all with the involvement of the mass of the population. Those responsible for plans and production are not even aware that this is missing. For them, the business of workers and peasants [poor people] is not to concern themselves about industry, bringing in to bear their accumulated experience, their practical knowledge, and their creative handling of the materials that they use every hour of the day. Their business is to work. (James 1981: 21)

By nation, C. L. R. James means what he calls "the West Indian nation" or "the Caribbean nation."

Organizing to win economic and social transformation should also go hand in hand with active support for the free movement of the people, whose increasingly massive migration across the region is a people's protest against its economic failures. Our job in response to it is not to support our governments in managing the migration, turning ourselves into gatekeepers, but to act in solidarity with those who are migrating. This means not just support for amnesties for those who have migrated "illegally," important though these are, but rejecting the very notion of "illegal" migration, campaigning for genuine free movement and for the measures which would facilitate it; providing support to those who are barred from entering a country to which they choose to migrate. That higglers were not among the first people to be officially allowed free movement and that we did not demand this is an expression of class and gender discrimination; or that we did not stand with domestic workers in their struggle for the right to free movement within CARICOM.[9] And if our failure to stand with higglers and domestic workers is a reflection of class and gender discrimination, it is a reflection of a complex class, race, religious and language discrimination that we do not join in fighting for Haitians to be allowed even the limited rights allowed other CARICOM citizens.[10] We must defend Haiti as a matter of priority. The whole world—and we in particular in the Caribbean—owes a great debt to the Haitian people, whose 1804 revolution paved the way for emancipation in the region and for liberation and anti-colonial movements everywhere.

In the face of the decline of "region" as exemplified by the decentralization of the University of the West Indies, the halting movement towards the Caribbean Single Market and Economy and yes, the fall of West Indies cricket, it is "ordinary" Caribbean people who are increasingly federating the region, daily, on the ground. Campaigning for free movement means campaigning on the side of those at the bottom across race, sex, sexuality, dis/ability and age, often led by women. It is on the side of micro-traders, domestic workers, small construction workers, agricultural workers, sex workers, mothers. It defends each sector that the present order of things assaults. Similarly, campaigning against SAPs is a campaign against their anti-working people and anti-women biases.

To quote Selma James, "We have to make demands that speak to people's needs and give them the courage to fight for them. The task is not to be modest because we think we can't get more (personal communication, undated).

I'm going to close where I started. We are far away from the spirit of resistance with which I began the presentation, resistance organized respectively by the labor movement in British Honduras, Jamaica, St. Kitts, St. Vincent, St. Lucia, Barbados, Trinidad and British Guiana—the independence movement in British Guiana, and the anti-racist Black Power movement in Trinidad. These movements were created out of courage and vision and leadership to confront the root causes of oppression and exploitation in the region as they manifested themselves during those decades. To stop sinking under the weight of our pessimism about our capacity to fight against capitalism we have to take inspiration from our own history and from the history of other countries, learn the lessons of their weaknesses, setbacks and failures and build on their strengths. We have to learn from the willingness of those who fought before us to take the risk of rising up against seemingly immovable forces.

POSTSCRIPT (GEORGETOWN, GUYANA, APRIL 2019)

Beginning in 2010, a year after this lecture was presented, what has now become an almost global phenomenon began to emerge. In material terms, this virulent ultra-right is partly a legacy of the policies of neo-liberalism, which led to increasing income inequality blamed not on the rich but on the "other"—most often racial and ethnic minorities, immigrants, and refugees. The angry resentment of its followers is also fed by the growing self-assertion of the LGBTI+, women's, Indigenous and anti-racist movements.

Globally, the ultra-right is not homogeneous but it tends to be characterized by anti-globalization, support for laissez-faire and extractive capitalism, militarism, and ultra-nationalism, a key element of which is intolerance of religious minorities. It is racist, xenophobic, misogynist, homophobic and, transphobic, and discriminates against people with disabilities. It is an expression of identity politics of the negative kind—one that is product and producer of separatism and a desire for supremacy or a return to what is nostalgically remembered as an earlier supremacy.

There are growing attempts to strengthen the ultra-right by connecting it across nations, and within countries, there is a merging of the traditional right and the ultra-right under the hegemony of the ultra-right. The strength of this rising force is a reflection of the failure of traditional parties and more crucially, of the failure of the separate movements for justice and equality to build a sustained politics that works to include all sectors of the oppressed and exploited.

NOTES

1. Kathleen Drayton was born and raised in Trinidad and Tobago. A political and social activist in different parts of the region for most of her life, she was a pioneer of gender studies at the University of the West Indies. Drayton retired as a Senior Lecturer in the Department of Education at the Cave Hill campus of UWI and earlier, was the head of Women and Development Studies on the same campus. She died on July 3, 2009.
2. A survey conducted by four Red Thread women among 101 other grassroots women across race/ethnicity who compiled diaries of their time-use hour by hour.
3. The study focused on Jamaica, Guyana and Antigua-Barbuda.
4. In 1984 at their Heads of Government conference in Nassau, CARICOM heads adopted "structural adjustment [as the] key to Caribbean transformation," and thereafter placed all sectoral and financial policies and programs within this framework. The framework was devised by Washington-based institutions like the International Monetary Fund (IMF) and the World Bank, under the influence of the US Treasury, to deal with the debt crisis affecting some Latin American countries, and Jamaica. This policy framework is referred to by different names (Washington Consensus, SAPs, neoliberalism) but its purpose is always to privilege the market (especially large corporations) over people (especially poor people). It does this by requiring governments to cut budgets (especially by cutting social services and subsidies to poor people), privatize assets (such as electricity and water), deregulate industries, open/liberalize markets and increase indirect taxes, such as value added taxes, which fall disproportionately on poor people.

5. The People's Progressive Party (PPP) was a strong force less because of its ideology than because of its base in the majority Indian-Guyanese population and the abiding respect and loyalty they had for Cheddi Jagan in particular. The party also had material resources, including through its links with the Soviet Union. For its part, for many years after the assassination of Walter Rodney in 1980, the Working People's Alliance remained a significant presence among the working people in the coastlands and extended its work into Indigenous communities in the interior. This continued until the 1992 elections when, as usual in Guyana's elections since the 1950s, Indians and Africans voted for the PPP and the People's National Congress (PNC) respectively.

6. My repeated criticisms of CAFRA since 2002 largely come out of the conviction that if our organizing had implemented its original goals, it would at the very least have been able to better address the needs and interests of all sectors of women, starting from women who are poor.

7. The Caribbean feminist critique of SAPs (influenced by the analysis of DAWN, the network of "feminists from the South" proposing Development Alternatives with Women for a New Era) was put forward as a politics of social transformation, grounded in an awareness of how a corporate agenda might be built on the unwaged work of women. Caribbean women, at their regional meeting held in Barbados early in 1985 in preparation for the end-of-Decade conference in Nairobi, were the first to challenge this policy framework. For writing by Caribbean feminists on SAPs, see, for example, Peggy Antrobus (2004: chapter 5).

8. Peter Hallward speaking at international gathering organized by the Global Women's Strike in London, January 2009.

9. Free movement was later extended to domestic workers in December 2009.

10. Rather than understand the practice of voodoo and use of *kreyòl* by millions of Haitians as strengths, we often use them as proof of backwardness.

REFERENCES

Antrobus, Peggy. 2004. *The Global Women's Movement: Origins, Issues and Challenges.* London: Zed Books.

Bonilla, Yarimar. 2009. "Guadeloupe on Strike: A New Political Chapter in the French Antilles." Diaspora column, *Stabroek News* April 27.

——. 2009. "Jobs and Justice in the Caribbean: Taking to the Streets in Puerto Rico." Diaspora column, *Stabroek News*, October 26.

Danaher, Kevin, ed. 2001. *Democratizing the Global Economy.* Monroe, ME: Common Courage Press.

Director of Central Intelligence. 1985. "National Intelligence Daily." October 26.

Ferguson, James. 2003. "Migration in the Caribbean: Haiti, the Dominican Republic and Beyond." Minority Rights Group, July. Retrieved from https://minorityrights.org/wp-content/uploads/2015/07/MRG_Rep_Caribbean.pdf

Gregory, Steven. 2014. *The Devil Behind the Mirror: Globalization and Politics in the Dominican Republic.* Berkeley, CA: University of California Press.

Hallward, Peter. 2007. *Damning the Flood: Haiti, Aristide and the Politics of Containment.* London: Verso.

Human Rights Watch. 2002. "Citizenship and Proof of Dominican Identity." Retrieved from www.hrw.org/reports/2002/domrep/domrep0402-04.htm

Jackson, Jason and Judith Wedderburn. 2009. "Gender and the Economic Partnership Agreement: An Analysis of the Potential Gender Effects of the CARIFORUM-EU-EPA." In *Caribbean Development Report*, vol. 2. Santiago, Chile: United Nations Economic Commission on Latin America and the Caribbean.

Jamaicans for Justice. 2009. "Another Hasty and Irresponsible Statement by the Minister of National Security." September 29. Retrieved from www.trinidadexpress.com/index.pl/article

James, C. L. R. 1981. "The Birth of a Nation." In *Contemporary Caribbean: A Sociological Reader*, vol. 1, Ed. Susan Craig. Maracas, Trinidad and Tobago: The College Press.

James, Selma. 1986. *Sex, Race and Class*. London: Housewives in Dialogue.

Merriam-Webster. Undated. "Identity Politics." Retrieved from www.merriam-webster.com/dictionary/identity politics.

National Workers Union. 2009. "National Workers Union Calls For Defence of Chinese Migrant Workers." Retrieved from www.workersunion.org.tt/where-we-stand/nwu-media/untitledpost-1 (accessed October 15, 2009).

The Observer. 2009. "UK Supermarkets Warned Over Banana Price War." October 11.

Puri, Shalini. 2004. *The Caribbean Postcolonial: Social Equality, Post-Nationalism, and Cultural Hybridity*. New York: Palgrave Macmillan.

Reddock, Rhoda. 1994. *Women, Labour and Politics in Trinidad and Tobago: A History*. London: Zed Books.

——. 2007. "Diversity, Difference and Caribbean Feminism: The Challenge of Anti-Racism." *Caribbean Review of Gender Studies* 1 (April). Retrieved from https://sta.uwi.edu/crgs/april2007/journals/Diversity-Feb_2007.pdf

Roelofs, Joan. 2003. *Foundations and Public Policy: The Mask of Pluralism*. SUNY Series in Radical Social and Political Theory. Albany, NY: SUNY Press.

Scott, David. 2004. "Counting Women's Caring Work: An Interview with Andaiye." *Small Axe* 15: 123–217.

Thull, Francoise and Pierre Mabut. 2009. "Guadeloupe and Martinique Workers Call General Strike to Protest Economic Racism." *BayView National Black Newspaper*, February 13.

Trotz, D. Alissa. 2008. "Gender, Generation and Memory: Remembering a Future Caribbean." Distinguished Dame Nita Barrow 14th Annual Memorial Lecture, Working Paper, Issue 14, Centre for Gender and Development, University of the West Indies, Cave Hill, Barbados.

LAST WORD

ESSAY 27
Walter Rodney's Last Writing on and for the Guyanese Working People
[2010]

I want to start with the first lines of *The Groundings with my Brothers*, which of course came out of Walter Rodney's experience not in Guyana, but Jamaica:

> In 1938, exactly one hundred years after the supposed Emancipation of the Black Man in Jamaica, the masses once again were driven into action to achieve some form of genuine liberation under the new conditions of oppression. The beneficiaries of that struggle were a narrow, middle-class sector whose composition was primarily brown, augmented by significant elements of white and other groups ... (Rodney 1969: 12)

I begin with this because in a few short lines, it shows how Rodney's world view orders his writing. He is speaking in 1968,[1] but opens with 1938 to introduce the point that the pattern of the modern history of Jamaica and the Caribbean is that the working people win a victory, that victory is appropriated by others, and they are then forced to wage a new struggle in their quest for "genuine liberation." Like all Marxists he believed that class struggle is what moves human history, but unlike those who define themselves as orthodox Marxists, misreading or never having read Marx, he connected class to race and so named which side he was on in terms of both. Thus, in the context of Jamaica he was on the side of the "Black Man," the oppressed African majority, and against the brown man who was part of the class forces ranged against the Black Man;[2] but elsewhere in *Groundings* he made clear that in the specific context of the Caribbean as a whole and therefore in countries like Guyana and Trinidad and Tobago, Black Power must encompass both Africans and Indians. Anything else, he argues, "would be a flagrant denial of both the historical experience of the West Indies and the reality of the contemporary scene."

*   *   *

I know most of Rodney's work on Guyana, but only Nigel Westmaas—unofficial WPA archivist—has a completely accurate count of all he produced in those years. I want to touch on selected elements of his output, including the last three texts written for publication which are normally categorized as either scholarly, *A History of Guyanese Working People: 1881–1905*; polemical, *People's Power, No Dictator*; or children's historical fiction, *Kofi Baadu Out of Africa*. By June 1980 he had almost finished a draft of *Lakshmi Out of India*, which was to be the second book in what he intended to be a series.[3] He also gave numerous speeches which were later printed. Of these, I'll discuss one of the most important—a speech he made at the corner of Louisa Row and D'Urban Street in about 1976, "In Defence of Arnold Rampersaud" (an Indian-Guyanese activist of the People's Progressive Party (PPP) accused of murdering an African-Guyanese policeman).

Before I go on I want to stress two major weaknesses in his telling of the history of the Guyanese working people: There is no serious treatment of Indigenous peoples (although he planned a children's book on the story of the Indigenous peoples in Guyana), nor is there any serious treatment of women (although in his research for *A History of the Guyanese Working People*, he spent time searching old documents for and recording the little he found about their participation in the struggles of 1881–1905).[4] While these are obviously fundamental limitations, it should be pointed out that 1980, the year he was killed, was before the movement of Indigenous peoples and the second phase of the women's movement stamped themselves on the politics of the region. Working with him both as an editor of his last written work and as the editor of the 1978–1980 Working People's Alliance (WPA), I saw that as stubbornly as he always argued for his views, he was so quintessentially political that his political thinking and action were constantly being informed and reshaped by the teachings coming out of the social motion of oppressed groups.[5] This, along with the other, related strengths of his writings (and his organizing) is what we should take from him and use, not cite each understanding he had arrived at as the last word on any issue.

Academics may choose to place Rodney's writings in categories; activists who want to see whether and how they may be of use today should not. There was really no clear line of demarcation between Rodney the political activist whose organizing was shaped by what he had learned and kept on learning from history, and Rodney the always-growing historian whose writing was based on the most careful research, but ultimately shaped—deliberately—by a political vision. He did not claim to be "objective," or try to be. In "The Birth of the Guyanese Working Class" he lamented the fact that what he considered one of the best studies on British Guiana, Alan Adamson's *Sugar Without Slaves*, was "a study from outside, about peoples living *there*, who tend to be almost reified ... a study about *systems* ... not a study of the Guyanese *people* living on the plantations" (Rodney 1981b: 2; my emphasis). What he wanted for us were studies/histories where we reflect on ourselves, from our own perspective, in our own interests. Both as intellectual and as organizer, then, the task he set himself was to contribute to transforming the world. Thus not only did each "type" of writing have the same fundamental aim as the other, but the writing had the same aim as the speeches or the bottom-house classes he conducted or the groundings—to advance the struggle of the working people for their own liberation. Put another way, what his writing and speeches were always doing was examining and recording the struggle of the working people, including the hidden struggle that is imbedded in their daily activities, the victories they win, the usurping of those victories by other classes or by sectors of their own class who become leaders; and how they struggle again to overcome what he calls in the quotation from *Groundings* with which I began, "the new conditions of oppression." And whether he was talking about Jamaica or Guyana or anywhere else, he located developments here within a global struggle.

Even the way he wrote in those last years in Guyana underscores the blurring of lines. As I wrote in a newspaper article called "Remembering Walter":

He wrote everywhere—in the car if he wasn't driving, standing on the street corner, on the stelling waiting to board the Berbice ferry, waiting for public meetings to begin in Linden, on the Corentyne, in Leonora, in Berbice, often surrounded by the police—he wrote everywhere … (*Stabroek News*, June 11, 2000)

Almost literally, then, as Rupert Roopnaraine (2010: 25) put it, he was "fighting as he wrote and writing as he fought," and by that I mean at the same time, within the same space, and with the same driven purpose.

Everything he wrote was steeped in a view of history as something to be put to use. In the period of civil rebellion starting in July 1979, Rodney led the WPA's campaign to create the political conditions for insurrection among working people whose previous resistance to the authoritarian and anti-working people regime of Forbes Burnham had been prevented from moving to a higher level by race division and a lack of self-belief. The centerpieces of this campaign were massive, multiracial public rallies—mass groundings with young and older participants across gender and class, fired by drumming, chanting, and call and response; and wherever appropriate, Rodney began his interventions by identifying the plantation that had stood on the ground where the crowds now stood, connecting us to our history. These rallies were examples of the public meeting as a school for politics.

The central themes of the last Guyana writings are the central pre-occupations of the struggle he helped lead from 1974–1980—racial unity, resistance, and the inter-dependence of the two. The use of history to make history.

By racial unity he meant in the first place, unity between Indian- and African-Guyanese working people. That was the rupture he believed had to be and could be mended.[6] In very different ways all that he wrote (and did) following his return to Guyana emphasized the unity of the Indian/African working people. "In Defence of Arnold Rampersaud" was a deeply personal and emotional speech where he located himself as a Guyanese of African descent speaking directly to other Guyanese of African descent, admonishing witnesses who had lied on the stand and appealing to them not to let themselves be used against another working class person of a different race. Facing the crowd at Louisa Row and D'Urban Street, he began by evoking their proud, common history as the children of women and men who had freed themselves from slavery:

> Now, I am an Afro-Guyanese. There are very many things about what I've been describing against which I rebel. I'm not rebelling just as an abstract citizen. I'm rebelling as a Guyanese with this particular heritage—as an Afro-Guyanese ...
>
> Whatever else we may have been in our history in this country, we have been a people with dignity. We came out of slavery with dignity and that was a tremendous achievement, because slavery is inherently degrading. But our people came out of slavery and we could stand tall. We fought after slavery to build the villages in this country. We fought to open the interior of this country. Our people—I'm speaking now specifically of the black Guyanese whatever may be our shortcomings—have managed to persist in this country with this basis of dignity. (Rodney 1982: 7–8)

Then from the post-slavery period he came to the present and to the neighborhood where he had spent his childhood, not far from where he was speaking, peopled by women and men he knew would be familiar to his listeners:

> I was brought up not very far from here in a typical range yard in Bent Street. And there, amidst the poverty, looking back now, I can see in my mind's eye ordinary black people who were worth everything, who were human beings, who had strength, who had character. Never mind that he may have been a cartman, never mind the woman may have been taking in washing. When you stop to think of it, they had character ... And now I cannot accept that such people must be put to do some dirty skullduggery—coming to court, lying, to get another man convicted of murder ... (Rodney 1982: 8)

With far less feeling but with the same confidence with which he made this appeal, in *History of the Guyanese Working People* he refuted "the notion of Guyanese *history* as one that is ridden with racial conflict." He did not deny the presence of race conflict in nineteenth century British Guiana. The key chapter on race in the text—chapter 7—is "Race as a Contradiction among the Working People." He described how the two groups had been set up against each other, and the cultural and residential separations between them. But for him, the argument that the movement towards the race violence of the 1960s was inexorable was simply wrong; "communal violence … [had come about] … in a context of both local and international class struggle … The specificity of the early 1960s," he added, "[could] hardly be used to characterize the entire history of Guyana." He preferred the judgement of Guyanese labor spokesman H. J. M. Hubbard with which he closed the chapter:

> It is by any standards a remarkable fact that in a competitive semi-feudal society such as British Guiana with restricted social and economic opportunities and less jobs than potential workers, very few serious physical inter-racial conflicts arose between the ethnic groups constituting the population. (Rodney 1981a: 189)

*   *   *

The second, related focus of Rodney's Guyana writings in 1974–1980 was resistance. In *History of the Guyanese Working People* as in the struggle outside books, his position was that in the worst of times there is resistance, even when hidden. Thus he began the chapter called "Resistance and Accommodation" with the dialectic between struggle and accommodation, with struggle ultimately asserting "itself as the principal aspect of the contradiction" (Rodney 1981a: 151; see also, ibid., "It takes a very jaundiced eye to read a people's history as a record of undiluted compliance and docility"). Since there is always resistance he searched it out everywhere. Much of his digging into old documents in archives and in people's homes was aimed at finding the invisible makers of history. The most important example of this was his hunt for the part women played in open acts of resistance. But race was what he was most concerned with, and the chapter not only debunked the myth of Indian-Guyanese docility, but knowing the misuse of this myth, was at pains to explain the material basis why the resistance/accommodation dialectic was easier to see in the history of the Indian indentured workers, and why African workers of the period had more scope for resistance. (As an aside, it seems to me that throughout our history, myths of Indian docility and of an African propensity to violence have fed on each other.)

The last chapter of *A History of the Guyanese Working People* is at once narrative and analysis of "The 1905 Riots," beginning with the following:

> Riots and disturbances punctuate the history of the British West Indies. Most were minor phenomena with little significance beyond the small circle of lives touched by a brief explosion of social violence. *But there were times when the disaffection was more wide-ranging and the scale of violence larger; and when*

the level of consciousness and organization of the participants carried these elements forward into a moment of challenge to colonial authority. In different degrees, these characteristics were present in the riots of November–December 1905 in the county of Demerara. (Rodney 1981a: 190; my emphasis)

I cite this paragraph often because it tells us something about Rodney's view of what constitutes a resistance higher than "riots and disturbances"—one that manifests a wider-ranging disaffection; a larger scale of violence; and a level of consciousness and organization sufficient to challenge the oppressors. Given the debates over his attitude to violence I will add that throughout his writing, including *Groundings*, he makes it clear that the conditions of struggle he describes often demand appropriate levels of what all of us in the global movement understood as revolutionary violence.

As disunity among African and Indian working people grew, Rodney began to emphasize that racial unity and effective resistance were product and producer of each other. The connection he made between the two was clearest in *People's Power, No Dictator*, written in 1979 as a call to action. As he explained in the last section, titled "Raise Up a Clear Alternative: National Unity and People's Power," "The firmest unity is unity in struggle" (Rodney 1981c: 20). In both *People's Power, No Dictator* and *History of the Guyanese Working People* he also stressed the other side of this coin: the consistent efforts of the authorities in every era to foster divisions among the working people to weaken their capacity for resistance.

* * *

I want to close with a footnote about Rodney's conviction that in Guyana (and other racially divided societies), racial unity and effective resistance are interdependent. The footnote arises out of the preface to *Kofi Baadu Out of Africa*. Unlike his other writing, the children's books did not make the case for racial unity but were an expression of his focus on the need for racial unity. The preface made this explicit when it said "This collective effort,[7] [of completing the book] hopes to make a modest contribution to revealing further aspects of our rich and varied heritage, so that the children, at least, might better understand themselves and each other." Re-reading that after his death, and again now, I am struck by the words "at least" and the sense the words convey that in 1980, in a period of downturn of the political resistance, his faith in the will of adult Guyanese to racial unity was at least momentarily shaken.[8]

The generation for whom he wrote his children's books would now be in their forties, and both racial unity and resistance are at their lowest point since the late 1980s. So the task is unfinished. It is as true today as it was when Rodney made the point, that working to build unity in struggle in the face of all that militates against it is a precondition of the continued work of enlarging our freedom.

ACKNOWLEDGEMENTS

This essay is edited from a talk prepared for the Guyana Institute of Historical Research Third Annual Conference on the theme "History and the Environment," Saturday June 26, 2010, Georgetown.

NOTES

1. This speech was presented to the Congress of Black Writers in October 1968, a few days before Rodney was banned from Jamaica and what came to be called the Rodney riots erupted.
2. At the 25th anniversary commemoration of Rodney's assassination, Nadeen Spence, a Jamaican woman, exclaimed "In Jamaica, brown is a race."
3. In addition to the planned story of the Indigenous peoples, the others in the series would have been the stories of the coming to British Guiana of people from China, Madeira, and Holland.
4. It also needs to be said that his treatment of women in *Kofi Baadu Out of Africa* shows a very traditional view of women.
5. For example, as the issues were raised by gay people themselves, I saw his views begin to change on the question of their rights. He also believed, as he often said, that if you are serious you publish as your contribution to an ongoing conversation. I understood what he meant during an incident in 1979 in the WPA center where a younger, African-Guyanese party member made a point with which I disagreed, to which he answered triumphantly that he knew he was right because Brother Walter had written this in *Groundings*. I said that then both he and Brother Walter were wrong. Unfortunately for him Rodney came in and when the matter was put to him he answered, "I changed my mind."
6. This focus on the imperative of crossing the Indian/African divide was part of the reason for the relative inattention in his writing to the Indigenous peoples.
7. He had tried very hard to make the writing of the narrative and the illustrations collective, with less success than he had hoped for.
8. This may help explain the level of priority he gave to the completion of these books in conditions that were difficult and dangerous.

REFERENCES

Andaiye. 2010. "Black Sunflowers: Reflections on the Life and Work of Walter Rodney, 1974–1980." Draft prepared for the 7th Annual Walter Rodney Symposium, March 19, Spelman College.

Rodney, Walter. 1969. *The Groundings with My Brothers*. London: Bogle L'Ouverture.

——. 1981a. *A History of the Guyanese Working People: 1881–1905*. Baltimore, MD: Johns Hopkins University Press.

——. 1981b. "The Birth of the Guyanese Working Class and the First Sugar Strikes 1840/41 and 1847." *Review* 4(4) (Spring).

——. 1981c. *People's Power, No Dictator*. New York: Black Liberation Press.

——. 1982. *In Defence of Arnold Rampersaud*. Georgetown: WPA Press.

——. 1990. *Walter Rodney Speaks: The Making of an African Intellectual*. Trenton, NJ: Africa World Press.

——. 2000. *Lakshmi Out of India*. Georgetown: Guyana Book Foundation; Trenton, NJ: Africa World Press.

——. 2004. *Kofi Baadu Out of Africa*. 2nd edition. Georgetown: Guyana Book Foundation.

Roopnaraine, Rupert. 2010. "Race and Rebellion: A Personal Interview with the Past—Writing and Making History in Walter Rodney, *History of the Guyanese Working People, 1881–1905*." In *The Sky's Wild Noise: Selected Essays*, Ed. Rupert Roopnaraine. London: Peepal Tree Press.

Afterword:
Andaiye and the Caribbean
Radical Organizing Tradition

Anthony Bogues

A MEETING

She stood there. Her face set in a reflective somber mood. Then she spoke without raising her voice, as she wondered aloud in a calm tone tinted with anger … "How could we in the room be thinking and talking about the revitalization of a regional Caribbean left without a proper accounting of the implosion of the Grenadian Revolution? How could we," she said, her voice rising a bit but still calm, "be talking about a new Caribbean left when we have not thought fully about what the West Indian man has not confronted—the patriarchy of the movement?" Myself and Brian Meeks as co-chairs of the event looked uneasily at each other. George Lamming sitting in the front row had a knowing smile on his face and all the male comrades in the room looked uncomfortable.

It was my first meeting with Andaiye. We were in Trinidad. It was 2001, and I, with others from Brown University in collaboration with the Centre for Caribbean Thought at the University of the West Indies (UWI) and the Oilfield Workers Trade Union (OWTU), had organized an international conference on the 100th anniversary of the birth of C. L. R. James. As we planned the meeting, Brian Meeks, David Abdullah from the OWTU and I agreed that one of the things we should try and do was to see if it was possible to convene a gathering of individuals who still considered themselves part of a radical left, in order to discuss the reconstitution of a Caribbean left, after the formal academic conference. We thought about this in a political conjuncture in which there had been the collapse of the nationalist projects in the region; the obvious decline of an organized left; the defeat of reformist projects and the implosion of the Grenadian revolution. All three of us agreed that the dominance of neoliberalism needed to be encountered as there was a dearth of radical thought within the region. We had discussed the implosion of Grenada but thought that the temporal distance of the implosion would create space where, even though it was a haunting specter, we could debate it as part of the process of re-forming a regional left. We never discussed patriarchy. And so, as Andaiye spoke, we were now confronted by a key figure of the post-colonial Caribbean radical moment, forcing us to come to terms with aspects of Caribbean left political practice and thought in the wake of constitutional decolonization within the Anglophone Caribbean.

The meeting did not discuss the matters raised by Andaiye in any great depth and it became clear, even with the intervention of Lamming, that on that day we were not going to be able to create even a semblance of a regional left. In politics there are moments when things cannot happen. I had learned a hard lesson years before this—that radical politics was not about any individual subjective push, but that action was also about balance of forces, the ways in which a moment might be closed or alternatively be open. That any opening or closing was both discursive and organizational, where matters which had been elided in previous moments, if not tackled, would stymie the politics of organization. I had worked in the mass movement in Jamaica in different capacities, had attended countless political meetings in London and Jamaica, had spent time as a young journalist and activist talking to Walter Rodney, but there was a quality about Andaiye I had rarely encountered. Here was a figure for whom radicalism was embodied in her very being, and in that embodiment there was a fierce commitment to radical forms of democracy and an under-standing that radical politics required a consistent opening to daily life of the most oppressed group.[1]

POLITICAL PREOCCUPATIONS

Talking to her after the event I realized that Andaiye's preoccupation in that meeting was not about who was responsible for the implosion in Grenada, which is how it was interpreted by many as recriminations went back and forth between individuals in the room. Rather, it was about democracy as a political and social form. How did we on the left after Grenada think about forms of democracy not just as a political but as a social form? And how could the left begin to think and practice forms of democracy without confronting patriarchy?

I suggest that these two political notions animated Andaiye's political thought and practice in ways which made her a critical Caribbean political personality of her time. The appellation of public intellectual or activist intellectual does not sit well on Andaiye. She was doing something else. In that doing her body, spirit and political ideas were themselves forces brought to bear on specific struggles.

Guyana is a unique Caribbean political site in the twentieth-century history of Caribbean decolonization. The major nationalist movements in the Anglo-phone Caribbean were not Marxist parties although some may have had a

Marxist wing.[2] In Guyana, the major political movement/party that struggled against British colonialism was the People's Progressive Party (PPP), a Marxist movement led by the late Cheddi Jagan. It meant that the political ideas of Marxism were in the public domain.[3] Thus growing up as a child and becoming politically aware she would have been surrounded by these ideas. She notes in an interview with David Scott, that "Rupert Roopnaraine, Walter Rodney and I talked about ... a kind of privilege to have been surrounded in a way that could not have happened to a child anywhere in the Caribbean now ... what came out of those men was real confidence that we were not too small or too poor to transform our world" (Scott 2004: 142).

Becoming politically active, then, Andaiye could take certain political things for granted. However, over time, the Guyanese context and the rule of Forbes Burnham would raise for her and others, issues which were not immediate ones on the Left's political agenda. For example, in the Jamaican case, the question of democracy was not given deep thought. For the People's National Party (PNP) left at the time, the issue revolved around the internal democracy of the party and the ability and capacity for party conventions to debate policy positions. For the Workers' Party of Jamaica (WPJ), democracy was generally understood as part of a bourgeois structure of rights which had to be overturned by a struggle for revolutionary democracy. However, within the Guyanese context the matter was different since the left faced the authoritarian structures of the People's National Congress (PNC) regime led by Burnham. Such a situation led Andaiye to be keenly attentive to democracy both as a form of political structure for rule, as well as a principal way of organizing. In the Scott interview she noted that, "these rights having been fought for and won by the working class; they were not rights that we were willing to turn our backs on, on the grounds that they were 'bourgeois democratic' rights" (Scott 2004: 183). For her, democracy was not a political concept but an organizing political principle of any radical state formation, political organization and social life. This in my view makes her one of the outstanding Caribbean figures of the period of decolonization. For her, living in the postcolonial Caribbean the politics of the native elite had created deep structures of domination within the region. This insight she quickly discerned and would write eloquently about in her remarkable analysis of Mr. Slime in George Lamming's classic novel, *In the Castle of My Skin*. For her, this meant that radical left politics had to pay attention to the ways in which the middle class quickly became the practical beneficiaries of rebellion.

Again we recall her at the James conference in 2001. Her account of the implosion did not foreground the political figures of the revolution, rather making the point that having visited Grenada many times, she noted that what struck her was the absence of forms of democracy. Not pro forma debates about the revolution within the revolution itself, but rather an openness to critique.[4]

EQUALITY

If forms of radical democracy were central to Andaiye's life, then a form of radical equality was another preoccupation and indeed for her they were inseparable. Beginning with her relationship with the Working People's Alliance (WPA), she made it clear that women were not equal in that organization. She notes in the Scott interview that when this was said it caused consternation. This preoccupation led her over time to create with other women the organization called "Red Thread." This was a different Caribbean women's organization than those which had been created by left parties and movements. The organization was not dependent upon the masculine authority of the political party. It was not a wing of the party which focused on "women's issues"; rather it was an organization which began in her words with a "politics of transformation, starting with women" (Scott 2004: 207). This was a different perspective of radical left politics. In other words, rather than beginning with the agency of an undifferentiated working class, or peasant class, or with the social group called the poor, or the "Wretched of the Earth" in Fanon's words, Andaiye, working in collaboration with others, begins to identify women as the catalytic agent for social change in the Caribbean. Again in the Scott interview, she notes:

> You can only change capital if you organize against all the work they make us do. Counting women's work means in the first place seeing where women's unwaged labour is the organization of capital ... [it] excites me ... as a way of understanding the world so you understand what the hierarches in the world are and the particular directions and intentions and kinds of exploitations. (Scott 2004: 212–213)

This was at the heart of what Andaiye was saying to us at the meeting in Trinidad in 2001. It was what she devoted her entire adult life to. This deep desire to understand the world and to change it was her reason for life. It gave her a rare strength of character and personhood. It made her a fierce critic and careful organizer, and in the end made her one of the finest radical personalities of the decolonization period in the Caribbean.

CONCLUSION

Andaiye belongs to a radical Caribbean organizing tradition in which political questions of democracy, radical forms of equality, and self-liberation were paramount. In this tradition the question is not so much the party as organizer; rather it is how ordinary people can organize themselves for their own freedom.[5] What she brought to that tradition was not only her political personality but a set of ideas which foregrounded the struggles of women not as subsidiary to the main struggle but as catalytic. Guyana's progressive politics is confronted with an ethnic divide and the ignoring of the indigenous communities. Andaiye's politics broke the barriers of difference and attempted to organize a distinctive political conception of possibilities. As she stood there in the room on the Trinidadian, St. Augustine campus in 2001 speaking to us with her sharp tongue, she was urging us to re-examine the entire scaffolding of our radical politics. It is something which remains to be done.

Anthony Bogues is a writer, scholar, and curator. He has published eight books in the fields of Black radical political thought, Caribbean intellectual history and Caribbean art. He is currently working on a book titled *Black Critique*. Other projects currently include analysis of the political thought of Michael Manley and Jamaica in the 1970s, co-editing some of the unpublished writings of Sylvia Wynter and editing a volume on Haitian Art. At Brown University he is the Asa Messer Professor of Humanities and Critical Theory and is the inaugural director of the Center for the Study of Slavery and Justice. A visiting professor and curator at the University of Johannesburg, he has also curated art shows in the Caribbean, South Africa and the USA.

NOTES

1. There was only one other political figure I can recall who had this kind of embodiment and that is the worker-intellectual, Joseph Edwards, who I met as a member of *Abeng*. Edwards formed one of the most important worker councils in Jamaica in the largest meat packing company in the Caribbean. He also wrote the seminal pamphlet published by the *Abeng* group, *Unions Versus Management* (1969). *Abeng* was a radical newspaper published in Jamaica for nine months in 1969. After the paper stopped publication it became a gathering place for radicals to coordinate radical political activity. It was dissolved in 1974 when members of the group moved to create various Marxist groupings including the Workers Liberation League which then became the Workers Party of Jamaica.
2. For example the PNP in Jamaica was led by a political group who could be described as socialist influenced by the political ideas of the British Labour Party. There was of course a Marxist Left in the party led by Richard Hart and others. For a discussion of this see Hart (1989). For a discussion of the Guyanese political context see Lewis (1998).
3. Although this was Marxism of a then Soviet variety it should be noted that when the PPP was destabilized by American and British power the Forbes Burnham regime, over time, developed a political ideology which was called Cooperative Socialism. The Guyanese political terrain created the conditions for some of the most important political commentary on state formation in the third world as well as that of a political economy of decolonization. For an analysis of state formation, see Thomas (1984), and for political economy and politics, see Rodney (1975).
4. I would suggest here that what was at work as well at this time in Andaiye's thought was her preoccupation with the struggles of women in the Caribbean and that part

of her radical understanding of democracy was rooted in her analysis of women's struggles within the Caribbean. Here I think it is critical to note her relationship with Selma James. If Rodney and others on the Caribbean left including groups like New Beginning in Trinidad were influenced by C. L. R. James, then we should note how Andaiye became influenced by the remarkable political practice and thought of Selma James, particularly her work in the "Wages for Housework" campaign.

5. Of course the Caribbean political tradition which opens up this debate is one in which the ideas and political practices of C. L. R. James are central.

REFERENCES

Hart, Richard. 1989. *From Occupation to Independence*. London: Pluto Press.

Lewis, Rupert. 1998. *Walter Rodney's Intellectual and Political Thought*. Detroit, MI: Wayne State University Press.

Rodney, Walter. 1975. "Contemporary Political Trends in the English Speaking Caribbean." *Black Scholar* 7: 15–21.

Scott, David. 2004. "Counting Women's Caring Work: An Interview with Andaiye." *Small Axe* 15 (March): 123–217.

Thomas, Clive. 1984. *The Rise of the Authoritarian State in Peripheral Societies*. New York: Monthly Review Press.

Index